Inside the Regiment

Inside the Regiment

The Officers and Men of the
30th Regiment During the Revolutionary
and Napoleonic Wars

Carole Divall

Pen & Sword
MILITARY

First published in Great Britain in 2011 by
Pen & Sword Military
an imprint of
Pen & Sword Books Ltd
47 Church Street
Barnsley
South Yorkshire
S70 2AS

Copyright © Carole Divall 2011

ISBN 978-1-84884-453-7

The right of Carole Divall to be identified as Author of this Work has been asserted by her in accordance with the Copyright, Designs and Patents Act 1988.

A CIP catalogue record for this book is available from the British Library.

All rights reserved. No part of this book may be reproduced or transmitted in any form or by any means, electronic or mechanical including photocopying, recording or by any information storage and retrieval system, without permission from the Publisher in writing.

Typeset in 11pt Ehrhardt by
Mac Style, Beverley, E. Yorkshire

Printed and bound in the UK by CPI Antony Rowe, Chippenham, Wiltshire

Pen & Sword Books Ltd incorporates the imprints of Pen & Sword Aviation, Pen & Sword Maritime, Pen & Sword Military, Wharncliffe Local History, Pen & Sword Select, Pen & Sword Military Classics, Leo Cooper, Seaforth Publishing and Frontline Publishing.

For a complete list of Pen & Sword titles please contact
PEN & SWORD BOOKS LIMITED
47 Church Street, Barnsley, South Yorkshire, S70 2AS, England
E-mail: enquiries@pen-and-sword.co.uk
Website: www.pen-and-sword.co.uk

Contents

List of Illustrations vi
Preface vii
Acknowledgements ix
Timeline x

1. Portrait of a Regiment 1
2. In Command 13
3. Scum of the Earth 32
4. Or Fine Fellows? 51
5. Raw Recruit to Rough Soldier 63
6. The Backbone of the Regiment 79
7. Officers and Gentlemen 96
8. An Officer's Life – Work and Play 111
9. Crime and Punishment 130
10. You Stand Charged 146
11. The Law of the Lash 163
12. Disease and Death 177
13. Women, Children and Other Miscellaneous Matters 197

Appendix: Surgeons and Assistant Surgeons in Order of Appointment 210
Notes 212
Select Bibliography 217
Index 220

List of Illustrations

30th Foot, sergeant, 1807
30th Foot, private, 1806
30th Foot, officer, 1806
30th Foot, company officer and private, 1815
30th Foot, colonel and officer, 1818
30th Foot, fifer, 1816
Recruiting party of the 33rd Foot
Major Charles James
Three depictions of infantry musket drill
Infantry Drilling
Royal Barracks, Dublin
Royal Barracks, Dublin, plan
Troops in Bivouac near the Village of Villa Velha
Camp Scenes
Baggage Wagon
Soldiers Marching

Preface

Spectamur Agendo, the motto of the 30th Foot, the Cambridgeshire Regiment as it was officially known, invites us to judge the regiment by its deeds. In 1793, when at Toulon the 30th Foot first encountered the French Revolutionary forces, and particularly the genius of Napoleon Bonaparte, they were found lacking. However notable their deeds, they could not rise above the inadequacies of an army that had been allowed to grow rusty with disuse after the disasters of the American War. Twenty-two years later they encountered Napoleon for a second time, a meeting with a very different outcome. At the crucial battle of Waterloo the second battalion of the 30th Regiment were in the centre of Wellington's line and, like the other units around them, stood their ground against cavalry, infantry and artillery attacks. If that battle was 'hard pounding', the 30th were one of the units who suffered the worst of the bombardment.

Just as the army evolved into a more efficient military machine, so the 30th also became a fighting regiment that could be proud of its deeds. In Egypt eight years after Toulon some daring and dashing behaviour earned the praise of those in command. Having done little to impress Wellington on their first encounter in Portugal, the second battalion later demonstrated the steady conduct that took them to glory at Badajoz, Salamanca and Villamuriel. Finally at Quatre Bras and Waterloo they stood their ground with the grim determination which was so characteristic of the British infantry of the day.

Yet behind the colours and the battle honours stood the men in the ranks, their sergeants and their officers. The structure of a regiment was a complex web of relationships, hierarchies and systems of command, all interdependent, from the youngest drummer boy to the lieutenant-colonel. Like all well-functioning bodies, every member had his purpose.

Whereas *Redcoats Against Napoleon* described the public deeds of the 30th, this study seeks to explore the private life of the regiment, the forms and arrangements, the castes and characters that enabled a typical regiment of the line to function efficiently. Obviously, much was imposed centrally. Thus such crucial issues as promotion, military law, recruiting, drill, medical services, were common to all the regiments of the line. One example, however, taken from the 101 British-based regiments which made up the infantry and explored in detail, reveals how the system worked in practice. By understanding the rules and routines of the time, we can appreciate why the ineffective army of 1793 became the efficient machine that served Wellington so well in the Peninsula, and played no small part in the eventual defeat of Napoleon.

Yet systems only work when individuals co-operate to make them work. The regiment was not a single entity but a collection of men of all kinds and from all levels of society, a much more stratified society than anything we would recognise today. Embedded in the official records, the muster rolls and the monthly returns, the discharge papers, the casualty returns and all the other documentation demanded by the War Office are the stories of the thousands of men who served King and Country during the Revolutionary and Napoleonic Wars. Some were rogues; others were honest patriots. Some were excellent soldiers; others were irredeemably bad. For some the army was a pathway to prominence and glory; for others it was the only escape from destitution. Whatever their motives, whatever their experiences, they were all members of the same regimental family.

Although the information in this study is specific to the 30th Foot, and particularly its two-battalion period (1803–1817), the conclusions which can be drawn from the efforts and experiences of the men who served in *The Old Three Tens* have far wider implications for our understanding of the army as a whole, and particularly its workhorse element, the infantry. For the first time Britain was a nation at war. The Royal Navy beat off the threat of invasion, but it was the army that finally took the war to the enemy. In doing so it became arguably the finest military machine Britain has ever produced. Delving 'inside the regiment' helps us to understand why.

Acknowledgements

Much of the research for this study has been undertaken in national and local archives. Once again my thanks are due to the staff of The National Archives, where all the official documents are deposited, and the National Army Museum, which holds the journals of William Stewart and Edward Neville Macready. In particular I would like to thank Juliet McConnell for help in accessing many of the illustrations for this book. Once again the staff at the museum of the Queen's Lancashire Regiment have been unfailing in their support and willingness to search through a mass of material for anything that concerns the 30th. On a local level, the librarians in Lowestoft proved most helpful in finding information about Thomas Walker Chambers and his family, while the record office in Leicester assiduously searched out the background of Sergeant Joseph Scotton. The staff at Mullingar library provided a wealth of information on the Irish militia, the barracks system and recruiting practices, all of which have helped me to recreate the life of the soldier in Ireland.

I also want to thank all the friends and fellow enthusiasts who have contributed their expertise and those vital snippets of information that have made it possible to produce this study of the 30th Foot. In particular, the enthusiastic support of Mick Crumplin FRCS enabled me to write about the medical services of the time, while Colin Yorke's research of his ancestor, John Yorke, provided valuable information about the life of the soldier in the ranks. Philip Haythornthwaite not only provided images but his book, *The Armies of Wellington* was the initial inspiration for this study. I also have to thank the re-enactors of the Napoleonic Association and the 33rd Foot. Some may think they 'play' at soldiers. Talk to them, however, and their wealth of knowledge about the soldier's daily life quickly becomes apparent.

Redcoats Against Napoleon was made possible by the enthusiastic support of Lieutenant-Colonel John Downham, which he has generously extended to my work on the private life of the regiment. Without his interest and assistance, much that I have been able to incorporate into this study would have remained undiscovered. Similarly, I must thank my husband for his patience, and also for his photographic and graphical skills which so often bring to life the words on the page. He is also an excellent proofreader and spots those points where the author knows what she means but few readers would.

Finally, this book is testimony to the fine qualities not only of the 30th Foot, but to all those units that fought against Napoleon in the early years of the nineteenth century – Wellington's far from infamous army.

Timeline

1789   The start of the French Revolution
1791   The 30th returned to Europe from Dominica
1793   The regiment was distributed by companies to serve with the Mediterranean fleet; some of the companies subsequently served at the siege of Toulon
1794   Part of the regiment took part in the invasion of Corsica
1795   The regiment was reunited in Ireland
1798   Rebellion broke out in Ireland. The 30th sailed to Sicily
1799   The regiment formed part of the force, under General Graham, that forced the French to surrender Malta
1800   The 30th joined Abercromby's force for the campaign in Egypt
1801   (21st March) Battle of Alexandria; (7th April) Cairo taken; (17th August) French surrendered in Alexandria
1802   The Peace of Amiens. The 30th returned to England
1803   The formation of a second battalion
1804   Both battalions sailed to Ireland
1805   1/30th joined Lord Cathcart's expedition to North Germany
1806   1/30th sailed to India
1809   2/30th sailed to Portugal, and then to Gibraltar
1810   (May) 2/30th joined the defending force at Cadiz; (September) 2/30th sailed to Portugal and joined Wellington's army behind the Lines of Torres Vedras
1811   The Anglo-Portuguese drove Marshal Masséna out of Portugal; (3–5 May) Battle of Fuentes de Oñoro
1812   (19th January) Fall of Ciudad Rodrigo; (6th April) Storming of Badajoz; (22nd July) Battle of Salamanca; (19th September) investment of Burgos; (21st October) siege of Burgos raised; (25th October) action at Villamuriel; (19th November) the Anglo-Portuguese army returned to Portugal
1813   (24th February) Six companies of the 2/30th returned to England; (29th August) four remaining companies returned to England; (September) the battalion was reunited on the island of Jersey

1814 (February) 2/30th joined Graham's Flanders expedition; (4th April) Paris taken, leading to the abdication of the Emperor Napoleon
1815 (March) Napoleon returned from exile; (15th June) French crossed the border into Belgium; (16th June) Battle of Quatre Bras; (19th June) Battle of Waterloo; (26th December) 2/30th returned to England
1816 (1st February) 2/30th returned to Ireland
1817 (24th April) 2/30th was disbanded
1818 Remnants of the 2/30th joined the 1st Battalion in India
1819 (18th March) Assault of Asseerghur
1829 (14th February) The 30th left India

Chapter 1

Portrait of a Regiment

On a fine spring day at the beginning of April 1814[1] the casual passerby on the road from Brasschaat to Antwerp might have wondered at the sight of 500 redcoated soldiers assembled in this green and wooded area of Flanders. He would not have been surprised by their actual presence. British and Prussian soldiers, in alliance, had been engaged in a struggle with the French since the beginning of the year, a struggle only concluded by the allied presence in Paris which would lead to the abdication of Napoleon Bonaparte in twelve days' time. On this spring day the second battalion of the 30th Regiment were not mustered in battalion order as a prelude to action. Instead, they were about to be inspected by Major-General Mackenzie, lately the commander of the reserve of the force General Sir Thomas Graham had brought to Flanders to drive the French out of Antwerp.

A month later, in very different circumstances, and rather earlier in the morning, the senior battalion of the regiment also underwent an inspection. Cannanore (modern Kannur) was a recently established cantonment on the Malabar coast, the wettest region of southern India. Situated in Kerala state, this area had originally been part of Portuguese India. Subsequently taken by the Dutch and then passed on to an Indian princely house, it had finally become part of British India in 1790. By the beginning of May the temperature was already 32°C, and although the monsoon period lay a month ahead the humidity was a constant factor, sufficient to sap the strength of the mainly seasoned men who made up the first battalion. Nevertheless, they had been in Cannanore long enough to become acclimatised, having arrived in November, 1811. Most of them had also served long enough to be thoroughly familiar with the demands of an inspection. Furthermore, they were about to be inspected by their own commanding officer, Lieutenant-Colonel Vaumorel, who was in temporary command at Malabar.

As both battalions of the regiment were serving abroad, a depot unit had been established, initially at Winchester and now at Colchester. Here they enjoyed the advantages of one of the most extensive barracks complexes in England. The men who waited there to be inspected by Major-General Acland were a mixture of raw recruits, volunteers from the militia, invalids from India and veterans from the Peninsula. This last group comprised some men who were awaiting discharge upon completion of their seven years' service, an option that denied them a pension, and others who had been judged unfit for service in Flanders.

Even before the day of inspection arrived, there were forms to complete, and these give us a clear impression of the 30th (or *Old Three Tens*) in the spring of 1814. The total strength of the regiment was 231 NCOs and drummers and 1,565 privates. This was under strength, but better than a year before when the total strength had been 1,443 all ranks, and only the enthusiastic activities of the recruiting companies had brought the regiment closer to its notional strength.

By 1814 a large proportion of the British army was Irish. When the three units are considered as a whole, this Irish presence is noticeable but not exceptional, constituting just under a third of the manpower. Within the units, however, a very different picture emerges. Most of the Irish soldiers were in the second battalion, making up nearly half its strength, and at the depot, where just under a third were Irish. The Irish presence in the first battalion, therefore, was relatively low, little more than a fifth of the total strength.

This discrepancy tells us something about the relative experience of the two battalions since the beginning of 1804, when the regiment was posted to Ireland. The first battalion stayed there only two years, before taking part in Lord Cathcart's abortive expedition to north Germany and then sailing to India. During this period there was some recruitment in Ireland, although most of the recruiting companies were still operating in England, with one in Scotland. After 1806, however, not only did recruiting activities become more concentrated in Ireland but volunteers from the militia were invited to join the regular army with enhanced bounty. As we shall see, the result was a flood of volunteers into the second battalion before they also left Ireland in 1809. Some of them were subsequently transferred to the first battalion, but this was never more than a trickle.

The Scottish element, despite the activities of a recruiting company, remained negligible, only forty men across all three units. The number of foreigners was even lower, seven in the first battalion and two in the second. One of the most interesting was Charles Dupree, a drummer with the first battalion. He enlisted in

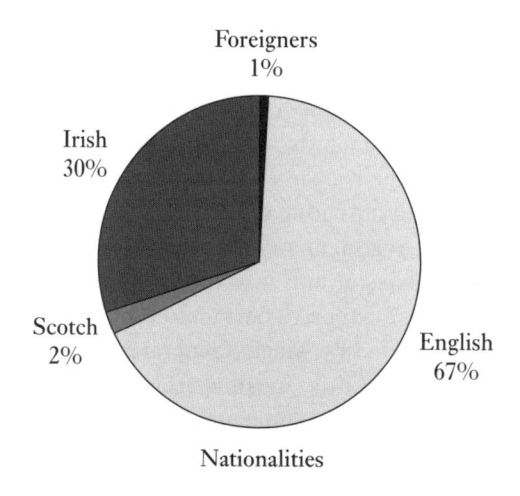

Foreigners 1%
Irish 30%
Scotch 2%
English 67%

Nationalities

Northampton, where he was working as a shoemaker, in 1802. He was born in St Eustia in the West Indies, however, and had already served in the Royal Irish and the Northampton Fencibles. When he was finally discharged in 1827, 'worn out', his good conduct earned him a well-deserved pension. He also chose to remain in India.

Length of service was obviously an important element in any unit, since experience in the ranks would normally translate into good conduct in action, a point later demonstrated by the second battalion at Quatre Bras. Not surprisingly, the largest number of inexperienced men were at the depot. Nearly a quarter had served less than a year and half less than four years. In contrast, only sixty-three men in the first battalion had served less than four years, while over two-thirds had at least eight years' service. Indeed, most of the surviving veterans of Egypt (1801) were in India. The second battalion, statistically, resembled the depot. Although there was no-one in the ranks who had served for less than a year, nearly a quarter had less than three years' experience and only forty-six had served for more than ten years. On paper, therefore, the junior battalion was less experienced than the senior, but these were the men who had seen action in the Peninsula, most of whom would fight at Waterloo.

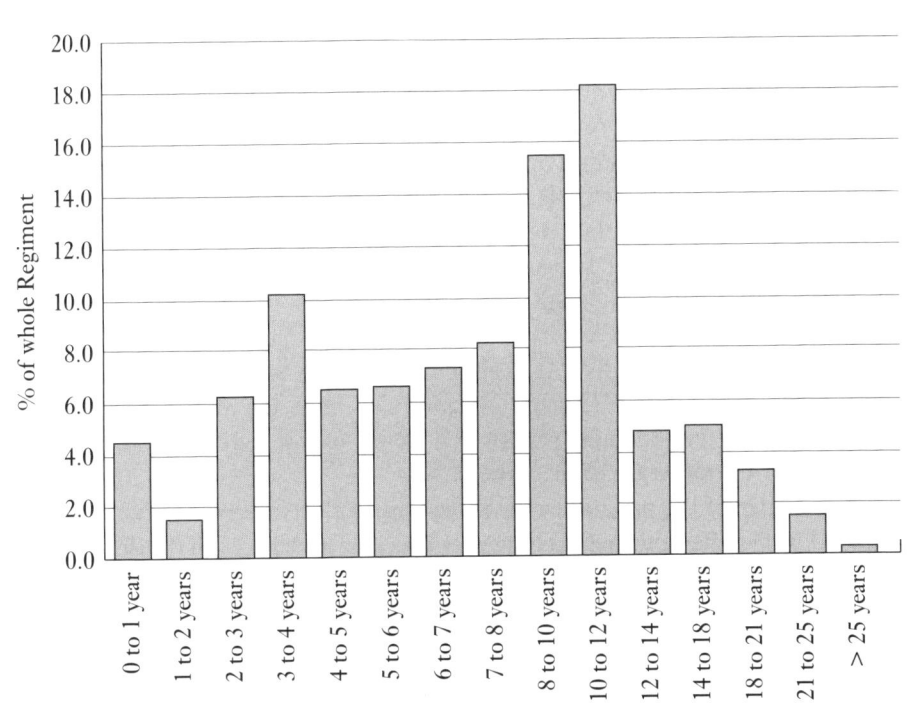

The NCOs and drummers across all three units were seasoned veterans. No sergeant had served less than six years, but whereas nearly half the sergeants with the first battalion and the depot had served between ten and twelve years, in the second battalion half of them had served less than eight years. However, all three units had as NCOs men of considerable experience. For example, Matthew Donnellan (of whom more later) had enlisted in 1795 and by 1814 had been a sergeant for sixteen years. Such men brought steadiness and a wealth of experience to an essentially young battalion.

The corporals in the three battalions followed much the same pattern as the sergeants. The first battalion and the depot had only one corporal each who had served less than six years, while well over half had served between eight and twelve years. In the second battalion, though, a third had less than six years' service. Taken in total, over a third of the sergeants of the regiment and half the corporals had served between ten and twelve years. As a statistic, however, this is somewhat misleading since some men were recognised within a year of joining the regiment as ideal NCO material, whereas others could stand in the ranks for a much longer period before their potential was recognised.

Just as length of service varied across the three units, so did age. Although the optimum age in all three units for sergeants was between 25 and 35, the first battalion had more at the upper end of this age group, the second more at the lower end, and the depot a more even spread. The greatest number of corporals, however, were aged between 25 and 30, consistently across the three units. The comparative youth of the NCOs of the second battalion was sufficiently unusual to attract a comment from an inspecting officer a year before: 'The greater part are very young. They perform their duty with promptitude and energy and attend to the best of their abilities the discipline of the Regiment.'[2]

When the drummers are considered, an apparent contradiction emerges. Only one drummer, in the first battalion, had served for less than four years. Of the total forty-one drummers, three-quarters had served for more than seven years, which suggests an experienced cadre across the three units. (Over half were with the first battalion, the other two units having only nine apiece.) The age of the drummers, however, tells a different story. Nearly two-thirds were under 25 and only the first battalion had half their number above this age. All the second battalion drummers were under 25, and all but two of the depot drummers, a reminder that boys, particularly sons of the regiment, were often trained up as drummers. When Sergeant Edward Laughron was hanged in 1805 for the murder of his wife, his two young sons were adopted by the regiment, and both served as drummers. To reinforce the point, when General Acland inspected the depot he made the suggestion in his confidential report that some of the boys 'might surely be considered for the situation of drummers'.

The age range of the privates in the three units reflects that of the NCOs. In the first battalion over half the men were aged between 25 and 35. Even the depot, which had been taking in recruits and militia volunteers, had a similar preponderance, over a third in the same age group, although just under a third were under 18. In the second battalion, however, over half the privates were aged between 18 and 25, against less than a quarter in the next age group. In other words, the battalion that would go into action at Quatre Bras and Waterloo was young in years, although by June 1815 every man in the ranks had served for at least two years. Perhaps it is not surprising that when the men who survived the disbandment of 1817 arrived in India they were not initially welcomed by the veterans of the senior battalion who had been denied the chance of action and glory.

The men who served in the 30th are individualised in a variety of official documents: muster rolls and pay lists, discharge papers, casualty returns and courts martial records, for example. In contrast, women and children exist primarily as statistics. In total, there were 101 wives and seventy-six children with the three units. This, of course, does not include irregular relationships and their offspring. Significantly, there were no children with the second battalion, since Lieutenant-Colonel Hamilton had chosen to leave at the depot men with young families. We know in general terms the age range and gender of the children. There was a preponderance of males under 10 (only one over) because this was the age when the regiment could enlist them as boys. Girls, however, were mainly over 10 with the first battalion and under 10 with the depot, a contrast which came about merely by chance.

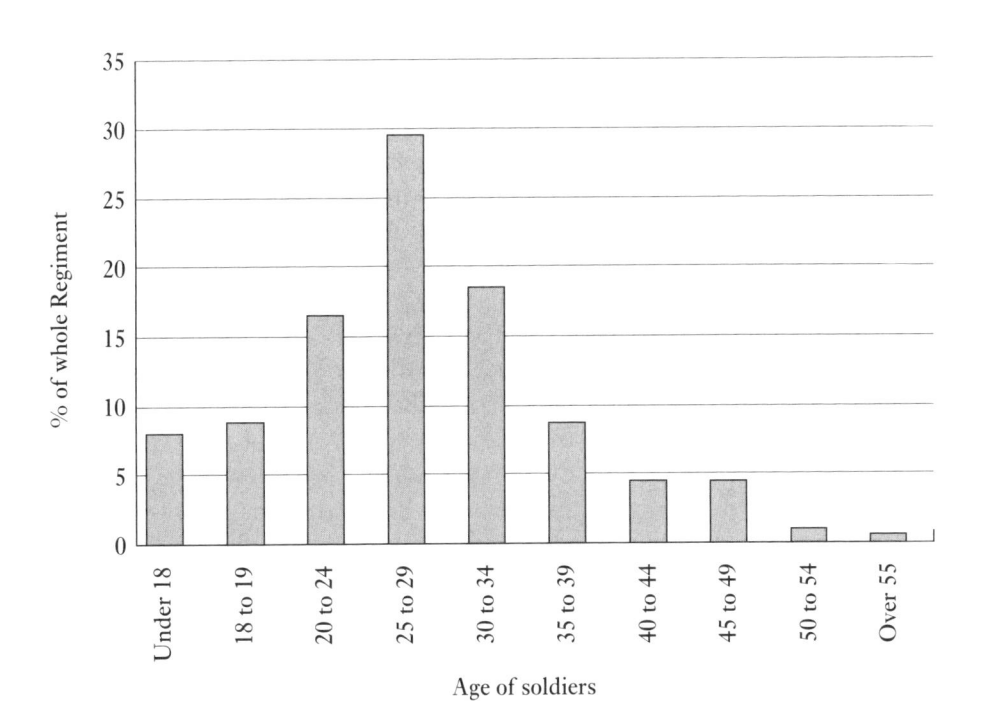

Two other sets of statistics are contained in the returns. One lists casualties during the previous six months, which reveals that the senior battalion lost ten men in that period against four in the junior battalion. Allowing for the different strength of the two battalions, these figures are remarkably similar. The second battalion, however, had lost two men to enemy action during the Flanders campaign, something the first battalion had not experienced since 1801 and the days when the 30th was a single-battalion regiment. Disease was a constant problem in India, as it had been for the second battalion in Spain and Portugal, but ten deaths in six months says much for the skill of the surgeon, Pearse, and his assistant. There had been five deaths at the depot, a higher rate than the other two units, but this is explained by the high proportion of invalids, many of whom were broken in health by the time they reached England.

Perhaps more illustrative of an essential difference between the two battalions and their relative experiences are the statistics for regimental courts martial. Although the first was nearly twice the strength of the second, that does not explain a discrepancy of seventy-two men on trial against twelve. (The depot returned none, the men being described as 'orderly and well behaved'.) The tedium of service in India was the problem, as will be discussed in more detail in the context of crime and punishment.

Before moving on to the three confidential reports, we can return to that scene at Brasschaat and consider what Major-General Mackenzie would have noted as he inspected the assembled ranks of the second battalion. He would have noticed, for instance, a disproportion of subalterns, twenty-four against the three captains and three staff officers. This had been a problem for the junior battalion from the day the senior battalion sailed to India, taking most of the more experienced officers with them. He would also have noticed the youth of these subalterns; only three were over 25 and the eldest of them was only 30. This was not a unit where men had grown old as lieutenants while younger, richer men had leapfrogged to higher rank. Service in the Peninsula had made dead men's shoes a sad but inevitable feature of life. Possibly he also realised that nearly three-quarters of the officers were Irish.

He might also have noticed that a fifth of the battalion was under the statutory height of 5 feet 5 inches, although most of these were the lads and very young men who still had growing to do. A similar number were over 5 feet 9, while the majority were between 5 feet 6 and 5 feet 8. He might also have noticed that only one of the drummers was over 5 feet 5, a reminder of their youth.

He was later to comment that the clothing and accoutrements were 'in strict conformity to His Majesty's regulations in clothing and appointments, which are in good condition as also the men's great coats'. As for the arms, 'They are serviceable, clean and marked.' In other words, the battalion was smartly turned out, presumably after a great deal of white-claying and black-balling, despite the harsh conditions they had experienced in the first three months of the year when a Dutch winter had caused considerable suffering, relieved only by generous helpings of gin. As for necessaries, they were 'of good quality & seem reasonably charged'. The general did notice, however, that the colours were bad. We learn from an inspection eighteen months later that:

> The colours are not now conformable to the Regulations: having been 12 years in use, they are worn out, & not capable of recovery, the Badges & names of locations in which the Battn has been engaged: as a substitute Lt-Col Hamilton has annexed silk streamers on which such names etc are placed.

No wonder Ensign Macready referred to the colours as 'our dear old rags', watching with relief as they were carried to the rear during the most desperate stages of the Battle of Waterloo.

The battalion would then have demonstrated for the general the field exercises and movements which were an essential part of the inspection, and he was able to write that 'The order of Reviews & Field Exercises is adhered to, & their Field Movements are good.' This was a definite advance from the situation in 1810 when Brigadier General Houghton had commented that although 'the men were steady in the ranks, sufficient attention however has not been paid to the drill of the regiment, and the field movements were by no means accurate'. Time and experience, to say nothing of a commanding officer who was famous for his ability to bring troops up to scratch very quickly, had effected commendable improvement.

It is unlikely there was anything about the first battalion in Cannanore that surprised Lieutenant-Colonel Vaumorel since he was already intimately familiar with the condition of his corps. The return does not identify the officers present, but the monthly return for April makes clear that the imbalance noted in the second battalion was not a problem shared by the first. Apart from the staff officers, there were six captains and eighteen subalterns present. Of these officers, ten (plus one of the majors and the quartermaster) properly belonged to the second battalion. On the other hand, nine first battalion officers were with the second, this being one of the practical problems which arose when both battalions were serving abroad. There had been some slight re-adjustment during the year between the second battalion's return from the Peninsula and departure to Flanders, but the problem remained insoluble during the two-battalion period. Furthermore, there were officers who had come back to England for recovery of health or personal reasons who had then joined the second battalion instead of returning to India. Captain Thomas Walker Chambers had set the pattern in 1810, choosing to join what was his rightful battalion instead of activating the resignation he had signed in India. By 1814 Lieutenants White, Sinclair and Nicholson, posted absent without leave by the first battalion, were serving with the second.

Vaumorel would be aware that nearly half his battalion was under 5 feet 7 and less than a fifth 5 feet 9 or taller, although it was so long since he had seen the second battalion that he probably would not have known that it was proportionately taller. He might have been surprised to discover this fact since there was a common perception that Irish soldiers were generally shorter than English or Scottish, yet the second battalion had many more Irishmen than the first. Nor did the first battalion have the high proportion of young men yet to reach their full height. Nonetheless, the difference was merely coincidental.

He would also have known that although the men's uniforms were the previous year's issue, they were still in excellent condition. Also, the 1814 issue had just been delivered from Europe, ready to be finished off by the battalion tailors. Accoutrements were 'all good, very little wanting' and arms 'clean and seviceable and regularly marked'. As for necessaries, they were 'charged at a fair price, and are of a good quality'. Unfortunately, selling one's necessaries was a favourite hobby in the battalion, so it is unlikely that a full complement was on display.

Not surprisingly, Vaumorel found no fault with the field exercises and movements, which were 'performed with precision: and the various formations made with correctness'. Even when the battalion was found wanting in this respect in 1809 the inspecting officer General Wilkinson, who had previously commanded the battalion, explained that

> two Hundred of the Men with a proportion of Officers and non-commissioned Officers were upwards of nine months at sea, and thirty above one Year and a half serving as Marines, and the whole of them only joined a short time before the review; in addition to which the Battn itself was near three months in the Field, most of the time on the March and only arrived in quarters a little more than three weeks before the Review.

A cynical observer might have commented that it was a definite advantage to be inspected by senior officers who had such a close connection with the regiment.

This advantage is reflected in Vaumorel's remarks on the personnel of the battalion which reflect his closer relationship with them. His judgement that 'every degree of attention has been bestowed on the Regiment by the Officers attached to it' and that 'every officer present with the battalion was fit for purpose' has to be respected because he knew the men he was evaluating. He also knew that 'The Field Officers and Captains have paid due attention to the instruction of the Subaltern Officers' and that 'The Subaltern Officers are active, intelligent and have acquired the information which by His Majesty's Regulations is declared to be necessary.'

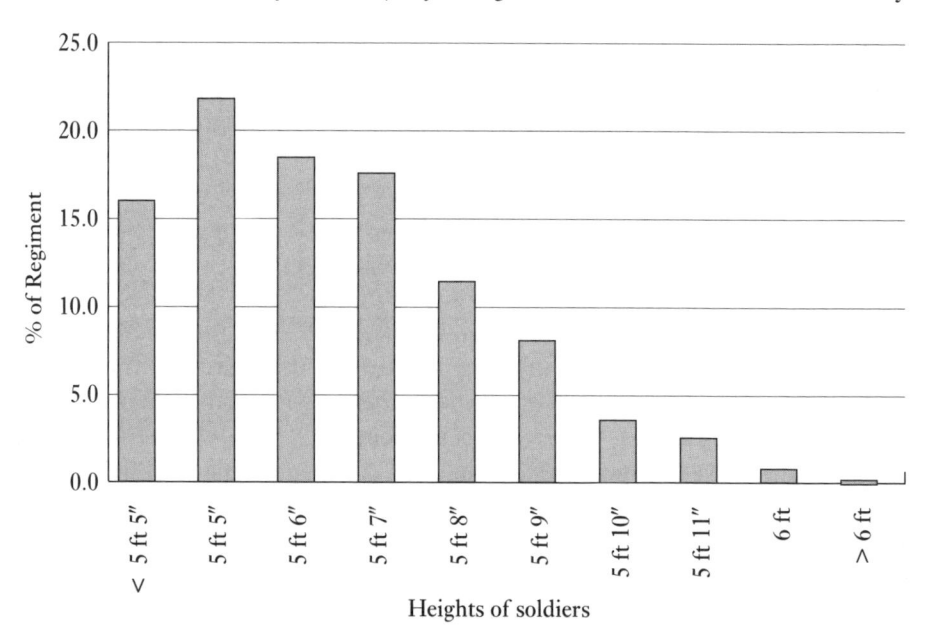

Similarly,

> The Captains are well acquainted with the interior oeconomy [sic] of their companies and competent to command them in the various situations of service. The Officers understand their duty in the field and quarters, and are intelligent and zealous in the performance of it.

He also commented on the 'perfect unanimity and good understanding of the Corps', adding that they had always 'afforded the Commanding Officer the support which he is intitled [sic] to require from them'.

There were similar commendations for the NCOs who were 'properly instructed, active, and intelligent, and they are obedient and respectful to their Officers, at the same time they support their own authority in a becoming manner'. Most importantly for the good conduct of the battalion, they 'promote to the best of their abilities, the Discipline of the Regiment'. Perhaps Vaumorel's comments on the privates are open to question, however. He described them as 'a good body of men, with an appearance of health and cleanliness: and they are of the proper standard:…they are well drilled, attentive, sober, and well behaved'. The last two points are somewhat at odds with the seventy-two courts martial, but it would seem that by the standards of India this was not an excessive number. Drummers and musicians also came in for praise, the former being 'perfect in the different beats of the drum: and they are attentive to their duty in the field and quarters', while the latter 'play in correct time' but were also 'trained and fit for the ranks'.

We can judge Vaumorel's evaluation of his corps against the next inspection, when the inspecting officer was General Wetherall, who had no connection with the 30th. He echoed many of Vaumorel's judgements, commenting upon

> the high state of discipline, order, and interior oeconomy [sic] which distinguishes this Corps…The present Commanding Officer, Lieutenant-Colonel Vaumorel, with Lieutenant-Colonel Maxwell and Major Bircham, are officers of talent and experience. I am also gratified in stating the attention shewn by the Captains and Subalterns in the discharge of their duty is highly creditable to them, and is attended with the most beneficial effects to the service.
>
> The non-commissioned officers are intelligent and conduct themselves with strictest propriety. The privates…are an efficient body of men perfectly drilled and full equal to field service.

Indeed, Wetherall's only criticisms concerned an addiction to drinking which he noticed among the men and the frequency of corporal punishment 'which I hope and trust will hereafter be superseded by a more lenient and less disgraceful measure, that of solitary confinement'. He concluded: 'In summing up the character of the 1st Battalion of His Majesty's 30th Regiment I have no hesitation in saying that I consider the general state of it calculated for the most excellent and enterprising service.' Unfortunately, the battalion would have to wait another four years before half of them saw some active service at the siege of Asseerghur.

To return to Vaumorel's inspection, in every respect the battalion emerges as an exemplary unit. Whether it is messing arrangements, for both officers and men, the keeping of company accounts, the conduct of the medical services, or attendance at divine service, everything is as it should be. Even 'The Sergeant School Master is very correct and attentive, and the scholars make much progress under his tuition.'

The confidential report of the second battalion is considerably shorter than that of the first, and adopts a much more detached tone, as might be expected when the inspecting officer's only connection with the battalion was a short period of command. Even then they had been given little opportunity to impress, only once coming under fire, when they had held steady against a battery from the French 74-gun *L'Anversoise*. Nevertheless, General Mackenzie's somewhat perfunctory comments create a convincing picture of a well-functioning corps. It also becomes clear that certain key words carried strong implications of approval. For example, the phrase 'zealous and attentive' is applied to Hamilton, whose 'Regt is in a good state of discipline, & is well versed in the prescribed manoeuvres', to Major Bailey and Lieutenant-Colonel Vigoureux, and to the captains of the battalion, who are also 'competent to command their companies both in the field & in quarters'. The subalterns were 'active and attentive', although only 'tolerably well instructed'. (Six months later another inspecting officer noted that attention had been paid to their instruction.) The adjutant was 'intelligent and well qualified'; the officer doing duty as quartermaster was 'attentive and competent'; the privates were 'a good body of men & are healthy and clean'. Indeed, there are no negative comments apart from the qualification 'tolerably' when describing the level of instruction given to the subalterns and NCOs. The latter, however, were also 'active and attentive'.

Thus it can be concluded that both battalions were fit for purpose, although only the second battalion had the opportunity to display a proper military competence in action.

The purpose of the depot was to support the two battalions, although the term depot is itself somewhat misleading. In a general military sense a depot was a place for the collection of military stores or a place for the reception of recruits, or detached parties, from different regiments. Thus the Isle of Wight was the depot for the infantry. Essentially, the depot of the 30th at Colchester was a collecting point for recruits and invalids, with the further responsibilities of sending detachments to the battalions and managing the two recruiting companies, whose detached parties were operating in various parts of England and Ireland. Consequently, what Major-General Acland found at Colchester on the 10th May was very different from the ranks assembled at Brasschaat and Cannanore. To start with, there were only eight officers present, Captain Stewart in command, six subalterns, and Quartermaster Kingsley, who was soon to sail to India. Kingsley had been invalided home from the Peninsula in 1812. Stewart was also an invalid, still recovering from serious wounds received while serving as brigade major with the second division at the siege of Pamplona the previous year. Nevertheless it is obvious from General Acland's comments that he was now sufficiently recovered to function as 'an intelligent and attentive officer' who was also 'attentive to the instruction of the soldiers'. This was necessary in order to send the two battalions men who were already versed in the basic exercises and manoeuvres.

Two-thirds of the men at the depot were under 5 feet 8 although, excluding the twelve boys, there were only twelve under the statutory height. Like the second battalion, there was a high percentage of lads and young men who were not yet full grown. General Acland commented that the privates were 'tolerably good, but there are several young and weakly lads'. He also noted that eight recruits and eighteen volunteers from the militia had joined since the last inspection. However, not all the recruits were 'conformable to the recruiting regulations, and have been taken on the strength of the Depot on the approval of the Field Officer who [illeg] them'. Furthermore, '27 men are unfit for service, and proposed to be discharged'. Since in Stewart's opinion only a third of the men were actually fit for service, the general's comments would not have been unexpected. Nevertheless, by June 1815 many of these newcomers, as well as some recovered invalids, and the prisoners of war who would return to the depot over the next six months, were in the ranks of the second battalion, holding square at Quatre Bras and standing against the French in the centre of Wellington's line at Waterloo.

In all other respects, Acland found much to praise in the depot unit. The NCOs, many of them seasoned veterans, were 'attentive', 'the interior oeconomy & cleanliness of the Barrack Rooms is properly attended to', while the officers' mess was 'established on that system of oeconomy which enables a subaltern officer to belong to it'. There were some complaints from the men concerning arrears of pay while serving in the Peninsula. Since pay was always in arrears in Spain and Portugal, these would be men who had been invalided home before the latest instalment had been made. Acland was able to report, however, that the claims 'have been duly investigated & transmitted to the battalion, & I have given directions that every attention shall be given to bring them to a final adjustment'.

That Acland had uncovered a widespread problem is borne out by the report on the second battalion. Mackenzie noted that 'One man complained of want of settlement when on board ship being invalided from Lisbon – which from the want of a proper certificate could not be charged. I have again ordered it to be written about.' There were also complaints in the first battalion, although the details were on a separate certificate which has not survived. Other inspection reports, however, indicate similar problems with pay. As far as the depot was concerned, pay was now well regulated: 'the men sign their accounts, which are witnessed by an officer, who is in the habit of settling in person with the men.' This was also the procedure in the two battalions, since regular payment was a problem neither in Flanders nor in India.

Obviously, clothing, accoutrements and arms were as important at the depot as in the other two units. Clothing was generally in good condition, although

About 200 great coats delivered in 1812 are much worn & nearly unserviceable. Capt Stewart having recently joined the Depot cannot account for their being in this state, but every attention is now paid by him to their care of the clothing & accoutrements.

Greatcoats were the only problem because 'The arms, accoutrements & other appointments are clean, good, & serviceable.'

The three inspection reports together create a clear picture of a well-regulated regiment, with officers and men who were fit for purpose, and which functioned appropriately in three very different situations, cantonment in India, active service in Flanders, and recruitment and training in England. The 30th was a typical infantry regiment of the line, and the comments passed on it were replicated many times over in the reports on other, similar regiments. For this reason, delving into the workings of the regiment, which is the purpose of this study, not only reveals the inner life of the 30th, but gives a comprehensive picture of how other infantry regiments, the backbone of the army, functioned in the first two decades of the nineteenth century.

Chapter 2

In Command

The Revolutionary and Napoleonic Wars (1793–1815) devoured men. In a worldwide war, all the combatant nations of Europe had to expand their fighting forces. Even Britain, trusting at first to the power of the navy and suspicious of the imagined dangers associated with a large army which stemmed from memories of Cromwell's major-generals, found itself caught up in the demands for men, and yet more men.

Of the three service arms, cavalry, artillery and infantry, one was romantic, one was highly specialised, and one was the often disregarded workhorse. Yet it was *the poor bloody infantry*, the least glamorous of the three arms, which not only did the footslogging but also won the battles. This is not to belittle the function of the cavalry and artillery but even Napoleon, a gunner at heart, who refined the use of artillery as a weapon to soften up the enemy, never won a battle without some significant contribution from his infantry. Indeed, the failure of the French artillery and cavalry at Waterloo to break the allied army makes the point. Wellington's campaigns in both the Peninsula and Flanders were critically dependent upon his infantry. His foot soldiers might be composed of the scum of the earth, but as he himself remarked: 'it really is wonderful that we should have made them the fine soldiers they are.'³

In 1790, when the 30th Regiment returned to Europe from Dominica and before the outbreak of the Revolutionary War, the infantry of the army consisted of three Guards regiments and seventy-seven regiments of the line. By 1815 there were 104 regiments of the line in the British establishment, as well as eight West Indian regiments, nine foreign regiments in British pay, nine colonial corps and five Canadian regiments. Furthermore, the infantry of the King's German Legion alone comprised ten battalions of the line and two light battalions, while in India the East India Company maintained its own army, in addition to the regular troops posted there. If not exactly a nation in arms, Britain, along with its colonies, was more militarised than at any period since the English Civil War.

Like all the armies of the day, the British army was organised into regiments, each regiment being a self-contained unit within the wider military establishment. Although the time had passed when a colonel literally owned his regiment, each regiment regarded itself as autonomous. When one officer described another as 'of ours', he was not making a distinction between friend and enemy but between an officer of his own regiment and any other. Co-operation between regiments was an essential element of military strategy, hence the significance of brigades and divisions, and close comradeship could develop. This is particularly evident in the regiments of the Light Division during the Peninsular campaigns but can also be observed in the relationship of the 30th and 44th, who several times found themselves on campaign together. Eventually in 1813 the two second battalions formed a provisional battalion. 'These two corps being thrown so much together in Spain, were almost like one regiment.'[4] On a more human note, Edward Neville Macready told of how the Peninsular veterans of the 2/30th, meeting a sergeant of the 2/44th, plied him with drink until he was rendered senseless. Similarly, when the 2/30th arrived at Quatre Bras, they passed the wounded of the 2/44th who immediately cried to them, 'Push on, old Thirtieth – pay 'em off for the poor 44th. You're much wanted, my boys. Success to ye, my darlings.'[5]

On the other hand, rivalries could run deep and resentment could fester. A man's first loyalty was always to his regiment, and he would defend its honour with his fists if necessary. When the 2/30th were awarded their Waterloo medals in Limerick in May 1816, their cock-a-hoop pride provoked such an aggrieved reaction from the 16th, who had seen no active service and already resented the boasting of the Peninsular and Waterloo veterans, that the officers of each unit were obliged to separate their wrangling and brawling men. Such was the kudos of being a fighting unit that General Barry, the local commander, sided with the veterans, even though, as Macready implies, they had started the trouble with their taunting of the men of the 16th.

Such was the perception the men had of their regiment, yet to talk about a regiment as if it were a fighting unit is actually misleading. It was, in reality, an administrative concept such as a bureaucrat would recognise, while what the commander in the field needed was battalions. Companies might sometimes be detached for specific purposes, as happened to the 5/60th and the Brunswick Oels Jägers in the Peninsula, but the battalion was the essential element of strategic planning.

If the 30th is typical, many regiments in the period between the War of American Independence and the outbreak of the Revolutionary War were less than exemplary. Although the acerbic recollections of a disgruntled private soldier must be treated with some caution, James Aytoun's observations still read like a catalogue of gratuitous punishment inflicted by brutal sergeants armed with rattan canes, and of inefficiency and drunkenness among those officers who were at least present. As Aytoun remarked, 'No wonder our armies were taken prisoner. No wonder our gallant generals, our hardy, determined soldiers were beaten when scarce a subaltern knew or did his duty'[6] – a criticism, incidentally, which is strangely similar to Wellington's castigation of his junior officers at the end of 1812, after the disasters of the retreat from Burgos.

Not surprisingly, the first British encounters with a nation overwhelmingly inspired by the concepts of liberty, equality and fraternity ended disastrously. The 30th were not a bad regiment by the standards of the time. Indeed, they may well have been more efficient than many; they certainly conducted themselves well at the siege of Toulon. They were, however, part of a military establishment which was in desperate need of reform. Not until 1795, after his failed adventure in Flanders, did the Duke of York become Commander-in-Chief of the army and begin the prodigious task of cleaning the Augean stables. It is ironic that failure in Flanders is remembered in a nursery rhyme, while the administrative success which played no small part in later British victories is less well known. Even the Duke of York, though, could not completely amend the damage of a decade or more when self-interest had been rampant and parliament had pursued its peacetime policy of keeping the army in financial straits against the unlikely threat of a military coup. Nor could he sweep his new broom through the antiquated system of military administration.

To understand why Aytoun could make such damning criticisms of the way his battalion functioned, it is necessary to consider how the army was organised, an army that was tarred with the stigma of defeat, low in public esteem, short of money and governed by an essentially corrupt administration. This last weakness was the root of the problem. In theory, the king was the commander of the army: in practice six different functionaries directly or indirectly controlled military affairs and were often in conflict with each other. For example, in the event of a war, a secretary of state assumed control but which secretary of state depended upon location. The foreign secretary was responsible if the campaign took place in a foreign country, but the colonial secretary took charge if India or the colonies were attacked, while the home secretary had to organise any defence against invasion.[7]

Although the regiment, subject at different times to all the different functionaries who comprised the military establishment, was essentially an administrative convenience, it is nonetheless relevant to consider what this 'paper' unit represented in both theory and practice. On paper each battalion of the regiment, itself under the command of its colonel, would have a staff of a lieutenant-colonel, two majors, an adjutant, paymaster, quartermaster, surgeon, two assistant surgeons and four staff sergeants. These last were the sergeant-major, armourer sergeant, paymaster sergeant and quartermaster sergeant. Later there was also provision for a drum major and a schoolmaster sergeant.

Again in theory, each battalion consisted of 1,000 men divided into ten companies, a grenadier company, a light company and eight battalion or centre companies. Traditionally the grenadier company contained the tallest men, and the light company, the smallest and nimblest. With the increased significance of light infantry, however, intelligence may have been equally important. 'The grenadiers and light infantry companies [were] to be completed with proper men out of their respective regiments, and to be kept as complete as circumstances will permit.'[8] A commentator described the light infantry as 'a body of active, strong men, selected from the aggregate of battalion companies, and made up of the most promising recruits that are occasionally enlisted.'[9] Each company was commanded by a captain, supported by three subalterns and a small cadre of NCOs. These would comprise a paymaster sergeant, not to be confused with the battalion paymaster sergeant, three to five other sergeants, two drummers, or a drummer and a fifer, and three to five corporals. If there was a pioneer company, one corporal and ten privates would remain unattached. Similarly, a small detachment might be specially trained to handle artillery, a skill which came in useful when the 2/30th helped to man the guns at Fort Puntales, Cadiz, in 1810.

So much for theory. A survey of the records of the 30th demonstrates the disjunction between theory and practice. By looking at the February monthly returns for four specific years we can see a rather different reality. Even without considering the number of officers attached to each battalion, a situation which quickly became complicated after the first battalion sailed to India, (at times nearly half the officers were attached to the wrong battalion), the numbers for sergeants, drummers and rank and file show considerable fluctuation which reflects the practicalities of service. In February 1804 the two battalions had been in Ireland a month, the first battalion headquarters at Tullamore, the second at Moate. At this point the strength of both battalions was close to the notional. The first battalion had 923 rank and file, with thirty-five sergeants and seventeen drummers, while the second had 887 rank and file, with fifty-one sergeants and eighteen drummers. There is no obvious reason why the junior battalion had so many more sergeants, but it was an imbalance which lasted until the beginning of the following year, when numbers were equalised by transfer.

Four years later the first battalion was in India and the second was still in Ireland, stationed at Longford. The strength of the senior battalion had risen to 1,126 (331 present fit, forty-two in hospital, 751 on command and two on furlough) with seventeen sergeants and twelve drummers. The junior battalion, however, was seriously under strength, 559 rank and file, although still possessing a good complement of sergeants (thirty-two) and drummers (nineteen). Nevertheless, with the anticipation of foreign service its strength steadily increased, reaching 771 rank and file by the end of the year, with thirty-eight sergeants and twenty drummers. Two months later most of them sailed for Portugal.

By the beginning of 1812 Peninsular service was having a detrimental effect on the junior battalion. Although the paper strength was 596 (which omits some invalids sent home), with forty-seven sergeants and nineteen drummers, only 391 rank and file, thirty-two sergeants and fourteen drummers were actually with the battalion at Ciudad Rodrigo, fourteen rank and file being returned 'sick absent'. At this point, the first battalion had 948 rank and file, of whom 129 were sick, thirty-nine on command and two on furlough, with forty-eight sergeants and twenty drummers. Since both battalions were now serving abroad there was also a depot at Hull. Its strength in February 1812 was six sergeants, two drummers and fifty-eight rank and file, while a further ten sergeants, six drummers and twenty-nine rank and file made up the various recruiting parties operating in England and Ireland.

The first battalion continued its loss of manpower so that by February 1816 its strength was 855 rank and file (674 present, 178 sick and three on command), with forty-six sergeants and twenty drummers. Less than a year after Quatre Bras and Waterloo the second battalion, which had returned 619 rank and file in May 1815, but had taken heavy losses in June, had recovered its strength to 592 rank and file, with fifty-three sergeants and twenty drummers. But its days were now numbered, and upon disbandment in April 1817 only 305 NCOs and privates were transferred to the first battalion. This had a welcome effect on the strength of the first battalion. In February 1820 it mustered 807 other ranks, with fifty-eight sergeants and twenty-one drummers.

The following table makes clear the differences in total strength between the two battalions.

	1st battalion	*2nd battalion*
February 1804	923	887
February 1808	1126	559
February 1812	948	596
February 1816	855	592

The colonel of the regiment from 1799 was General Sir Robert Manners. He was appointed *vice* the recently deceased General Thomas Clarke, and remained with the regiment until his own death in 1823. A Lincolnshire landowner whose principal residence was at Bloxholme, near Sleaford, he was a grandson of the second Duke of Rutland. Since his own father had risen to the rank of general, his military career was predictable. After a short period with the 3rd Dragoon Guards he transferred to the 86th and saw service in the West Indies, where he was briefly a prisoner of the French. Changing regiments with each purchased promotion, he was in Flanders in 1794 with the 3rd Foot Guards and in Holland in 1798 as lieutenant-colonel of the 9th and brigadier of a division. He had been promoted to major-general in 1796 and after the Holland expedition his career was essentially that of a staff officer, with first the Eastern Division, then the Southern Division before he returned to Eastern Division. Although he was colonel of the 30th for twenty-four years, until his death, it is doubtful that the regiment saw much of him. He was definitely present at an inspection by the Duke of York in 1803, and may well have presented colours to the second battalion in the same year. There is also some suggestion of his concern for members of the regiment. In 1807, when Brevet Lieutenant-Colonel Wade of the 30th died at Sleaford while on recruiting service, Manners arranged for him to be buried in the family vault at Bloxholme. As for

Manners himself, his private life was somewhat bizarre since, instead of marrying, he took as his mistress a certain Mary Ann Goodchild, also known as Mansel, by whom he had five children. His social status, though, meant such irregularity was tolerated.

According to Charles James,

> A colonel of infantry should understand something of fortifications, and be well acquainted with field-engineering. He cannot be too careful to maintain union and harmony among his officers; and, to succeed in this, he must acquire their esteem and confidence, and conduct himself so as to be respected. The true way to succeed in this, is to keep up subordination with unalterable firmness; to do justice to every one, to employ all his credit to procure favours to the corps in general, and to the officers in particular, without ever losing sight of the health, comfort, and contentment of his men.[10]

In practical terms, however, these responsibilities devolved on the lieutenant-colonel, who commanded on a day-to-day basis.

The 30th during the period under consideration was particularly fortunate in its commanding officers. Although their careers, and what the records tell us about them, belong properly in a study of the officers of the regiment, they are worthy of particular comment because of their extended periods of service and the influence they exercised. They also tell us much about the men who commanded British battalions during the Revolutionary and Napoleonic period.

Sir William Wilkinson, third son of a gentleman of extensive property in Northumberland and County Durham, joined the 30th as an ensign in 1773, was promoted through to lieutenant-colonel (1795) and did not leave the regiment until 1815. His first experience of action, after five years in Ireland, was in the later stages of the War of American Independence. At the outbreak of the Revolutionary War he served as a marine in the Mediterranean, in which role he accompanied a large detachment of the regiment to Toulon where Admiral Hood was supporting the Royalist rising against the newly-formed Republic. Captain Wilkinson was appointed town major. This made him responsible for the evacuation of the town when the Republicans, aided by a rising gunnery captain, Napoleon Buonaparte, finally overwhelmed the Royalists and their British and Spanish allies. He managed this task so successfully that he was personally recommended to Sir David Dundas, in command of the land forces, although this did not lead to his name being mentioned in despatches, a bitter disappointment for a conscientious officer.

From Toulon Hood redirected his energies to Corsica and Wilkinson was involved in the campaign which took possession of Bastia. After another period in Ireland, where he served with a brigade of Irish militia light companies during the rebellion, he then accompanied the regiment to Sicily, from where they sailed to Malta under the command of Sir Thomas Graham. As a further testimony to his competence he was offered command of a newly-formed Maltese corps and although he turned it down he must have been gratified by the compliment. To him fell the honour of receiving the keys of Valletta when the French finally surrendered. He also saw action in Egypt, although his active service was disrupted by attacks of dysentery and ophthalmia.

When a second battalion was established in 1803, Wilkinson was second lieutenant-colonel in the regiment. He was attached to the senior battalion, and took command a year later upon the departure of Charles Green, who had been absent for some time in Grenada. When the battalion went to India in 1806 Wilkinson was on the general list but, as he himself explained in his statement of service, being unable to get employment he rejoined his regiment and served with them in India until 1815. While in India he dealt firmly but fairly with a mutiny by officers in the service of the East India Company; as a result of his decisive action, the men of the regiment in question did not join the general unrest. When he left for Europe, he received fulsome thanks from the governor and council of Bombay

> for the cordial and zealous co-operation which we have invariably received from you in the promotion of the important interests committed to our charge, a sense of which we shall not fail to report to the Honourable Company, for the Information of His Majesty's Government.

Wilkinson's military career ended in frustration. The reduction of the army after Waterloo meant there was no position for a superannuated general. Twenty years later his health began to give way; by 1840 a severe attack of dropsy was causing him constant pain and sleepless nights. On the 17th March, towards midnight, a single pistol shot indicated that this strong-minded man, in his eighties, had made a decision to end his suffering.

As for Wilkinson's relations with the officers of the 30th, two contrasting pieces of evidence convey something of the nature of the man. Both come from 1810, when he was in command of the Southern Division in India. His refusal to accept the lenient sentence imposed by a court martial on Lieutenant Nicholson, whom he had accused of fomenting tension within the officer corps, indicates that he was a stickler for proper conduct. At the same time, he wrote a generous testimonial for Brevet Major Sir Charles Burdett, in which he described him as 'intelligent, active & zealous in the performance of his military duties, and that few officers can be better entitled to promotion than he is, nor any more likely to do credit to whatever rank he is preferred to'. These words could almost be a description of Wilkinson himself.

William Lockhart began his career with the 33rd Foot in 1781, remaining with them until the end of 1783, by which time he had been promoted lieutenant and had seen active service in North America. After two months on half-pay he exchanged into the 30th, with whom he spent the next twenty years. Although not involved in the events at Toulon because he was with that part of the regiment which was still in England, he saw action in Corsica in 1794. He experienced further action at the capture of Malta (1800) and was commended for his distinguished conduct in the Egyptian campaign a year later. As he reported in his 1810 statement of service, having fought at the Battle of Alexandria and the 'Affair of Rahmanieh', he 'Commanded the regt at the affair of the Green Hill near Alexandria 17 Aug when it charged & repulsed a superior body of the enemy, under the fire of their own batteries.' General Hutchinson, in command, wrote in his despatch that the action

> afforded one more opportunity to display the promptness of the British Officers, and the heroism of the British soldiers…The enemy [about 600 men] advanced in columns with fixed bayonets, and without firing a shot, till they had got very close to the 30th Regiment, to whom Col. Spencer gave an immediate order to charge though they did not consist of more than 200 men, he was obeyed with spirit and determination worthy of the highest panegyric.[11]

Having risen to captain in 1793 and major in 1795, he was promoted to lieutenant-colonel in 1803, and as the junior at this rank assumed command of the newly-formed second battalion. By the end of 1804, though, he moved to the first battalion as a result of Lieutenant-Colonel Green's promotion to the general list. He served with Lord Cathcart's abortive expedition to North Germany, before sailing to India in 1806. That same year he was in command of a detachment from the battalion serving with Admiral Pellew's squadron in the Far East. In this capacity, at the end of the following year, he was involved in the successful surrender of Gressie, held by the Dutch, and the seizure of four ships and various stores. Admiral Pellew, in his despatch, expressed 'his Approbation of the Zeal and Perseverance manifested by the respective Officers and Men employed upon the Service above mentioned'. This included Lockhart 'commanding the Troops'.

From this point onwards his presence with the battalion in India was intermittent as he fulfilled various staff roles before his final promotion to the general list in 1814. A year later, though, aged 61, he found himself on the retired list. Three years later his widow was receiving a pension in his name for herself and their children.

Lockhart was succeeded in command of the first battalion by Philip Vaumorel, who had purchased the position of captain-lieutenant with the 30th in 1793, after thirteen years with the 57th Foot. He had served in North America but his first taste of action with his new regiment came at Toulon, where he demonstrated both personal courage and strict obedience to orders. Vaumorel was at Fort Mulgrave, an entrenched position crucial both to the defence of the town and to the safety of Royal Navy and Spanish vessels in the Inner Harbour. When evacuation became a necessity, the commander of the fort received written orders to do his utmost to hold the position; if the defenders exhausted their ammunition they were to resort to the bayonet. The fort had suffered from well-directed Republican artillery fire for several days when the first concentrated attempt to take it was launched, on the night of the 16th December. The 500 defenders, British and Piedmontese, repulsed an initial attack by about 900 Republicans, and then a second by a greatly augmented force. The officer in command, however, fled during the first attack, leaving Vaumorel to hold the fort in obedience to orders.

The next day yet a third assault was made which quickly overwhelmed the Spanish artillery in the fort. The Spanish rapidly retired, and the assailants swarmed through the embrasures of the entrenchment, leaving the defenders with no choice but to surrender. For Vaumorel and the other survivors, the consequence was a twenty-month imprisonment in France, slightly sweetened perhaps by the realisation that much of the fleet had been able to weigh anchor and move out of range of the Republican guns. He also earned the respect of his enemies, and the commendations of the British command. General Hislop, who had been General Dundas' D.A.G. at Toulon, later wrote in a testimonial for Vaumorel of a 'gallant though unsuccessful defence', and that 'you and the brave soldiers who were with you nobly did their duty'.

Vaumorel was also involved in the successful blockade of Valletta which gave the British possession of Malta, and fought in the Egyptian campaign of 1801, during which he was promoted to major. Like Lockhart, he was with the first battalion as part of Cathcart's failed expedition, and then sailed with them to India, where he spent the rest of his career. Because of Lockhart's involvement with staff duties, Vaumorel was signing the monthly returns from the spring of 1809, and from October of the following year he was listed with the army rank of lieutenant-colonel, followed by regimental rank two months later. Although Lockhart briefly returned to the battalion in 1811, Vaumorel was effectively in command from the beginning of 1809. In 1818, however, he was granted two years' leave for recovery of health. There was no recovery, and he died in 1820, aged 55, a victim of the Indian climate.

When Lockhart transferred to the first battalion, William Minet took his position in the second. He had served briefly with the 30th as captain in 1783 before going on half-pay, and then by purchase into the 4th Foot. When he rejoined the regiment in 1804 he had seen some service in Holland, in 1799; otherwise his experience was mainly confined to garrison duties. Having gained the rank of lieutenant-colonel by brevet in 1798 he was later appointed at his own request to the command of a newly-formed West Indian corps before transferring to the 30th.

At first this must have seemed like another inactive appointment because only the first battalion was expected to go on campaign. Once the senior battalion was in India, however, the junior corps was called into action. In 1809 they sailed to Lisbon under Minet's command. Although they were almost immediately sent on to Gibraltar, a year later they were involved in the defence of Cadiz, and by October 1810 were part of the fifth division, holding the Lines of Torres Vedras.

Minet left the battalion early in 1811, initially on a temporary basis as president of a court martial, but in June he was promoted to the general list. Officially, he remained as lieutenant-colonel with the regiment until 1815, but his association was severed by the promotion. He died in 1821 with the rank of lieutenant-general.

Although his period of command had been relatively brief, to him must go much of the credit for making the second battalion the efficient fighting unit it eventually became, at Badajoz, Salamanca and Villamuriel in the Peninsula, and later at Quatre Bras and Waterloo. According to the adjutant, William Stewart, Minet's departure for Lisbon was generally regretted.

The last of the officers to assume command during the two-battalion period was Alexander Hamilton, in many ways the most distinguished, and certainly the most colourful of them. He had reached the rank of major (1808) when Minet departed, and immediately assumed command of the second battalion. Like Wilkinson, he had joined the regiment as an ensign, in 1787, so that by 1810 he had a wealth of service to look back on. At Toulon he was prominently involved in the storming of Mount Faron, and was severely wounded in the leg at Cap Brun. He recovered to serve in Corsica, leading the successful storming of the Convention redoubt in the early stages of the campaign. While serving as a marine he quelled a mutiny, for which he received the thanks of Captain (later Vice-Admiral) Campbell. Having been Sir John Moore's brigade-major in Malta, he then accompanied the 30th to Egypt and was thanked by General Doyle in brigade orders for his part in the action on the 17th August which won such commendations for Lockhart. Even before he took command of the second battalion he had already been 'Employed in the Command of Sundry Light Battalions in Ireland & in the Expedition to Portugal' (Statement of Service 1810), receiving thanks and certificates for his services, which seem to have been exceptional.

Minet's departure meant that Hamilton commanded the battalion during the successful pursuit which drove Masséna out of Portugal, and at Fuentes de Oñoro (May 1811) where he was yet again wounded.

He was to be wounded a third time at Quatre Bras where, to quote his obituarist,

> with that generous solicitude he always evinced for his officers and men, but forgetful that his duties as commanding officer demanded he should not expose himself, ordered the battalion to stand fast, while he singly approached [a] hedge to reconnoitre. The cavalry were not visible; but two tirailleurs who had posted themselves in a tree, both fired at the Colonel: one of their shots hit him in the left leg, the ball obliquely passing between the bones.

Before this, he had led the battalion into action at Salamanca and Villamuriel, as well as commanding them through Graham's Flanders expedition in 1814. Yet his career with the 30th might have ended in 1811, when he was promoted to lieutenant-colonel in a West Indian regiment. Because his replacement had been severely wounded at the first siege of Badajoz, the promotions were cancelled and Hamilton returned to the 30th at his new rank.

Upon reduction, Hamilton went to India in 1818 with the remnants of the second battalion, assuming command of the regiment upon Vaumorel's death. He returned to England after ten years in India during which he was given the brevet rank of colonel and served as brigadier to the Hyderabad Subsidiary forces. A year later he retired from the army.

He died in his seventy-third year, 'worn out', to use the term found on so many old soldiers' discharge papers. As his obituarist wrote indignantly in the *United Services Journal*, 'although twice *severely* wounded' he retired '*without any pension*, although until the date of his decease he was suffering for a series of years from a constitution broken down by the vicissitudes of climate to which he had been subjected in his arduous career.' According to Macready, the decline had set in before Hamilton left India. His command had become so lax that

> he – an officer of 40 years standing – who had proved himself a gallant soldier by land and sea – been often wounded and who bore upon his breast four honourable testimonials of his service – reduced himself to the degrading predicament of being cautioned before a body of the Company's officers by a fellow 'that never set a squadron in the field nor the division of a battle knows more than a spinster.'[12]

However, this is not to detract from a career distinguished by forty-three years of dedicated service and two exceptional talents. The first was his ability to bring a battalion rapidly and effectively to a high state of discipline and efficiency, as he demonstrated when in command of the provisional battalion formed by combining four companies of the 2/30th and four of the 2/44th, in the spring of 1813, and again in the same year in Jersey, when the ten companies of the second battalion were reunited. His other talent, less tangible but equally valuable to a commanding officer, was his ability to endear himself to his officers, NCOs and men, to whom he became a talisman. A man who spent only seven months absent with leave in a career of such longevity and of whom it was believed that '*nothing* will hit him' could indeed be described as an 'ornament of his profession'.

Some differences are perceptible in the command strategies of these men. Wilkinson believed in strict discipline. He was once invited to complain when drafted into marine service in the Mediterranean, but replied, 'If a soldier supposes he has a right to choose his service, there will soon be an end of discipline.' What he demanded of himself, he expected of his men, although his humanity was also much in evidence, demonstrated for example by his visits to the plague hospital in Egypt for as long as men of the 30th were patients there. He also recognised the importance of *esprit de corps*, advising a young relative who was about to join the 30th, 'Be always respectful and obedient to your commanding officer, and never enter into cabals, either with or against any of your brother officers.' It would seem that Vaumorel took the tone of his command from Wilkinson, and also from Lockhart, who had firmly disciplined the newly-formed second battalion. Vaumorel certainly had a reputation as a martinet, a fact commented upon several times by Macready (who seems to have hovered constantly between a desire for strict discipline and resentment of it). Nevertheless, a survey of the variety of punishments imposed by courts martial suggests that Vaumorel came to believe in the lash as a last resort.

It would be easy to conclude that Minet and Hamilton opted for a more relaxed style of command to judge by the consistently lower court martial figures in the second battalion. It is tempting to suggest that the discrepancy is explained by different service: India, where the men had too much time and too little to do other than drink the local arrack; and active service with its demands on the men's time. The first half of that statement is undoubtedly true, but active service was often equally inactive, and it does seem that the second battalion was uncommonly well-disciplined, a fact commented upon in all the inspection reports. The musters, taken on the 25th of each month, provide some evidence of the difference between the two battalions since they record the number of prisoners on that date. These statistics, looked at over time, suggest the overall picture. Using the same four years that demonstrated the fluctuating strength of the two battalions, it is notable that in 1804 the figures are remarkably similar, thirty-one in the first battalion and twenty-six in the second. Four years later both battalions recorded much lower figures, seven in the first and only one in the second. In 1812 the musters show twelve prisoners in the first and none in the second. A similar return for the second battalion four years later is in sharp contrast to the sixty recorded by the first. Although this number includes a minority of men who were serving sentences in solitary confinement, it is still difficult to explain why there had been such a rise in wrongdoing.

There seems little doubt that the 30th were fortunate in their lieutenant-colonels, judged by the less fortunate experience of some other regiments. All five of the men who commanded during the two-battalion period were distinguished by, and commended for their zeal, while four of them had the opportunity to display that gallantry which was the other quality so highly valued by their contemporaries.

Immediately junior to the lieutenant-colonel were the two majors of each battalion. According to James, the

> MAJOR *of a regiment of foot*, the next officer to the lieutenant-colonel, [is] generally promoted from the eldest captain: he is to take care that the regiment be well exercised, to see it march in good order, and to rally it in case of being broken in action: he and the adjutant are the only officers among the infantry that are allowed to be on horseback in the time of action, that they may the more readily execute the colonel's orders.[13]

A battalion was organised into two flanks (or wings), the left being the headquarters flank under the direct command of the lieutenant-colonel, with the junior major as his second-in-command, while the senior major had responsibility for the right flank. In the absence of the lieutenant-colonel, however, the senior major assumed command of the whole battalion, as did Major Bailey after Hamilton was wounded at Quatre Bras. Interestingly, Bailey should have been with the first battalion, who were functioning with just one major, while the second had three. Sometimes both the lieutenant-colonel and the senior major might be absent, whereupon the junior major would take command. This was the situation when Grey led the second battalion into action at Badajoz. If all the field officers were absent or incapacitated, command passed to the senior captain. Thus Bamford after Badajoz and Howard after Waterloo assumed temporary command.

The first of the non-combatant staff officers was the paymaster. He needed to be a man of substance, or at least enjoy the financial support of men of substance, since the first requirement for entering the service as paymaster was a substantial down-payment of £2,000. He had to submit to Horse Guards details of his situation in life, two sureties and the names of four referees. The money was security for his financial probity and, bearing in mind the sums of money that passed through the paymaster's hands, it was probably a necessary insurance against fraud.

Michael Jones joined the regiment in 1797 as an ensign by purchase, becoming paymaster without purchase a year later. In 1803 he was appointed to the first battalion and accompanied them to India in 1807, remaining until 1818, when he transferred to the 80th Foot. Initially, the second battalion was not allowed a paymaster on its establishment but this changed in 1808 when Hugh Boyd Wray joined the regiment. He was an Irishman from Birr, presumably a man of some substance, and 28 upon appointment, which suggests some experience, presumably financial, in civilian life. He also obtained his commission without purchase. Having served with the battalion in the Peninsula and in Flanders, for which he was awarded a Waterloo medal, he went on half-pay upon reduction, but rejoined the regiment when Jones' replacement died in 1819, after only a year's service. His arrival seems to have been greeted with considerable pleasure, which suggests that he carried out his responsibilities beyond what was normally required of a paymaster.

Indeed, there is evidence to this effect in a letter Wray wrote to Lieutenant Lancelot Machell, brother of Captain Richard Machell of the 30th, who had been invalided home after receiving a severe wound at Badajoz. The subject was the

> Sale of Capt. Machell's Horses, which he informed me, were left in Lisbon to be disposed of under your directions, and the Amount to be appropriated to the discharge of some demands due in this Country – since which, I have not had the pleasure of hearing from you. I shall therefore esteem it a favor [sic], your giving me the earliest information respecting the business as your brother must be under some degree of anxiety in it, and I should wish to communicate him, what has been done – I beg leave to add, that the demands, which I believe, Captn Machell to be most anxious about, are due to officers. One of whom (Lieut. Eager) has lately been transferred from the 30th to the 13th Vetns, his Amount is

one hundred & seven Dollars, the other is Lieut. Garvey (now here) whose Amount is one hundred & thirty two Dollars.

Presumably, Machell was not the only officer to entrust his financial affairs to the paymaster.

Wray remained with the regiment until his death, which occurred in 1830, while he was on leave of absence after the regiment returned from India. Like so many officers and men, his health had been broken by the alien climate and conditions.

The first duty of a paymaster was to organise the battalion finances, a function which brought him into close contact with both the pay office and the regimental agent. Just how onerous this responsibility might be in terms of time and travelling, particularly when on active service, is indicated in General Orders. In 1812, for example, the following general orders were addressed specifically to paymasters. On the 16th January they were requested 'to wait upon the Paymaster General at Malhada Sorda to receive the balance due on their estimates to 24th December, 1811', irrespective of where their battalion was posted. Twelve days later they were required to make the same journey to receive payment for their December estimates. That journey was then repeated on the 17th February. Because of the financial problems of the army in 1812, the next order to travel came on the 1st August, with Cuellar as the destination. At the beginning of September there was a sharp warning to paymasters, since 'The Commander of the Forces knows no reason why the accounts of regiments should not be settled as regularly by the Paymasters of regiments in this Army, as by the Paymasters of regiments in England.' This was in response to a complaint from the Secretary at War. The 30th were one of the units specifically instanced, as were most of the other battalions in the Peninsular Army, which suggests that settling such accounts was rather more difficult when battalions were on campaign. Twice in six weeks during the Burgos campaign and subsequent retreat, Villa de Toro was the destination where 'the balance on their several estimates to the 24th May and the 24th of June' would be paid. What happened the second time is not clear, but on the 31st October a general order was received instructing paymasters to report to the Paymaster General at Olmeda where the money for June would be distributed. The last summons for the year came on the 29th December to Malhada Sorda, to receive monies up to the 24th September.

Although it is impossible to calculate how far these various summons required Wray and the other paymasters to journey, particularly at times when the various divisions of the army were widely scattered, it is obvious that in a year of hard campaigning the paymasters were obliged to travel even further than the rest of the army. Thus it is easy to understand why paymasters were granted an allowance for forage for their horses.

Whereas the paymaster had the notional rank of captain, with implications for his pay, the adjutant had specific rank within the battalion, either as lieutenant or as ensign. Indeed, if the 30th are typical of regiments of the period, the adjutant would have this rank before he was appointed to his staff position. There is just one exception to this, as we shall see.

James sums up the duties of the adjutant as easing

> the major of part of the burthen of his duty, and [performing] it in his absence. He receives orders from the brigade major, if in camp; and when in garrison, from the town major. After he has carried them to his colonel or officer commanding the regiment, he then assembles the sergeant-major, drum-major, and fife-major, with a sergeant and corporal of each company, who write the orders to shew to their respective officers. If convoys, parties, detachments, or guards, are to be furnished, he gives the number which each company is to furnish, and hour and place for the assembling: he must keep an exact roster and roll of duties, and have a perfect knowledge of all manoeuvres, etc.[14]

Although the lieutenant-colonel signed the various returns which were then sent to the adjutant-general's office, the adjutant, assisted by the battalion clerk, actually completed them. In his journal, William Stewart complained of the difficulties he faced when his clerk was detained in Lisbon. Sergeant Matthew Donnellan, battalion clerk in 1812, was able to remember exactly the details of a certain Private John Riley's disappearance in Spain four years later, on the occasion of Riley's court martial, because he had recorded them in the muster roll at the time.

According to general orders of 1805 the list of returns required from each battalion included the monthly return, the half-yearly casualty return, the return of women and children belonging to the regiment, also half-yearly, a monthly return of officers, a weekly state, embarkation returns, and returns of recruiting parties. The adjutant was also required to countersign muster and pay lists. In his mind would be the awareness that according to the Articles of War

> every officer who shall knowingly make a false return to the King, to the commander in chief of the forces, or to any his superior officer authorised to call for such returns, shall, upon being convicted thereof before a general court-martial, be cashiered.

Furthermore, 'Whoever shall be convicted of having designedly, or through neglect, omitted sending such returns, shall be punished according to the nature of the offence, by the judgement of a general court-martial.'

Nor did the adjutant's duties end with carrying orders and overseeing the meticulous completion of forms. As Stewart's journal makes clear, he had responsibility for the minutiae of battalion life, including the training of new subalterns, which explains why he had to possess 'a perfect knowledge of all manoeuvres'.

Stewart was the first adjutant to serve with the second battalion. He had joined the 30th in 1802, from the Londonderry Militia and transferred to the second battalion as ensign and adjutant in December 1803. He was promoted to lieutenant a year later, but remained as adjutant until April 1811, when news of his promotion to captain reached the battalion in Spain. Officers of this rank did not serve as adjutants. Two months later, however, Stewart was appointed brigade major to the second division, a position for which his staff experience made him eminently suited and which he held until he was seriously wounded at the blockade of Pamplona in 1813.

Stewart's successor in the second battalion was John Garland, appointed adjutant in May 1811. Like many officers of the period, he had transferred between regiments to effect promotion, beginning his career in 1805 as an ensign in the 44th, then moving as lieutenant to the 27th a year later, and joining the 30th in 1807, still as lieutenant. He learnt of his appointment to adjutant in July 1811, and remained in this post until promoted to captain in the 73rd in November 1813. This promotion was a reward for meritorious services, and the recommendation undoubtedly came from Hamilton, who often drew the attention of Horse Guards to officers of outstanding ability. Garland stood with his old comrades at Waterloo when the 30th and 73rd formed square together.

With the departure of Garland, Matthias Andrew filled the post of adjutant in the second battalion until its reduction. Like Stewart, he was 'home-grown', having joined the regiment in February 1808. In September 1809 he was promoted to lieutenant and then, four years later, appointed adjutant. He demonstrates that the adjutant was not immune to the risks of his fellow officers. Having already been wounded during the action at Villamuriel (25th October 1812), he took a wound at Waterloo while serving as adjutant, not surprisingly, since he was on horseback and his white horse (commented upon by the surgeon, Elkington, in his journal) must have made him quite literally a sitting target. Although no longer adjutant, Andrews went to India with the remnant of the second battalion and remained with the 30th until 1827, when he was promoted to captain in the 44th.

In April 1803, just before augmentation, the adjutant, Alexander Young, was appointed to the Renfrew Militia, and his place was taken by Lieutenant Benjamin Nunn, who had joined the regiment as ensign two years earlier and quickly gained promotion as a result of the need for more officers. In India he served for a period as Assistant Quarter Master General with the Southern Division before being promoted captain. During his time as adjutant he had to deal with a period of unpleasantness among the officers; he even had the responsibility of persuading two officers to sign resignations. Nunn, who died in India in 1813, was succeeded as adjutant by George Stephenson. Unlike the others, he was promoted from regimental sergeant-major to ensign *and* adjutant, and held the position until he died in 1818, when Lieutenant William Atkinson was appointed in the more usual manner, having joined the 30th in 1811. Because of his position on the list of officers, he was one of those obliged to go on half-pay in 1817, but returned a year later as adjutant.

Quartermasters, like paymasters, carried considerable responsibility in material terms, but unlike paymasters quartermasters were not men of substance, although their 'principal business [was] to look after the quarters of the soldiers, their clothing, bread, ammunition, firing, etc'.[15] The temptation towards peculation must have been strong at times, as court martial papers indicate. Their biggest problem, however, might well be their social standing in the mess. It was normal practice for the quartermaster to be a promoted quartermaster sergeant, against whom there could be some prejudice.

The 30th possessed two long-serving quartermasters, Arthur Poyntz and John Foster Kingsley. Poyntz, like most quartermasters, had risen through the ranks, and was promoted from quartermaster sergeant (the usual route) in 1796. He held the position until his death, serving with the first battalion after augmentation, in Ireland and in India. The monthly returns suggest that he was suffering from the effects of the climate by the spring of 1811, when he was recorded as having the commander-in-chief's leave to go to Europe for recovery of health. Why he never left India is unclear, but he died at Madras in February 1812. He seems to have enjoyed the confidence of his superior officers, who were probably instrumental in obtaining commissions for two of his sons (Arthur and Samuel Robert), while his youngest son, James, studied at the Royal Military Academy before also being commissioned into the regiment.

Poyntz was succeeded by Nicholas Wilson, who had served with the 50th Foot as quartermaster since 1805 and whose death in January 1814 led to the interesting appointment of William Ledge, a long-serving soldier with the regiment. Ledge does not appear in the list of officers in *The Historical Records of the XXX Regiment* nor in Bannatyne's *History of the Thirtieth Regiment*. Yet he is identified as quartermaster with the first battalion from April 1814 until December 1815. Since it would have been impossible for the regiment to have organised this appointment through Horse Guards we must surmise that on this occasion, and probably on others, the appointment of a new quartermaster did not necessarily go through this channel. Meanwhile, the death of Poyntz meant that Kingsley had become senior at that rank. In January 1814, when the rest of the second battalion sailed to Flanders, Kingsley remained with the depot in England, waiting for Wilson to arrive from India and replace him in the junior battalion. In October of that year he finally sailed to Flanders, news of Wilson's death having reached the second battalion by this point. A month later, though, the monthly return shows the second battalion with two quartermasters, Kingsley and John Williamson, who had been promoted from quartermaster sergeant on the 27th October. Kingsley now sailed for India, to join his rightful battalion, at which point Ledge became surplus to requirements and his appointment was cancelled, although he was subsequently promoted to ensign.

There is no doubt that a quartermaster could crucially affect the comfort of the men. Kingsley, who features several times in Stewart's journal, is a case in point. For example, on one occasion Captain Bamford reclaimed for his men a proportion of their tobacco allowance which we can only assume the quartermaster had appropriated for his own purposes, presumably financial ones. Kingsley, however, was something of a law unto himself. Again the evidence comes from Stewart's journal. When visiting Lisbon on leave, which meant he had to provide for himself, Stewart was somewhat taken aback by the ease with which Kingsley, also on leave, had been able to make himself comfortable at no expense to himself. As he rather cynically commented: 'Commissaries and Q Masters however are one and the same Family, alike in Honesty and Honour.' (To make the point, he crossed out the last three words.) This did not prevent him from enjoying Kingsley's hospitality, which suggests that the weaknesses of quartermasters were generally recognised and accepted. On another occasion, Kingsley took himself to Lisbon without first obtaining the permission of Hamilton, who was in command of the battalion during Minet's absence. Everyone waited for the inevitable explosion of wrath, since Hamilton had threatened to put Kingsley on a charge, but in the event nothing happened. Perhaps even Hamilton recognised that Kingsley was not a man with conventional notions of service.

Nevertheless, there were times when Kingsley undoubtedly had the good of the battalion at heart, although on one occasion, at Moito on the 1st June 1811, his irascible Irish temper got the better of him. He had been charged with the responsibility of bringing shoes from Lisbon for the battalion, which was stationed on the Spanish-Portuguese border. By the time he reached Moito, he was short of carts. An argument about the availability of carts with Mr Dankerts, a commissary, became a fracas in the streets. This eventually involved an officer of the Royals, Lieutenant Rae, who accused Kingsley of insubordination. Things were made worse when the men of the 30th who were acting as escort attempted to take possession of some commissary carts by stealth. The result was that a month later Kingsley found himself standing a court martial at Campo Mayor. Before giving an outline of what happened from his perspective, he opened his defence with the following plea to the court.

> I shall trespass as little as possible on the attention of this honourable Court, in recapitulating the circumstances so unhappily connected with the situation I am placed in; I trust that in doing so it will appear that however my feelings and judgement have been led astray, I have not with intention acted in any way Criminal, but that the Injuries I had suffered by Robberies committed on the Property I was answerable for, and the serious difficulties I experienced by the Commissary having refused all Assistance to me, together with the very urgent necessity there was for my arrival at the Regiment, with the supplies I had for its use, will I trust be fully considered by this honourable Court, so as to ameliorate the apparent Irregularities alleged against me.[16]

He also presented to the court a testimonial from Hamilton:

> I hereby certify that I have known Quarter Master Kingsley for nearly Eight Years, during which period I have ever considered him, as an Officer and Gentleman, and have known him to have done the most Generous and Kind Acts.

Kingsley was actually charged on three counts: that he had disobeyed army orders by taking possession of bullock carts intended for public service, that he had disobeyed the orders of Lieutenant Rae, his superior officer, and that he had behaved in a disrespectful and insulting manner towards Lieutenant Rae. He was found guilty on the first and third charge but not the second, and was sentenced to be suspended from rank and pay for three months, and receive a public reprimand. This took the form of a general order, to be read to him on parade, in which Wellington made the point that when the commissary 'declined to supply him with the means of conveyance which was necessary to enable him to perform the duty on which he was detached from his regiment, he ought to have reported the circumstance to his Commanding Officer', rather than lose his temper. Yet it is difficult not to sympathise with Kingsley, who undoubtedly believed his first duty belonged to his regiment. Indeed, so effectively did he perform his duty (despite the little matter of the tobacco) that he was particularly commended in an inspection report of 1813 for the excellent care he took in providing the men with the very best food supplies.

And on the subject of quartermasters and food, we have a tale from that disgruntled soldier, James Aytoun, which demonstrates the problems a less efficient (or honest) quartermaster might cause.

> Our pay being as above [5d a day], we were supplied by Quartermaster [Henry] Craig with beef at about 3 1/4d. lb. and when it was boiled it was as dry as chestnut and as brown. We were obliged to make our salt wet with soup or water that it might adhere to the nutbrown beef and our bread was in competition with the beef for colour and quality.

In this situation, some enterprising men in the light company, who had discovered that excellent bullocks' heads could be purchased for two shillings,

> prevailed on the pay sergeant to advance them money and having obtained a pass they went to the victualling office and purchased bullocks' heads at the above price and the meat was rich and less than half the price of Quartermaster Craig's contracted carrion. The consequence was, as our company had supplied themselves, that they refused the contract beef I called carrion...The next step was for the quartermaster to send for the pay sergeant of the company and he was made prisoner and tried by court martial because the men bought provisions better and cheaper than Quartermaster Craig supplied them with.[17]

The remaining three staff officers were all medical men, the surgeon and the two assistant surgeons. Since the medical aspects of their duties warrant extended discussion, and since they were appointed by a different route from the other officers of the regiment, they will be considered separately.

Chapter 3

Scum of the Earth

Were the private soldiers under Wellington's command merely the scum of the earth, the dross of early nineteenth-century society fitted for no other role in life than to serve as cannon fodder? Or do we hear in this acerbic comment the frustration of a man who had led his army to a notable triumph at Vitoria, only to see it frittered away in the swinish rush for money and goods that could be turned into drink? Whatever the truth, there is no doubt that Wellington's judgement on his troops generally echoed popular opinion of the soldier at the time. It has also passed into the mythology of the British army of the Napoleonic period. Yet any attempt to test the accuracy of this prejudice is hampered by the anonymity of the men themselves. True, they have names, dates of enlistment, brief records of service. Their background can be identified from these records, but their motives for becoming soldiers can only be surmised. Nevertheless, something may be learnt about the conduct of these men and the lives they lived by trawling through the records.

Their geographical origins can be identified with certainty. Monthly returns and the returns prepared for inspection reports state exactly the composition of every regiment in terms of national identity. Discharge papers, casualty returns, and attestation papers where they exist, give place of birth and place of enlistment. As a result there are very few men who cannot be placed exactly, and that tends to be because they were discharged without being recommended for a pension, had enlisted for the limited period of seven years, or died before the keeping of detailed casualty returns.

In the broadest geographical context, three circumstances determined the composition of the 30th Regiment. Recruiting parties could not recruit at will. Indeed, a recruiting party of the second battalion was taken to task in 1814 for recruiting in Hungerford, the preserve of another regiment. Consequently, the location of their activities determined the origins of the men they brought into the regiment, numbers varying from a steady stream to a flood. In 1804, for example, in a period of eight months, the first battalion added ten recruits and the second, fifteen. Four years later the first battalion, in India, gained only three recruits, all boys, sons of the regiment, while the second battalion acquired ninety-eight recruits, four of whom deserted, as well as 219 volunteers from the Irish militia. In

1812 the numbers from the depot were 166 recruits (plus forty-five still to join from the recruiting parties at the end of the year) and eighty-seven militia volunteers. By 1816, however, the need for men had eased, and the numbers dropped accordingly, one boy in the first battalion and fifty-three recruits, three of whom deserted, in the second. During the three decades which cover the Revolutionary and Napoleonic Wars the principal areas for recruitment were the east and south-east Midlands and Ireland. In 1803, however, the year of augmentation, there was an inflow of over 1,000 men, the vast majority of them from the Army of Reserve. Three years later there was another influx from the Army of Defence. Both these units were raised in a geographically concentrated manner, similar to the process by which the militia regiments were raised. As a result, those taken in by the 30th came from the Eastern Counties and East Midlands. The transfer to Ireland led to an increase in the number of recruiting parties operating in Ireland, and it also placed both battalions in an ideal position to accept volunteers from the Irish militia regiments. Despite the occasional activities of recruiting parties in Scotland and Yorkshire, the 30th during the two-battalion period was predominantly composed of men from the east of England, labourers, framework-knitters and other textile workers for the most part, and Irishmen, mostly classified as labourers, although weavers constitute a sizeable group.

The discrepancy between the numbers of Irish in the two battalions has already been noted. The difference can be explained by considering the service of the two battalions. When the first battalion went to India in 1806, they took with them their pick of the regiment, many of whom were long-serving English soldiers (including most of the veterans of the 1801 Egypt campaign), and the cream of the men who had come in from the Army of Reserve. It was only after their departure that men from the Irish militias were invited to volunteer for general service, and these were used to complete the strength of the depleted second battalion. These were the men who fought in the Peninsula and at Waterloo, adding to the strong Irish presence in both these theatres of war.

Although nationality conveys something of the nature of the regiment, since there were thought to be marked differences of temperament between soldiers from the different nationalities which made up the British Isles, it does not reveal motives for enlistment. There are two generally accepted reasons, however, why men did not enlist: a prosperous economy and the dire reputation of the army:

> Men of a nation of shopkeepers could not be expected to fly from their desks, benches or counters to the ranks of the worst reputed institution in England. Bad as some of the conditions of industrial life were, there was not present the danger of a public disciplinary flogging; and hard as an employer might be, he did not exercise a control over one's clothing, appointments and mode of walking. A merciless employment might be left; the penalty of desertion was death.[18]

This definitive statement, however, may be as much a simplification as that all soldiers were scum of the earth.

Two social factors suggest motives which go beyond the merely personal. Other than labourers, the most common occupations within the 30th were textile-related. Weaving was a declining occupation. Instead, highly mechanised and centralised alternatives offered considerable reward to entrepreneurs who sank their capital into the new machines but passed little of the profit on to their workers. Similarly the hosiery industry was being transferred from a domestic occupation centred on the family and controlled by middlemen into an industrialised enterprise where again the profit rested in fewer and fewer hands. One way to show one's frustration was to become a Luddite machine-breaker. Another, less drastic option was to volunteer for the army.

A second great social change was brought about by the enclosure movement. Impelled by revolutionary changes in agriculture and justified by the need to feed a growing urban population, it was an inevitable development. Furthermore, it could be justified when the country was at war and under threat of blockade. The interests of tenants whose forebears had farmed small parcels of common land for centuries but who had no documentation to support their claims were easily set aside. Such families might well find themselves 'on the parish'. For men too proud to accept such grudging charity, becoming a soldier might well appear preferable to becoming a pauper. No wonder the 30th found so many willing recruits in the Eastern Counties, where enclosure acts were dispossessing families at an accelerating rate. As with machine-breaking, rick-burning might relieve a man's feelings but it would not feed his family.

There remain, however, the generally accepted motives for enlistment. Recruits were likely to be

> the usual raw stuff swept in by the recruiting sergeant – all those restless spirits who were caught by the attraction of the red coat, country lads tired of the plough, or town lads who lived on the edge of unemployment, and to whom a full stomach had been for some time a rarity.[19]

Then there were men lured into the army by the promise of money, which meant the promise of drink, or to escape the shotgun wedding, and others who reckoned army life preferable to prison if given the choice. Personal circumstances might also drive men into the army, particularly apprentice lads serving harsh masters who did not have the option of simply walking away.

John Shipp, an enlisted man who was twice commissioned, remembered how, while standing in a frozen Norfolk turnip field trying to warm his fingers by placing them in his mouth, he heard the sound of martial music. He ran to see the sight:

> Just at this moment the whole band struck up *Over the Hills and Far Away*, which kindled a flame in my bosom which nothing but death can extinguish, though I have long since had my fair share of the reality of the Scotch melody.

This experience motivated him to escape a cruel master and join the army.[20]

As has already been noted, there was an appreciable influx from the militia after 1807. These, like the men of the Army of Reserve (also known as the supplementary militia), either volunteered for service or were chosen by ballot if there was a shortfall in numbers. Substitution was possible on payment of a fine, and there were enough exemptions to prevent the system too closely resembling conscription. The county-based units were regularly officered. The period of service was four years, and was confined to the British Isles. This could explain the readiness to transfer into the regular army because life in a home station was not exciting, nor was there any chance of action once the threat of invasion had passed. Service in a fighting unit promised adventure. Furthermore, there was the bounty offered, between £16 and £40. For those who had originally volunteered into the militia, this was a second bounty. Private William Wheeler, for example, wrote to his family:

> I have at length escaped from the Militia without being flead [sic] alive. I have taken the first opportunity and volunteered together with 127 of my comrades into the 51st Light Infantry Regiment. I had made up my mind to volunteer but into what regiment I cared not a straw, so I determined to go with the greatest number.[21]

To take a less cynical view, and one justified by some surviving soldier accounts, a sense of duty and patriotism was not unknown among the men in the ranks. Sergeant Morris, for example, described in his *Recollections* how, at the age of 16 he joined the Loyal Volunteers of St George's Middlesex, not to secure exemption from being drawn to serve in the Militia, the motive of many of his comrades, but from a sense of honour:

> ...other motives influenced me. I was particularly fond of reading the heart-stirring accounts of sieges and battles; and the glorious achievements of the British troops in Spain, following each other in rapid succession, created in me an irrepressible desire for military service; so, as the first step towards it, I became a Volunteer, and, oh! How proud did I feel when having gone through my course of drill, I was permitted to join the ranks.

He later joined the 73rd (Highlanders), the regiment with which his brother served, having 'felt at times almost ashamed of being only half a soldier'.[22]

Men from the militia were generally regarded as a benefit to the regular army; thus Castlereagh's decision to allow the regular army to draw in volunteers from the militia had an immeasurable effect upon the strength of the Peninsular army. These men had drilled for at least twelve months, in a corps which had been training men for many years: they were, therefore, preferable to the raw recruits who had been obtained by the recruiting companies. The influx from the militia certainly worked in favour of the second battalion; these volunteers could not serve outside Europe which meant they could not be transferred to the first battalion. Instead, they strengthened the junior battalion and were contributory to its good performance in the Peninsula.

Far less favourable was the reputation of the men who came in from the Army of Reserve. As Fortescue demonstrated, taken overall they did not provide the influx that was hoped for. By concentrating on the 15,000 who died, deserted or proved unfit for service, however, he tended to underrate the 30,000 men who proved effective soldiers, two-thirds of whom transferred into regular units.

For the 30th, the men from the Army of Reserve were crucial to augmentation, and it is instructive to examine the records in order to establish what became of them. The judgement that 'sickness and desertion were very great'[23], even when supported by precise figures, is open to question. Of the 1,595 men from the Army of Reserve who were transferred into the 30th in 1803, only 418 had left the regiment by the end of 1806, a period long enough to constitute reasonable service. This date also avoids the heavy death rate suffered by the first battalion during their first two years in India, and the number who transferred into garrison battalions in 1807 when they were given the choice of garrison service or general service. Even 418 is a misleading statistic, since it includes 136, surplus to requirements, who volunteered for other units, forty-five who were rejected and sent back to the Army of Reserve, six claimed as deserters and one claimed as an apprentice. Seventy-three deserted and eighty-six died in the period under consideration, but both figures represent a small part of the total desertions and deaths. As for the 171 men who were discharged, although this is all but fifty of the total, it still represents a good return on the original intake. Indeed, the 30th can be said to have benefited from the Army of Reserve; without it, there could have been no second battalion.

Although economic necessity, a taste for adventure, a sense of duty, even the lure of the bounty offered, represent positive motives for enlisting, there still remain the king's hard bargains, recruits drawn from the semi-criminal classes, or those corrupted by such men. There were individuals for whom the army represented a chance to disappear from the attention of such law enforcers as existed in Georgian England. Sir John Colborne claimed that most regiments had about fifty such characters, men who could not be tamed even by the ferocity of military discipline. Oman went further, suggesting that the majority of men brought before courts martial were Irish, thus ascribing the delinquency disproportionately to Irish soldiers.

The 30th, as a finely balanced Anglo-Irish regiment, provides an interesting study in this respect. Although crime, punishment and courts martial are considered elsewhere, the matter of nationality is relevant to this discussion of *the scum of the earth*.

The second battalion, with its roughly equal numbers of English and Irish soldiers provides a relevant example, even though there were fewer offenders than in the first battalion. In a period of four years when regimental courts martial were included in inspection returns there was a ratio of 3:4, English to Irish offenders. This would suggest that the Irish were indeed more likely to offend but not to the extent that would justify them being regarded as the source of most indiscipline in the battalion. Furthermore, of the four most regular offenders in this battalion, three were English.

Harsh punishment was not the only discomfort for the men in the ranks. To borrow Gibbons' comment, the life of the average soldier could prove nasty, brutish and, if sent to an unhealthy or dangerous posting, short. However, this may be a modern perception. If the soldier is considered contemporaneously, he enjoyed certain advantages, particularly if he came from the impoverished classes. Army discipline was brutal (although civilian punishment was not exactly gentle); it might be sharper but it was definitely shorter. The army could not afford to keep its trained soldiers in disease-infested prisons, so a more immediate form of punishment was required. Similarly, the soldier might suffer the lash for crimes which would be likely to earn the death penalty in the civil courts. Transportation was an option for both civil and military courts, but was used more rarely by the latter. Even when the soldier had been transported, he still functioned as a soldier in a penal corps.

In a period when the only welfare system, if such it can be entitled, was a random charitable lottery, the soldier could at least depend upon receiving clothing, food and shelter. Although the military medical services were still rudimentary in many respects, they were probably no worse and may well have been better than what was available to the great mass of the population, and they were given freely to the soldier.

Military accommodation was an ongoing problem for the authorities at a time when the army was expanding rapidly, from 40,000 men in 1792 to 250,000 in 1814. A scattering of purpose-built barracks supported by a system of billeting in inns could not house this increase. Encampment, such as the 30th experienced at the Curragh during the first period of Irish service, was a possibility in summer but as soon as the weather deteriorated something more substantial was required.

Before 1792 the Ordnance Board had beds for 40,000 men in their permanent establishments, more than enough for soldiers on home service. Much of this accommodation, however, was in the north, north-west and Scotland, against the Jacobite threat of earlier times. The Revolutionary Wars posed a different geographical threat. Once the Low Countries were under French control, both the south and east coasts were recognised as possible invasion points, but they lacked accommodation for the troops needed to guard the seaboard approaches to London. Indeed, the pressure of billeting and the resentment it aroused was so great that landlords in Kent and Sussex removed their inn signs, an action which could have cost them their licences.

Significantly, there were at least twenty-one petitions to parliament urging the building of barracks, and in response a building programme commenced. Initially durable materials were used but by 1803, when the threat of invasion seemed imminent after the collapse of the Peace of Amiens, a more temporary approach was adopted. The barracks at Chelmsford and Woodbridge, where the two battalions of the 30th spent the second half of 1803, were built of wood, Chelmsford having been constructed in 1794 to hold 1,700 men. Nearby Colchester expanded in 1803 to accommodate 7,000 troops. Thus the 30th formed part of a concentration of military units guarding the coast between the Thames and the Ore.

Barracks, as with everything else military, were controlled by the minutiae of regulation; and the rules which related to supplies and allocation of space give some idea of the life of the soldier. Coal, candles and fuel were all regularly provided, as was the basic furniture (beds). The barracks were also supplied with sheets, blankets, towels, chamber pots, ironmongery, cooking utensils, coal buckets, bellows, candlesticks, and cleaning implements, which may have represented luxury for some men. As for space, whereas field officers were allowed two rooms, and company officers one room each, with another two rooms to serve as the mess dining room and an ante-room (Chelmsford was the first barracks where the officers of the 30th definitely enjoyed this arrangement), the men in the ranks were as many as twelve to a room. Since the size of rooms in different barracks varied greatly, the men suffered varying degrees of overcrowding, although this was something many of them would have been familiar with. They might find themselves sleeping in bunks, but the more usual arrangement was two men to each wooden bed.

Throughout their time in England and Ireland the 30th Regiment, particularly the second battalion, experienced a wide range of barracks. The junior battalion mustered at Bromswell camp, then moved to the hutted accommodation of Chelmsford before moving to the new, temporary camp at Woodbridge, which was also hutted. Here they experienced timber-framed and weather-boarded buildings, constructed on site since prefabrication was yet to be discovered. They may well have slept in two-tier bunks, or hutches, rather than beds, as this was the preferred sleeping arrangement in the newer barracks. The Woodbridge barracks lasted two years and the only evidence of their existence is a Barracks Road on the outskirts of the modern town. Since the battalion spent only two months there it is unlikely the place made much impression on the men, although the officers may have appreciated the entertainment offered locally by the small theatre.

By the beginning of 1804 both battalions were in Ireland, where they found a very different situation from the one that pertained in England. Since the reign of William III government policy accommodated soldiers in barracks, and few towns of any size lacked such facilities. Many of them were old and dilapidated, and there was much rebuilding at the end of the eighteenth and beginning of the nineteenth century. Furthermore, the rebellion of 1799 and the subsequent French invasion made secure accommodation for soldiers in strategic places an urgent necessity. These Irish barracks, old and new, were built of durable materials to house what many Irish regarded as an army of occupation, and what at best might be described as a supernumerary police and revenue force.

During their first period in Ireland, the second battalion was posted at Mullingar, Moate, Longford and Athlone in the Irish Midlands, Dublin (George

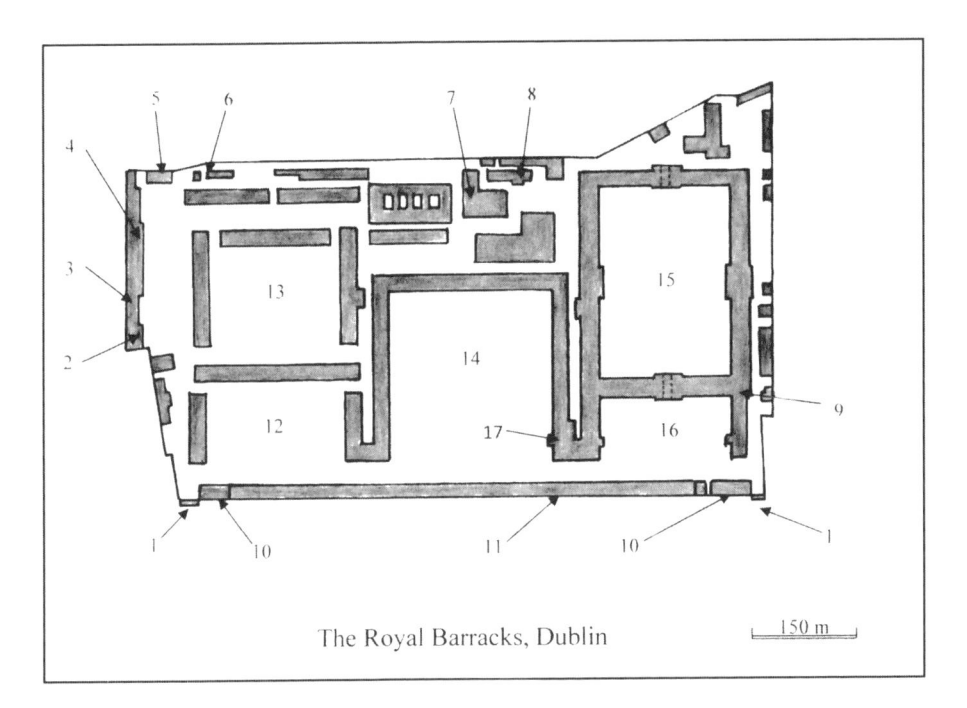

The Royal Barracks, Dublin

1 Entrance	9 Barrack master's quarters, stores and office
2 Barrack sergeants' Quarters	10 Guardhouse
3 Armourers workshop	11 Barrack master's quarters
4 Officers' stables	12 Cavalry square
5 Washhouse	13 Stable square
6 Soldiers' privies	14 Royal square
7 Canteen and cookhouse	15 Palatine square
8 Barrack sergeants' quarters	16 Brunswick square

Street and Royal barracks), and Strabane, Londonderry and Omagh in the north. The first battalion, during a briefer stay, were at Tullamore and Dublin. The Royal Barracks in Dublin are particularly well documented. Sanctioned by the Irish parliament in 1700 and completed nine years later, they were designed in a style to rival the royal military hospitals at Kilmainham and Chelsea. Not surprisingly considering their grandeur they were known in the mid-eighteenth century as the Grand Barracks, becoming the Royal Barracks in 1803. By the time the second battalion were in occupation, however, they were no longer the magnificent buildings of the early eighteenth century. Although the edifices were still impressive, the jerry-built construction was causing serious interior decay.

Most of this first Irish sojourn was spent in the Irish Midlands, in the towns and villages around Tullamore. There was a general belief that the French still planned to invade Ireland, so 'permanent and temporary barracks… accommodated men that could quickly be deployed to assist in the defence of the line of the Shannon, or take the offensive against an enemy force'.[24] Second battalion headquarters were at Moate, with detachments at Clara and Kilbeggan. This last had a notable distillery, Locke's, so they also served as revenue men. The barracks in Tullamore could accommodate twenty-two officers and 1,026 men, while the smaller barracks at Moate and Kilbeggan could hold eleven officers and 360 men, and twelve officers and 400 men respectively. It is probable that the detachment in Clara was billeted in inns and private houses, which must have increased the feeling among the local population that they were being occupied by a foreign power. There are no records of any disturbances, however.

The first battalion left Ireland in November 1805, initially to join Lord Cathcart's expedition to North Germany, and when that was aborted, to sail to India, where they remained for the next twenty-three years. Much of their time was spent in Madras, in Fort St George, which Macready described as

> a regular fortification composed of three full and two demi bastions, the latter works appiu'd on a line wall, which runs *en cremaillères* along the beach. The curtains are covered by cavaliers and lunettes. The ditch is wet, except between the curtain and the ravelin of the north face which are connected by a strong caponnier, and the former cut by a tenaille. In this part a cunette is cut. The counterscarp is faced with a revetment and defended by a palisaded covered way and a glacis, which I believe is mined.

So much for the technicalities of military architecture. Macready also commented upon practicalities, such as that the fort

> had more to fear from the ocean than from the enemy, as the surf, which was once half a mile from it, in bad weather breaks against it, notwithstanding a vast pile of stones which has been thrown between them at the expense of eight shillings a pebble. There are provisions for years, and numerous reservoirs of water, together with an admirably supplied arsenal within the Fort, so that its capture by anything but a European army is impossible.

None of this, however, could compare with his reaction upon arrival from Europe:

> The first day I passed thro' the barracks amid swarms of half-naked drunkards tumbling over or laying [sic] sleeping in their cots, I was surprised to see hundreds of black and yellow concubines, and doubly so when I was told the Honourable East India Company allowed each of them a pagoda per month for prostituting herself to an European soldier.[25]

The second battalion, after a stay in Ulster where a detachment had been engaged in suppressing illicit whiskey stills in Omagh, returned to the Irish Midlands and the barracks of Longford and Athlone, the former too small to accommodate the whole battalion but the latter roomy enough for 160 officers and 1,452 men. In March 1809 the battalion sailed to Portugal, before moving on to Gibraltar, a British garrison town for nearly a century. The South Barracks, which had been completed in 1730 in Palladian style, offered rather better accommodation than anything the battalion had so far encountered. At the end of the previous century Gibraltar had been notorious for the laxity of military discipline and the unruly behaviour of the underemployed soldiers. By the time the second battalion arrived, the Duke of Kent had transformed the situation by the imposition of extreme discipline.

> He placed all but three of the wine shop out of bounds to soldiers and opened 'Canteens' selling weak beer brewed by the British Army Brewery. He also imposed a working day of dawn to half past four in the afternoon: it was a diet of drill, drill and drill again – officers and soldiers alike.[26]

The punishments he imposed were also draconian, with the result that there were plots against his life. As a result, he was quickly recalled, but the legacy of his approach to discipline lived on.

The second battalion left Gibraltar for Cadiz in September 1809, and did not experience barracks life again until 1813, when six skeleton companies augmented by recruits were posted to Berwick, some of the roomiest military accommodation in the British Isles. Each soldier was allowed 450 cubic feet, against the usual range of from 196 to 448 cubic feet. There was a notional capacity of 642 men but when the six companies arrived they mustered only 237 men, with eighteen officers. Since the surgeon, Elkington, remarked in his journal that they 'had but little society' in barracks which he described as 'very old but substantial', there must have been room to spare.

The six companies did not enjoy this superior accommodation for long, however. After a couple of months they were posted to Jersey where they were joined by the remaining four companies, recently returned from the Peninsula. Apart from some detachments posted to various coastal points to watch for a French invasion, the men were engaged on the King's works, which may have involved the road-making programme initiated by General Don, the governor, or the construction of Fort Regent, the extensive fortifications designed to protect St Helier and only completed, somewhat ironically, as the Napoleonic Wars came to an end. Accommodation was at Grouville in 'wooden barracks built some years before for the Russians'.[27]

It was back to the *ad hoc* arrangements of active service in 1814 and 1815, which meant anything from being billeted on local householders to being squeezed into barns when not in camp. January 1816 saw the battalion back in Ireland where they were accommodated in barracks at Limerick and Tralee. Elkington described the barracks at Limerick as 'not good, the mess room so small that nearly half were obliged to dine in the reception room'. Tralee barracks, on the other hand, were considered good. It is interesting to note this meticulous recording of barrack conditions in the surgeon's journal, since it conveys the importance of accommodation to the officers. Whether the men were quite so nice in their requirements probably depended on their background; backgrounds more varied than might perhaps be expected.

James in his *Regimental Companion* provides a valuable source of contemporary information on the subject of barracks and quarters. He outlines not only the rules and regulations of barrack life but also suggests what he obviously regarded as desirable changes. These would undoubtedly have been endorsed by the soldiers of the day since they included such humanitarian suggestions as the belief that soldiers' wives should receive a reasonable allowance and weekly pay for the work they did, as well as decent berths, whether in camp, barracks or quarters. At the time husband and wife rarely enjoyed more privacy than a blanket suspended between their marital bed and the next. Furthermore, women and children could stay in barracks with their menfolk not as a right but as a privilege expressly granted by the barrack master.

James also included considerable detail about hygiene. For example, before quitting the barracks for a new posting the men were expected to leave everything in good order. After their departure the rooms would be thoroughly fumigated, while the incoming men would be supplied by the barrack master with a pair of clean sheets, at 3d a man for a two-man bed, and 2d a pair for a single bed. These were changed and washed every month. There was also one round towel per room, fixed on a roller, and this was changed every week, at a charge of a penny for washing. Against this, however, was the absence of latrines in many barracks, which meant each room was supplied with a communal chamber pot which had to be emptied every morning. This was essentially a wooden tub, unpleasant enough, but familiar to those men who came from homes where several families occupied the same floor of a building. The army was at least insistent upon the regular removal and disposal of waste matter.

Any furniture or utensils wantonly destroyed were charged to the regiment, which probably encouraged commanding officers to observe the regulation requiring them to send a junior officer each day on a tour of inspection, to include each room occupied by NCOs and privates, as well as the kitchens and infirmary. The regimental courts martial of the 30th contain only one reference to wanton damage, which suggests that the regulation was taken seriously. There were also restrictions on the men's time. Lights out was nine o'clock, by which time all fires (used for cooking when there were no kitchens) and candles had to be extinguished.

The situation in billets was similar. Quarters were inspected on a daily basis to record any damage. Instead of receiving their supplies from the barrack master, though, the men were entitled to candles, vinegar, salt, use of fire and utensils for the dressing and eating of meat from the landlord. The actual food, as in barracks, was supplied by the regimental quartermaster. Alternatively, a landlord might choose to board his military lodgers, in which case he would receive 1/- a day for a subaltern, and 10d for a man in the ranks. The men received no extra money for being outside barracks, but officers were granted a weekly allowance which ranged from 10/6d for field officers to 6/- for subalterns.

On campaign, of course, the situation would be very different. In the short period covered by the journal of William Stewart, adjutant of the 2/30th, there are references to encampment, behind the Lines of Torres Vedras, for instance, when tents appear to have been used as shelter, and billeting in a variety of circumstances, ranging from Portuguese hovels to monasteries and castles. The hovels, in the general opinion, were worse than the habitation of the Irish, made even more unpleasant by the habit of the retreating French of leaving their dead inadequately buried. Wellington's general orders make clear that certain levels of respect were required for the properties the men found themselves occupying. For example:

> The Commander of the Forces requests that the General Officers and Commanding Officers of Regiments will take measures to prevent the soldiers from using the doors and windows, and pulling down the timbers of the houses for fire wood. The consequences will be that the soldiers will be without quarters, besides the serious injury that these practices occasion to the inhabitants of the country.[28]

Property was not just the buildings because the Commander of the Forces felt the need to 'inform the Soldiers that the *wine casks* are a most valuable property to the people of this country, and he desires that they may not be destroyed'.[29]

These orders were repeated at regular intervals, but soldiers were notorious for thinking in the short term. Indeed, they did not hesitate to cut down the olive and fruit trees to fuel their fires as another general order makes clear. This time Wellington suggested that

> parties on fatigue from each regiment should be sent out every morning to cut the quantities of wood required for fires; as there is no want of fire wood in the neighbourhood of all the cantonments, there can be no occasion for cutting the olive trees for that purpose.[30]

The cleanliness and health of the men was also an issue to which Wellington gave his attention. He requested 'that now the troops will have arrived in their positions [behind the Lines], the General Officers commanding divisions will order them to clean themselves'.[31] He intimated further that he would be carrying out inspections to make sure that the order was observed. He also arranged a supply of rice to the men, a pound to eight men, since this was thought to protect against flux and fever. Perhaps most significant, though, was his concern about the conditions of quarters after the French had abandoned them. He requested, a polite synonym for *ordered*, that

> the Officers commanding Regiments will be very cautious in occupying the *quarters* in which French troops may have been quartered, to make their men clean them well out before they sleep in them; and, if possible, to have fires lighted in them, but care must be taken not to burn the house. These precautions will be found to contribute much to the health of the Soldiers.[32]

Much of a soldier's time, whether at home or on campaign, would be spent on the march. Inevitably, a good many regulations covered the departure and marching order of a battalion. Even before the march commenced, the commanding officer, the quartermaster, and the sergeant responsible for billeting (if this was to be the men's accommodation at the end of the march) needed copies of the route. On home territory this would be a routine matter. Abroad, as Stewart complained, routes could be mistaken and the men would find themselves tramping through vineyards or struggling across wild country with little more than goat tracks to guide them. A nominated route might save them from trouble, however. The fifth division avoided the worst excesses of the retreat from Burgos when their route took them through Cordovilla rather than Torquemada and its tempting wine vats. It is probable that their conduct at Villamuriel soon afterwards would have been less distinguished if they had been suffering from the collective hangover which seems to have been the condition of the French troops who had enthusiastically mopped up what the Anglo-Portuguese army had left behind.

Under normal circumstances captains of companies were required to check the dress, accoutrements and necessaries of their men. This might be extended into another duty which James recommended:

> Among other arrangements for the interior government of the companies before the commencement of a march, the adjusting or fitting the straps of the knapsacks, so as not to incommode or fatigue the soldier unnecessarily, is a most material object. The regular complement of a soldier may be carried with ease, but while bits of cord or packthread are allowed to supply the deficiency of proper straps, and the men are suffered to let their knapsacks rest upon their pouches, galled shoulders and oppressed loins must inevitably ensue.[33]

The straps of the knapsack, which were separate from the knapsack itself (hence James' reference to substitute arrangements), passed under the armpits and across the chest. This constriction caused considerable discomfort, or even death in sickly men. During the light company's dash for Quatre Bras, the officers cut the straps when some of the men fell out, black in the face. It was generally agreed that French knapsacks were more comfortable, and after every action they would become highly-prized battle trophies.

Shoes and stockings also needed attention, to prevent sore feet and corns. New shoes should not be worn on the march, in James' opinion, and wherever possible men should be made to wash their feet after the march.

The knapsacks, which could cause such discomfort to the soldiers, were made of rough leather or painted glazed canvas and contained a man's necessaries, which meant in practice his worldly possessions. Fully loaded, with his musket, the marching soldier was carrying about 60lb weight. After six years the knapsack became his property, but if it was lost in the meantime stoppages would be imposed. This was a grievance which annoyed two men of the second battalion who were subsequently transferred to the first. Having lost their knapsacks during the Waterloo campaign, they were without them in India. Their complaints reached the inspecting general, who commented:

Privates Michael Lynch & John Twite state that they lost their knapsacks & necessaries when carried off the Field of Battle, wounded on the 16th and 18th June at Waterloo…the two men's claims are to be sent to Europe where no doubt the remuneration they expect to receive will be granted them.

On the morning of the march there were three 'beats': the first was general; the second, assembly; and the third, the order to march. Unless the situation was urgent, half an hour elapsed between each beat. In a critical situation, however, the routine which the soldier had been trained to observe and which was automatic to him, had to be abandoned. This in turn could lead to a further breakdown in discipline, as was observed when the army was in retreat.

Departure from Lisbon might take the following form:

To my great joy we paraded in the grand square…and marched in sections, to the music of our bugles, to join the army, having got our camp equipments, consisting of a camp kettle and bill-hook to every six men, a blanket, a canteen and a haversack to each man. Orders had been given that each soldier on his march, should carry alongst with him three days' provisions. Our mess of six cast lots who should be the cook the first day, as we were to carry the kettle about. The lot fell to me. My knapsack contained two shirts, two pairs of stockings, one pair overalls, two shoe brushes, a shaving box, one pair spare shoes, and a few other articles; my greatcoat and blanket above the knapsack; my canteen with water was slung over my shoulder on one side. My haversack with beef and bread on the other; sixty round of ball cartridge, and the camp kettle above all.[34]

Apart from the bugles, which denoted a light infantry regiment, this procedure would have been familiar to the men of the second battalion.

The normal procedure for the conduct of the march placed the commanding officer with the first division of the battalion, the right wing, which had the colours, the adjutant, quartermaster, surgeon, drum major, drill sergeant, recruits and heavy baggage. The rear division, the left wing, was commanded by the junior lieutenant-colonel or senior major, and was accompanied by the assistant surgeons, sergeant-major and quartermaster sergeant. Should the battalion be divided into three divisions, the last would be accompanied by an acting sergeant-major and a steady sergeant, acting as quartermaster sergeant.

A mile outside the town where the battalion was to be quartered the billeting sergeant, who was sent ahead for the purpose, met his commanding officer and gave him details of the pre-arranged billets. These were allocated by company before the battalion entered the town.

Once the battalion was in the town, the quartermaster waited on the chief magistrate. He had to show the route the battalion had received which was, in effect, its passport into the town. He also made a request for the required number of wagons required to convey the regimental baggage, at the rate of one wagon and four horses per company. This was probably a formality on home service but, as Quartermaster Kingsley's court martial in Portugal proved, it could be a problem when on campaign. In the Peninsula there were never enough carts and the Commissariat were rarely helpful, being too aware of their own requirements. It is unlikely that Kingsley was the only quartermaster, desperate to get supplies to his battalion, to take the law into his own hands.

On the march itself certain regulations had to be observed such as a distinction of seniority among officers. It was also crucially important, according to James, that flank officers should be active and intelligent. Battalions formed in column and deviation from the orders of the day was permitted only in the direst necessity. Neither officers nor men were allowed to quit their post during the march unless the commanding officer's permission had already been obtained. A man who needed to relieve himself could do so only by obtaining a ticket of leave from his company commander, and even then he was expected to return to his place as expeditiously as possible. This explains why Private Cox was so anxious to rejoin the column when Private Riley, who was under an arrest and Cox's responsibility, fell out during a march in Spain. Riley, complaining of a violent flux, may have counted on Cox's unwillingness to stay with him as a means to make his escape. On the other hand, he may have been genuinely unwell.[35]

The undesirability of straggling became horribly apparent when the enemy was close enough to harry a retreating army, as happened in the autumn of 1812. Stragglers and sickly men were picked off by the pursuing French and made prisoners of war in great numbers. As early as 1810 Wellington issued a reprimand to the Royals, 9th and 35th, who made up the fifth division, for straggling on the march as they retreated from Buçaco. He also took the officers to task for neglecting their duties:

> There are more stragglers from these three regiments, than all the others in the British army taken together, which must be occasioned either by the neglect of the Officers, or by the soldiers being unable to keep up with the march. In either

case, these regiments are unfit to do duty with the army, and if the Commander of the Forces should observe any more of this straggling on the march, he will send the regiments into garrison, and report their conduct especially to His Majesty.[36]

It is possible that the ill-disciplined conduct of the three battalions which were about to become the first brigade of the fifth division, as well as the Portuguese brigade (which General Leith was required to rebuke by the same general order) gave Wellington a prejudice against the whole division and kept them in a secondary role until they redeemed themselves at Badajoz.

Closely related to straggling, often its motivation, and equally dangerous when the enemy was near, was marauding, which might be dignified as foraging but was often undertaken without orders even when it was not downright plundering. Stewart reported two occasions in his journal when men wandered too far in search of supplies, legitimate or otherwise. On the 23rd March 1811 rolls were called and all absentees were confined to the bivouac upon their return to prevent marauding, which had broken out among the men. Two weeks later, two men were taken prisoner by the French while foraging.

On a less serious note, James warned against allowing the light bobs to up the pace during a march. This seems to have been a point of honour with all light companies since it was a way of demonstrating their superiority over rival light companies, and the bacon bolters (grenadiers) of their own unit. This latter rivalry was traditional between the two elite companies of the battalion, and took the form of a race in Flanders when Macready found himself involved in a 7-mile dash which saw off all but three of the grenadiers and left him gasping for breath as he was belaboured by the congratulatory pats of the 'greasy rogues' of the light company. In Spain the rivalry between regiments became apparent when the light companies of the battalions in the fifth division raced with full packs between Peñaparda or Navas Frias, where the division was stationed, and Valverde in order to establish their regimental superiority. Left to their own devices, the light bobs would always try to quicken the normal 3-miles-an-hour pace of the march, a pace which allowed marches that started at first light to finish at ten o'clock in summer and twelve noon in winter.

In one respect the soldier enjoyed some advantage over the more impoverished of his civilian contemporaries, and that was in the matter of dress. He may have been obliged to wear what the army dictated, but the army clothed him. He might find himself looking like a tatterdemalion at the end of a year's hard campaigning, his uniform patched with any kind of cloth that came to hand, but at least he knew that a new uniform would eventually be supplied to him.

Shoes, however, were a more serious problem. Those supplied by the army were of notoriously poor quality, and for the man on the march this was a more uncomfortable deficiency than a threadbare and patched uniform from which the dye had long since run out so that military scarlet had become brick-dust brown.

Desperate situations required desperate measures, and one solution was to make sandals secured by thongs in imitation of the Iberian peasants. Even when shoes survived the march in dry weather it only took mud like that encountered in the final stages of the retreat from Burgos to suck them from the men's feet:

> the state of the roads, if roads they could be called, was such, that as soon as the shoe fell off or stuck in the mud, in place of picking it up again, the man who had thus lost one kicked its fellow companion after it.

There was always the opportunity to replace lost shoes, however:

> several soldiers had died during the night from exhaustion and cold, and those who had shoes on them were soon stripped of so essential a necessary; and many a young fellow was too happy to be allowed to stand in 'dead man's shoes'. Others were so crippled as to be scarcely able to stand to their arms. Ague and dysentery had, more or less, affected us all; and the men's feet were so swollen, that they threw away their shoes in preference to wearing them.[37]

This explains how a man in the 30th managed to develop frostbite, more likely what today would be called trench foot, during the retreat from Burgos.

Tracing the developments of the uniform worn by the men during the period of the Revolutionary and Napoleonic Wars reveals some significant developments which must have made campaigning more comfortable. In 1808 the regulation hairstyle of clubbed hair, powdered and secured in a black bag was abandoned. Similarly, the breeches and gaiters of the earlier period were replaced by blue-grey trousers which were worn with short boots, known as shoes. The older style of coat was swallow-tailed and styled to reveal the waistcoat underneath. In 1806 this was replaced by a shorter coatee, closed to the waist, where it formed a broad, inverted V. An even shorter coatee was introduced in 1815, straight across the waist but still with vestigial tails. All three versions had a stiff, upstanding collar which supported a black leather stock, the most uncomfortable and most detested item of the soldier's uniform. Not surprisingly, it was often abandoned when going into action. Broad white leather crossbelts which went under cloth epaulettes were a constant in all three versions of the uniform. The crossbelts supported the bayonet and cartouche box, and were worn with a brass plate at the crossover point, embossed with the regimental number. The facings of the jacket in the case of the 30th were yellow, the colour which gave the nickname, Yellowbellies, a title going back to the early eighteenth century when the open cut of the coat revealed a yellow waistcoat. Since the nickname is associated with Lincolnshire, where the regiment was first raised, a geographical origin is also possible.

Overall, the soldier was adequately clothed, at a cost of £1.16.6d in 1811. The regiment provided him not only with his jacket, trousers and shoes, but also with a kersey waistcoat and a cap, the last being replaced every two years, whereas the rest of the uniform was renewed annually. This headgear changed from a tricorne to a shako in 1806, the original stovepipe shako being replaced by the Belgic, with its raised front, by the time of Waterloo. Both were topped with a feather cockade. Since shakos were made of stiffened felt, they rarely retained their shape in wet weather. It was possible, however, to cover them with an oilskin protector which extended over the neck, thus offering some slight protection against rain.

The soldier was stopped 1/6d a week for what were termed his necessaries. These comprised in part the rest of his uniform: three shirts, one pair of gaiters while these were still worn, three pairs of worsted or yarn socks, worsted or yarn mitts, the much-hated black stock, and a foraging cap. Some other necessaries were required to maintain smartness: a clothes brush, three shoe brushes, black ball, hair ribbon and leather bag (while still required), two combs, and straps for carrying a greatcoat. This last was also regarded as a necessary and was renewed every three years. The other necessaries were all related to the upkeep of the musket: turnscrew, brush and worm, emery, and brick oil. They were paid for at public expense. The final necessary, of course, was the knapsack, which carried all this paraphernalia.

Necessaries were easy to lose, exchange for ready cash, or steal, and as a result they figure frequently in regimental courts martial records. For example, in the regimental courts martial recorded in the November 1814 inspection of the first battalion twelve men were recorded as having made away with part of the regimental necessaries, for which they received punishments which could be as much as three months' solitary confinement or as many as 300 lashes, with stoppages.

Not only was the soldier clothed by the army; he could also rely on being fed by the army, except under the most severe campaigning conditions or when the commissariat failed. These two difficulties came together during the final days of the retreat from Burgos when the supplies took the wrong route. No wonder men of the third and fourth divisions resorted to shooting pigs while others scrambled for acorns as their only hope of sustenance. Nor was this an isolated incident. The Commissary attached to the third division during the Waterloo campaign also failed in his duty. As a result, on Wellington's order, 'Mr Deputy Assistant Commissary General Spencer [was] removed from the Commissariat, for quitting the 3d Division to which he was attached, without leave during the important operations recently carrying on.'[38]

The official daily ration was one and a half pounds of bread, a pound of meat (half a pound if it was pork), a quarter of a pint of pease, an ounce of butter or cheese, and an ounce of rice. Since not all of these were always available, considerable variations within this restricted diet are recorded. In addition, some battalions encouraged officers to supply their men with vegetables. Bread and meat were the most predictable items, but although the quantity remained the same the quality varied greatly. There were many horror stories of adulterated food, particularly bread. As for meat, a pound might be more bone than flesh.

Inspecting generals in the two-battalion period often commented approvingly on the quality of the meat supplied. In November 1813, while the second battalion was stationed in Jersey, it was reported that 'The meat and bread are furnished by contract, of a good quality', while sixth months later, in Flanders, 'The men's messing is well attended to, & the meat and bread issued is generally good.' In Vaumorel's inspection at Cannanore, we read that 'The men's messing [is] strictly attended to, and good as the supplies on the Malabar Coast will possibly admit of.'

On campaign, the meat was likely to be on the hoof until shortly before it found its way into the men's camp kettles, or alternatively it might be salted. As in so many aspects of military life which related to the comfort of the soldier, the French organised things rather better for their conscript army, so it is no wonder that the chance to eat what the French had left behind in the course of a hurried departure was eagerly accepted. This was the good fortune of the 2/30th along with the 2/44th, when they crossed the river into Sabugal in 1811, and broke into the recently vacated castle.

The daily drink allowance was five pints of small beer, which on campaign would be converted into whatever happened to be the local drink. The Portuguese wondered at the British soldiers' capacity for drinking the rough red wine which they themselves were reluctant to touch; while in India the native arrack was the cause of much indiscipline. There is evidence to suggest that some soldiers would willingly have starved themselves in order to have more money for drink, but for the system of messing which put men into groups who cooked and shared their food in rotation. This made it impossible for the individual soldier to forgo his food. Furthermore, the officer of the day, as part of his duties, was required to inspect kettles at the hour appointed for cooking, while supervising messing arrangements was one of the general duties of all company officers.

Finally, there was the question of pay, a shilling a day for the first seven years of service, rising to 1/1d after seven years, and 1/2d after fourteen years. This needs to be compared with civilian rates. For example, agricultural labourers earned an average of 2/- a day, while skilled textile workers might earn as much as 4/- a day. In addition, the soldier received a penny a day as beer money, and sixpence for subsistence when on the march, twopence of which remained his after fourpence had been paid to the innkeeper who fed him. Since food, clothing and accommodation were all provided, he might well feel satisfied with his lot – were it not for the deductions the army demanded. Stoppages for necessaries, as we have seen, could amount to 1/6d a week maximum, while a further 4/7d maximum might be taken for messing expenses, including the supply of vegetables. If the full amounts were exacted, the soldier would be left with 1/6d a week, hardly a princely sum. And yet some men managed to leave a considerable sum upon their death, anything between five and ten pounds not being unusual.

In conclusion, although it may be surmised from much of the evidence that the life of a soldier could indeed prove nasty, brutish and short (appropriate for the scum of the earth, some would have said), there were those who made it a positive experience. Indeed, for the men who rose to sergeant, or even earned the rare reward of a commission, the army offered the chance to reveal talents that would almost certainly have remained unfulfilled in civilian life.

Chapter 4

Or Fine Fellows?

When the men of the 30th are considered beyond their geographical origins, a fairly predictable picture emerges. There were 2,147 soldiers who survived to claim a pension or figured in the casualty returns (discharge, transfer and desertion as well as death) and whose former employment is known. Of these, 1,404 were labourers, both agricultural and general, a proportion that would be replicated in most regiments, although in the 30th they tended towards the agricultural because of the rural or semi-rural location of most of the recruiting parties. The next largest group were workers in the textile industry, 212 framework-knitters or hosiers from the East Midlands, 101 weavers mainly from Ireland and a further seventeen in related trades, including cotton-spinning and silk manufacture. These numbers reflect the growing importance of the textile industry as a source of wealth. A useful eighty-six were cordwainers or shoemakers; their expertise was often called upon as the poor quality shoes (actually short boots) failed to survive the rigours of campaigning. Similarly the fifty-four tailors, the next largest group, finished the uniforms to provide some sort of fit. The other notable groups of workers were those connected to building and agricultural skills, fifty-one in each case, thirty-three metal workers of all kinds, including four silversmiths, and thirty-one connected to the supply and sale of food. This last group included thirteen butchers who were particularly valued on campaign in the Peninsula when the meat arrived on the hoof and was slaughtered once camp had been established.

Some of the trades found in the records reflect the economic structure of early nineteenth-century Britain. For example, craftsmen made and sold direct to their customers such objects as baskets, brushes, chairs and pipes. On the other hand, there are some occupations which, although typical of the period, might not have been expected in the ranks of the army. Apothecaries, clerks, engravers, gunsmiths, musicians and a tutor might all have been thought to have little to do with military life, except possibly by patriotic choice or for less admirable reasons which are not revealed in the records.

Equally interesting is the age at which men enlisted. A quick survey reveals that most joined the 30th as their first regiment in their late teens or early twenties, but an appreciable number enlisted in their late twenties or even in their thirties. Some of these older men had already served with other units, been discharged upon reduction or for some other reason and then re-enlisted. This previous service was not always in army units. A certain Joseph Bell joined the 30th in 1806 at Moate, in Ireland, aged 36. He was a button-burnisher by trade, but he had also served for twelve years in the Marines. He stayed with the 30th for twenty-one years, four years as corporal and eleven as sergeant. Not surprisingly, he was finally discharged as 'worn out'.

There were several men who joined in their forties, but the oldest appears to be William Irwin, a weaver from Kilmore, County Armagh, who enlisted in 1812 aged 56. Not surprisingly, he served only four years with the second battalion. He was discharged suffering from chronic dysentery and general debility, but even in the short time he was with the battalion he had obviously impressed Hamilton, who described him as a 'good and faithful soldier'.

Length of service varies greatly, as one would expect. A small number of men (other than those who died or were killed in action) managed two years' service or less. For example, Charles Adams had to be discharged after only two years, aged 20, having been houghed while on guard duty. William Bristow completed two and a half years, but was then discharged for being 'blind in one eye and other not good'. Similarly Peter Farrell, William Tinsley and William Rutland were all discharged suffering from ophthalmia. Tinsley had also received a wound in his left leg at Waterloo, while Rutland had a rupture. He had served for twelve years in other regiments, however, before he joined the 30th. Wounds and accident were often the reason for these premature discharges. Michael Morrisey had a 'fracture of spine from an accident', Robert Ramsden lost his left leg at Waterloo, while William Fielding was discharged because of an 'accidental gunshot wound and ill health'. The shortest period of service, nine months in 1815, was brought to an end because of the hand and back injury Thomas Cochrane suffered at Waterloo. The remaining man to be discharged in his second year of service was George Jackson for ulcerated legs.

At the other extreme, 121 men (out of the 977 in the pension records) served for at least twenty-four years, ten of them for more than thirty. Some of these men are worthy of comment. Thomas Bibby, a weaver from Lancaster, who enlisted aged 19, and John Sharpe, a labourer from Henley-on-Thames, who joined from the Army of Reserve aged 18, suffered very different fates. Bibby rose to colour sergeant; his conduct was good and he was discharged as 'worn out'. Sharpe, however, was in the asylum at Fort Clarence and was discharged for 'mental alienation'. Andrew Black, a long-serving sergeant, completed thirty-three years in the regiment, while William White, thirty-two years, remained in the ranks despite his conduct being described as 'very good'. Both were labourers, Black from Dumfries and White from Essex, but the former presumably showed NCO qualities which the latter lacked. The longest-serving man, though, was Samuel Ramsey, a labourer from Stafford, who enlisted as a boy in 1802 aged only 8 and was discharged thirty-five years later. Unfortunately, his conduct left a little to be desired since it was only 'generally good'.

Perhaps the most interesting of these long-serving soldiers, however, is John Laughron. He enlisted on the 12th January 1805 as a boy of 10, days after his father had murdered his mother. He served as a drummer with the second battalion, sailing with them to the Peninsula. Like all the boys attached to the battalion, however, he remained in Lisbon when the rest of the battalion moved north in pursuit of Masséna. By the time of the Flanders campaign he had been transferred to the first battalion. He was later promoted to corporal, then to sergeant, and finally he was appointed colour sergeant. When he was discharged in 1837, aged 42 and officially 'worn out', he was described as 'an excellent NCO, trustworthy and exemplary in every respect and always efficient'. He was identified as a labourer, the 'trade' given to all the boys and lads who enlisted.

These were the men who fought for their regiment and, possibly as a secondary motive, for king and country during the thirty years of the Revolutionary and Napoleonic Wars, which contemporaries called The Great War. Whether life for a soldier was any more unpleasant than for the majority of his fellow-Britons is at least open to question. Similarly, his chance of survival may have been little worse than in civilian life, although any attempt to evidence such an assumption is beyond the scope of this study. By focusing on one company of the second battalion, it is possible to reach some tentative conclusions about soldier survival rate for the period 1803–1817, but only if it is accepted that one company can be taken as representative of the second battalion as a whole, and that death rates were similar across the two battalions. This second point of comparison might seem unlikely, because only the junior battalion saw active service, in the Peninsula and Flanders. Deaths in action, though, were the exception, and it can be postulated that there is a fair correlation between the effects of the Indian climate and the diseases encountered in Spain and Portugal.

In 1813, when the second battalion was divided into four strong companies which remained in the Peninsula and six weak companies which returned to England, there was inevitably some re-organisation, making it impossible to follow a single company through the period of the battalion's existence. However, by concentrating on the fourth company of the original battalion and then focusing on the ninth company, into which the largest number of men from the fourth company transferred in 1813, as well as tracking other men from the fourth company, it is possible to get a representative idea of survival rates in the battalion.

The junior battalion of a regiment was essentially a feeder unit for the senior battalion (except when on active service), so that a good many men stayed only a few years in the second battalion before being transferred to the first. Consequently, the men of the sample company represent every experience of the regiment, including service in India. On the other hand, many men remained with the second battalion, and even with the same company from augmentation to reduction. If they were not discharged in 1817, they sailed with the remnants of the battalion to India and its harsh climate.

A total of 509 men served with our sample company between 1803 and 1817 and of these 116 are recorded as having died of natural causes while serving with the regiment. At first glance, India would seem the more dangerous posting since fifty-nine men died there compared with thirty-three in Spain, Portugal and Gibraltar. The picture changes, however, when the period spent in India (twenty-three years) is set against the four years in the Peninsula, giving average figures of just over two deaths annually from natural causes against eight a year in Iberia. This can be explained by the rapidity with which the first battalion became acclimatised. Within three years the death rate had dropped to something approaching the European norm. Although there is similar evidence of acclimatisation in Spain and Portugal, the death rate was then accelerated by the rigours of the retreat from Burgos.

The other stations in which the second battalion served were much healthier. Thus, in the sample company there were no natural deaths in the Netherlands and Flanders (1814–1815), one in Jersey (1814), and two in France during the occupation after Waterloo. There were three in England in 1803, but these coincided with an outbreak of smallpox, and eighteen in Ireland during the seven years the battalion served there. Again these deaths seem to have been occasioned mainly by specific outbreaks of disease, particularly typhus-type fevers.

Some of the deaths recorded were more unusual. Two men of the company were returned as drowned in the wreck of the *Queen* off Falmouth in January 1814, although one of these, George Rawdon, apparently came back to life to claim a General Service Medal in 1848. Another man hanged himself in India after being transferred to the first division. This last, Thomas Rodwell, a hosier from Syston, had joined the second battalion as a boy along with men from the Army of Defence in July 1805. He was transferred to the first battalion in April 1806, in time to sail with them to India. This transfer suggests that he was seen as promising soldier material, since the senior battalion was entitled to choose the best men for their ranks. There is no explanation as to why he hanged himself nine years later. He does not figure in any courts martial records nor was he in debt, a factor which seemed to motivate some men to take their own lives. He was not alone, however, in choosing suicide as an escape from the misery of service in India. There were no attempted or successful suicides in the second battalion during its period of existence which would suggest that whatever the tedium of home postings or the extreme discomforts encountered on active service, they never sapped a man's spirits like India. Obviously, only a small minority were desperate enough to kill themselves, but it is at least plausible that drunkenness was the route taken by many to find temporary escape.

Compared with the incidence of natural deaths, the number of men from the sample company killed in action or who died of wounds seems remarkably low, only twenty in total for a battalion which boasted Fuentes de Oñoro, Badajoz, Salamanca, Quatre Bras and Waterloo as its official battle honours, to which can be added the sharp and bloody action at Villamuriel. The largest number of casualties for the company, seventeen, were taken at Quatre Bras and Waterloo. Thomas Vipond, the drum major who was killed during the Flanders campaign of early

1814 had initially served with the fourth company. A further two men who had formerly been with the company were killed at Badajoz (where the battalion took its heaviest casualties after the two battles of 1815). There might have been more losses from this company, but for the prevalent sickness which kept so many of them out of action.

Even if the natural and violent deaths are combined the resulting figure of 136, out of over 500 men, is not particularly high. This suggests that for the majority, although the soldier's life could be unpleasant, it was not necessarily short.

There were two other significant reasons why men left the company: transfer and desertion. The latter was a serious cause of wastage throughout the army, and the 30th suffered from it, if not to the extent of some other regiments then certainly to a notable degree. There could be considerable variation year on year, however. In 1807 the second battalion lost thirty-six men to desertion while in 1813 only seven deserted. There was a circumstance that caused desertion to rise, however. In both battalions, the first at the end of 1805 and the second at the beginning of 1809, there was an upsurge to forty desertions in each as the units prepared for foreign service.

Thirty-three men deserted directly from the sample company, but where they deserted is significant. Only two men deserted from the Peninsula. One returned three days later. The other, William Sloane, absconded with 130 dollars belonging to Lieutenant Mayne. Two men disappeared in France in 1815, although one returned six months later, and three men disappeared in England, one from the depot in 1815 and two in the early days before the first departure to Ireland. This means that the largest number of desertions took place in Ireland where desertion was a constant and chronic problem. Only one of these deserters had served more than a year; most of them stayed considerably less than a year. All of them were Irish. Some managed a few months' service (possibly because they found it impossible to take to their heels any sooner) but the majority remained only a matter of weeks, or even days. Michael Farrell, who joined as a recruit on the 20th February 1807, deserted four days later after muster. John McQuain, another recruit, who joined on the 26th October 1807, and John Knede, a recruit who had enlisted a month earlier, both disappeared within two days of joining the battalion. The suspicion has to be that some of these short-stay men were what might be termed professional deserters, since the practice was common at the time.

The lure was the bounty paid to recruits. Once this had been handed over, and presuming he did not drink it away, the recruit could make his escape with a sizeable sum of money in his pocket. He could then lie low for a while before presenting himself as a recruit to another regiment. In the days of uncertain identification it was a get-rich-quick scheme which could be repeated several times, although the penalty for serial desertion was death. That such men could be caught is illustrated by the cases of Lawrence Moore and Julian Pearse. The former enlisted as a recruit in 1807; the latter joined the second battalion upon its formation. Both were quickly claimed as deserters by other regiments.

Desertion might, and often did, prove a merely temporary affair. Francis Fahey is a typical example of apparent desertion. Fahey, an Irishman, was already serving with the 30th before augmentation. He was transferred to the second battalion upon its formation but when the regiment sailed to Ireland the following January, he was left sick in England, and was returned sick for the next nine months. By November he was back with his company. A month later he was returned as a deserter. Then in January 1805 this was amended to: 'supposed to have deserted, detained by sickness.' He eventually rejoined, and all was well until the 13th September, when he disappeared for an absence which lasted four weeks. Whether he was punished with a flogging is impossible to ascertain, since there are no regimental courts martial records for this period. He certainly spent the next three months in the regimental hospital, a protracted period for recovery from punishment, so he may again have been absent because of illness. Thereafter his career returned to normality. In March 1808 he was selected for service with the first battalion and was one of many to succumb to the Indian climate, dying in April 1810.

Desertion, with its attendant risk of capture and punishment, was a decision made by the individual soldier. Transfer, on the other hand, was officially sanctioned and only happened on specific occasions. The first of these occasions, as we have seen, was immediately after augmentation. The influx of men, from the Army of Reserve and as recruits, proved surplus to requirements, and some were encouraged to volunteer into other regiments. Of the original 110 men who mustered as the fourth company, one was transferred immediately into the Guards, and three went two months later, one into the Guards and two into the 47th Foot.

In 1806 there was an isolated case of a man transferring into the 43rd Foot, although no reason is given. The men who transferred into the Garrison Battalions are easier to explain. Originally formed in 1802 and comprising invalids, including Chelsea out-pensioners who were judged unfit for active service, after 1803 these battalions absorbed men from the Army of Reserve who were not transferred to regular units. They were disbanded and re-formed in 1805. By the end of 1806 there were nine battalions, and supplementary militia men still serving with the regular army were given the choice of opting for general service, with implications of serving abroad, or transferring into a garrison battalion. Nineteen men transferred from the fourth company, and 306 in total (although four subsequently returned).[39]

The third occasion when men transferred from the 30th into other units was in 1828, when the period of service in India was coming to an end. Of the 509 men who had served with the sample company at some time, five transferred into other regiments, four of them into the 26th Foot. This is a small number, but by 1828 very few second battalion men were still serving with the regiment. Of those that had survived until 1817, and had not been discharged, most had subsequently been invalided out. It would be sensible to suppose that most of the men from the company who were still serving in 1828 and opted to remain in India had joined the second battalion towards the end of its period of existence. There are some notable exceptions, however. For example, John Lilley came in from the Antrim Militia in 1808. He saw action in Spain, Portugal, Holland and Flanders, was a recipient of the Waterloo medal, and joined the first battalion upon reduction. He had served ten years in India when he decided to transfer into the 26th Foot, probably because like many men he had domestic ties which made a return to Europe undesirable. As several wills make clear, soldiers in India often entered into long-term relationships with Indian women and subsequently fathered children. Such irregular families could not be brought back to Britain, so a man had no choice but to remain in India if he wished to stay with his family.

Obviously, transfers could work in both directions and in September 1806 the second battalion received thirty volunteers from the single-battalion 47th Regiment. No reason for their arrival is given in the monthly returns, but in 1806 the 47th were posted to the Cape of Good Hope, so it is possible these were men from either the Army of Reserve or the Army of Defence who had not volunteered for service abroad.

In total, thirty-four men from the sample company transferred into other regiments for positive reasons and at their own choice, while three men went elsewhere because they had no choice. John Goodship, an 1803 recruit, deserted in December 1807. He returned in February 1808 and was transferred to a foreign corps for life a month later, an unusual punishment for an absence of only two months. Michael Reynolds deserted in 1807 and returned in December 1808. He was also sentenced to serve in a foreign corps for life, which is not surprising given the length of his absence from the battalion. William Moore, who joined in 1808 as a volunteer from the Carlow Militia, served in the Peninsula, Holland and Flanders. He fought at Quatre Bras and Waterloo. Although he was awarded a Waterloo medal, he was not with the battalion when they were distributed in Limerick in 1816, having been allowed to commute the sentence of a court martial to service abroad for life.

There remain the men who survived to claim a pension, and, not surprisingly, their conduct is generally described as 'good' or 'very good', with the frequent qualification of 'gallant' or 'zealous'. For example, on Joseph Brown's discharge papers Colonel Hamilton wrote: 'Conduct very good, behaved well at Waterloo', while for Matthew Donnellan, nineteen years a sergeant, he wrote, 'Conduct most excellent and behaved most excellently in Egypt'. Colour Sergeant Robert Mills was commended for 'Conduct most excellent and who from his long service as a serjeant has been a most trustworthy and useful one…recommended for a good pension'. The highest encomium went to Robert White who, in addition to comments similar to those which praised Mills, was described as 'one of the best and most honest & worthy no. com. Officers in the service'. He was recommended for 'the highest pension possible to give him'. White had been a prisoner of war for eight years. When he returned to England in 1814 he was quickly appointed colour sergeant, and later, quartermaster sergeant, so it is no surprise that he received such a commendation. Even a humble soldier like John Yorke, however, who served all fourteen of his years with the second battalion as a private, could be described as 'zealous'. This reminds us that not all those who took the king's shilling were 'the scum of the earth'. Yorke was a labourer who came to the 30th via the Army of Reserve as a substitute, accepting money to take someone else's place. Since there is no evidence that he was destitute, it must have been a free choice. Even at his lowly rank he was obviously able to impress his commanding officer by his dedication to duty, 'zealous' being Hamilton's preferred word for such a man.[40]

The conduct of a few men was described as 'indifferent' and there remained those who could only be labelled 'bad' or 'very bad'. This was more common of men discharged from the first battalion with chronic liver conditions. In the second battalion the only man who earned this comment was Anthony Callinan. He had joined as a boy and was only 17 when he volunteered for a trench-digging working party at Ciudad Rodrigo, dangerous and back-breaking work. As the bars on his General Service Medal indicate, he went up the ladders at San Vincente and fought at Salamanca. Although it was not acknowledged as an official action, he was also at Villamuriel. In Flanders his conduct seems to have deteriorated. In September 1814 he was found guilty of being absent without leave and making away with his necessaries for which he was sentenced to 300 lashes and received 200 of them. Although there is no further reference to specific misbehaviour, a negative impression had obviously been created. He received a pension, though, because he had been wounded at Salamanca.

Bryan Nowlan, also of the fourth company, turned out to be even worse than Callinan. Like Callinan, he had joined the regiment as a boy, enlisting in February 1805. He remained with the second battalion for two years, before being transferred to the first battalion in April 1807. Thereafter, his career followed a downward path, clearly evident in a sequence of courts martial. In 1814 alone he stood five regimental courts martial, for unsoldierlike conduct, three instances of drunkenness, two of which included abusive language and rioting, and stealing silver. His punishments totalled 900 lashes, all of which he received, as well as two weeks in solitary confinement. It had little effect because the following year there were another three court-martial appearances, all for unsoldierlike conduct, and a further 500 lashes. There must have been considerable relief in 1816 when he completed the seven years for which he had signed up, and which was dated from when he became a man in military terms.

Three men from the sample company suffered a fate that was rare for the 30th when they became prisoners of war. The first of them, William Uncle, was a labourer from Hertford who enlisted in September 1803, aged 22. Like Robert White, he was to spend eight years as a prisoner of war in France. Initially with the second battalion, he was transferred to the first battalion in December 1804. A year later he had the misfortune to be aboard the ill-fated transport ship, *Jenny*, as the battalion set sail for north Germany. Blown by a violent storm onto the French coast at Gravelines, Uncle found himself a prisoner. Although he and his companions were well-treated by the people of Gravelines, they would not have enjoyed their long incarceration at Valenciennes. Upon release in 1814, he joined the depot in Colchester and then, in April 1815, he arrived in Flanders as part of the last detachment to join the second battalion before the Waterloo campaign. Having survived two battles unscathed, he must have felt some satisfaction that he had finally been able to strike a blow against the French. He remained with the second battalion until reduction. At this point he had fourteen years' service, plus two years for Waterloo, and was entitled to a pension of a shilling a day. On his discharge papers he was described as 'worn out in the service', although there is no reference to his long period of imprisonment. His conduct, though, was 'very good'.

Less fortunate was the experience of William Cleavely, a tailor from Northampton who joined the 30th in October 1803 from the Army of Reserve. In 1807 he was one of the men who transferred into the 9th Garrison Battalion rather than sign up for general service, although he was back with the second battalion by March 1808. He spent the next four months recruiting, but by September he was with the rest of the battalion in Strabane. In March 1809 he embarked for the Peninsula, leaving behind his wife, Mary. Since she was returned as staying in Ireland, it seems probable that Cleavely married her after he joined the army.

Cleavely himself did not have a particularly happy time in Spain and Portugal. Indeed, notes in the muster rolls suggest that the climate and hard soldiering broke his health. In March 1811 he was returned as 'sick in the general hospital', where he remained for the next three months. He returned to the fourth company in June, but August and September saw him back in the general hospital. After this his health improved for a while but in April 1812 he was again returned sick. This latest period of sickness lasted until June. He fought at Salamanca and also took part in the advance on Madrid, and then onto Burgos. He survived the first part of the retreat, but on the 25th October, the day of the action at Villamuriel, he was taken prisoner by the French. He was subsequently returned as prisoner of war until December 1815, when he disappears from the records. By that time it could be assumed that he would not return to the regiment. The obvious conclusion is that he did not survive the rigours of a French prison, or even the march to France. It is strange, however, that he remained on roll for over a year after all the other men came back from captivity, since they could have reported what happened to him. Was he mortally wounded when taken on the 25th? Did he simply collapse and die, abandoned by his captors? Or is it just possible that he made his escape but never returned to the regiment (like the supposedly drowned George Rawdon)? Unfortunately, the records provide no answer.

Arthur Clinton, a labourer from Templemore, Tipperary, had a similar experience to Cleavely, but with a different ending. Clinton enlisted in May 1810, aged 16, and after a period of training at the depot joined the second battalion in Cadiz four months later as part of a detachment brought out by Captain Chambers. Like Cleavely, he suffered extended periods of sickness, from October 1811 to January 1812, and from April to September 1812. He was not so incapacitated that he was unable to take part in the advance on Burgos, however, and in the subsequent retreat, including the action at Villamuriel. On the 16th November, during the final stages of the retreat, he went missing and was subsequently returned as a prisoner of war, one of the many stragglers who fell into French hands when they were too weak to keep up with the main body. Unlike Cleavely, he survived the march to France and the rigours of a French prison. By July 1814, after the exchange of prisoners which followed Napoleon's first abdication, he was at the regimental depot. Three months later he joined the second battalion in Flanders. He fought at Quatre Bras and Waterloo, and remained with the battalion until reduction. He was one of the men retained by the regiment and subsequently went to India, where he served until 1827. He was then invalided home to be discharged as 'worn out' with the comment that his conduct was 'good', which was sufficient to gain him a pension. After seventeen years' service, which included the climatic and campaigning rigours of the Peninsula, nearly two years in a French prison, and nine years in India, it is no wonder that he was, indeed, worn out, although he was still only 33 on discharge.

He was still alive in 1848, one of the 136 officers and men who claimed the General Service Medal. His single bar for Badajoz tells us he was one of the few men in the fourth company fit enough to ascend the ladders at San Vincente. He had also, of course, received the Waterloo medal in 1816.

On the subject of medals, one man stands out as unique in battalion records. John Hill claimed seven bars on his GSM which suggest that his was a different experience of the Peninsular War. In 1803 two men by the name of John Hill joined the 30th, one as a recruit and the other from the Army of Reserve. Later there was a third John Hill, who died in March 1811. At this point the two other men of that name changed identity, so it is difficult to know whether the man with seven bars was a brickmaker from Atherstone, Warwickshire or a labourer from Aylesbury, Buckinghamshire (or even a labourer from Barfield, Essex, although this is probably the third John Hill). His service record is clear enough, though. He began his military career as a drummer with the fourth company before returning to the ranks. He sailed to Portugal in 1809, then on to Gibraltar. In 1810 he was in Cadiz with the rest of the battalion but at this point his situation changed. When the rest of the battalion sailed back to Portugal and the Lines of Torres Vedras, he remained in Cadiz as General Graham's servant. By 1812 he was General Murray's servant, which meant that he remained in the Peninsula when the rest of the battalion returned to England. As the servant of two generals he was later able to claim bars for Barossa, Ciudad Rodrigo, Vitoria, San Sebastian, Nive, Orthez and Toulouse. He did not return to the second battalion until July 1816, thus missing Quatre Bras and Waterloo, but the general service medal he received in 1848 must have been some (very belated) compensation.

One other man from the sample company was also unique, in that he never left England from augmentation until shortly before his discharge in 1816. Thomas Stone, a hosier from Beeston, Nottingham, had enlisted in 1797, aged 16, and had seen action in Egypt four years later. He was transferred to the fourth company of the second battalion in October 1803, and a month later was returned as being on recruiting service. He continued as part of the recruiting party in Sleaford until 1813, when he was returned as being with Captain James Fullerton, recruiting superintendent in Derby. A 'paper' transfer to the first battalion took place in January 1814, whereupon he disappeared from second battalion records for a couple of months. In April, though, he was 'on command' in Derby, obviously never having left. It can be assumed that his transfer to the first battalion had been cancelled, either because he was absent when the other nominated men were marched off or simply because Fullerton requested his presence in Derby. From January 1815 he was specifically described as Fullerton's servant and, although on the depot muster roll between October 1815 and March 1816, there is no reason to believe he was actually at the depot. By April 1816 he was once more being described as 'on command'. At some point after July 1816 he must have crossed to Ireland because he was discharged at Kilmainham in October 1816, suffering from an asthmatic complaint and a rupture. By this time he was 35, and had spent half his time with the 30th on recruiting duties. Nevertheless, he received a positive testimonial from Hamilton who wrote that he was 'wounded in Egypt and always conducted himself as a very good man'. Since Hamilton would have seen nothing of him after the first muster of the second battalion in October 1803 he was either remembering the man from ten years before (as he did for several others who served in Egypt) or basing his comment on Fullerton's testimony.

A straightforward but unexpected story belongs to Thomas de Joseph, as he was initially returned in the muster roll. His presence in a British regiment is surprising since he might more predictably have been found in the ranks of his own country's forces. Tomas de Jose, to give him his rightful name (which the regimental clerks never learnt to spell accurately) was a Portuguese national, a vintner, born in San Rouger, Lisbon. He enlisted, aged 18, in May 1809, during the second battalion's brief initial stay in Portugal. His motives, of course, are impossible to determine. He was with the fourth company throughout the Peninsular period and presumably saw action at Fuentes de Oñoro, Badajoz, Salamanca and Villamuriel since he suffered no periods of sickness and was never returned as absent from the battalion. He remained with the four companies in January 1813, returning with them to Jersey in the summer of that year. He saw further action in Graham's Flanders campaign but missed Quatre Bras and Waterloo through sickness. He remained with the second battalion until 1817, and then served in India until 1829. He was finally discharged in 1834, having served twenty-five years with the 30th. According to his discharge papers he was suffering from 'chronic rheumatism...a case of disease contracted in the Peninsula and the East Indies without being attributable to neglect, vice, misconduct, design or intemperance but from accidental causes'. The only Portuguese soldier to serve with the regiment, whose conduct was described as good, was 5 feet 7 and a half inches tall, with black hair, black eyes and a black (dark) complexion. Whatever his motives for joining a British regiment as it passed through Lisbon, he certainly gave sterling service and deserved his pension.

Such are just a few of the stories of the men in the ranks. There is a further variation, however, which could be told many times over, the story of the man to whom the army gave the opportunity to demonstrate that he possessed talents which would probably have remained undiscovered in civilian life. Charles Haughey enlisted as a recruit at headquarters in Strabane in May 1807. He was a labourer from Camms, County Tyrone, a grey-eyed, fair-haired 18-year-old youth, 5 feet 6 inches tall when he was full-grown. In all probability he did not have much of a future to anticipate, but he had talents which the army appreciated. By September 1807 he had been promoted to corporal, and five years later he was made sergeant. He was present at Badajoz and Salamanca according to the bars on his GSM, and presumably also fought at Villamuriel. Because he had initially volunteered for seven years' service he was discharged in February 1815, but rejoined in October, still with the rank of sergeant. The rest of his service, which lasted until 1835, was with the first battalion where he rose to quartermaster sergeant, a position he held for ten years. He was discharged at his own request, aged 46, to go to Chelsea. In his discharge papers he is described as 'active, brave and trustworthy', the prime qualities for a non-commissioned officer that were unlikely to have been valued, or even recognised, in a labourer.

Haughey was certainly not alone in achieving distinction from humble beginnings. Others rose even higher. These careers, however, are a necessary corrective to the view that men in the ranks were the scum of the earth. Many of them, the majority if we judge by the complimentary remarks on their discharge papers, were the fine fellows Macready so often referred to in his journal and remembered with such affection from his days in the second battalion.

Chapter 5

Raw Recruit to Rough Soldier

In my opinion the principal cause of our reverses, though one which has never been pointed out by any soldier who has written on the Peninsular War, was the immense superiority of the English Infantry in accurate shooting, a superiority which arises from their frequent exercise at targets, and in great measure also from the formation in two ranks…It is asserted that two ranks do not offer sufficient strength to resist Cavalry, but the English Infantry can in a moment form four deep to receive a charge, and our squadrons were never able to catch it in two ranks, though as soon as it had to fire it quickly resumed this formation.[41]

Thus wrote Marbot of the men he encountered in Spain and Portugal, basing his observations on actual experience.

General Foy somewhat unkindly commented that

The English soldier is stupid and intemperate. A rigid discipline turns some of his defects to advantage, and deadens the effects of others. His constitution is robust from the exercises of strength to which his youth has been accustomed. His soul is vigorous because his father has told him, and his officers have never ceased repeating to him, that the sons of Old England, plentifully replenished with porter, and with roast beef, are each of them equal to at least any three individuals of the pigmy races which vegetate on the Continent of Europe. Although of a sanguine complexion, he has no extraordinary ardour, but he stands firm, and when reasonably propelled, he keeps marching forward. When in action, he looks neither to the right nor to the left. The courage of his co-operators does not sensibly add to his own; their discouragement may diminish, but will not extinguish his ardour.[42]

He subsequently commented that

The infantry is the best portion of the British army. It is the *robur peditum,* the expression applied by the Romans to the *triarii* of their legions. The English do not scale mountains, or skim along the plain, with the suppleness and rapidity of the French; but they are more silent, more quiet, and more obedient, and for that very reason their fire is better directed and more destructive...The infantry, although on system formed three deep, like the other infantries of Europe, is most frequently drawn up only two deep. When making or receiving a charge, it is drawn up four deep. Sometimes it has made offensive movements and even charged columns, when in open order. In a retreat it stands firm, and commences by vollies [sic] from the battalions, followed by a well supported fire of files. It turns round coolly to keep off those who are hanging on its rear. While marching it fires without separating.

The English infantry is not afraid of charging its enemy with the bayonet. The leader, however, who would wish to use without compromising it, must move it seldom and cautiously, and reckon more upon its fire that upon its manoeuvres.[43]

A British NCO expressed a similar estimation of the man in the ranks, although what to a French general was reason for a certain amount of scorn became a more positive evaluation.

The British Soldier, fortunately for himself is a dunce in politics; it is a subject which he heartily despises. To keep his arms in serviceable condition, as well as clothing and appointments: to be patient under privations; cool and steady in danger; brave and daring in action; to be obedient to orders and to have an honest and cheerful heart form the perfection of his character.[44]

The point that emerges from these comments is that the British infantryman was trained specifically to meet the battle conditions of his time for which his temperament was ideally suited. It is an accepted truism that the musket of the day lacked accuracy beyond a minimal distance, but an unbroken line of muskets fired steadily and regularly was a daunting deterrent to an advancing army, even if only a small proportion of the bullets actually found their mark. Furthermore, if the men holding the muskets were trained to stand their ground and hold their fire until the enemy was within accurate range, the result would be even more devastating. Add to that Marbot's observation that a British battalion could move rapidly from two-line formation into the four-deep square in order to resist cavalry, as the 2/30th demonstrated at Quatre Bras, and the superiority of the British infantry becomes even easier to understand. But how did the raw recruit attain the proficiency which proved crucial on so many battlefields?

As a starting point, we can consider the composition of the 30th, which was replicated in many other regiments of the line. Between 1803 and 1817 both battalions consisted of seasoned soldiers, who exerted a steadying influence on the less experienced men. Even in 1803, when the regiment acquired its second battalion by taking in over 1,000 men from the Army of Reserve, it was acquiring a good many former soldiers as well as the younger, rawer material. Some of the seasoned soldiers were men who had been discharged in 1802, as a result of the Peace of Amiens, and now found their way back into the regular army. In the following years, other discharged men did the same. For example, Joseph Scotton, who eventually became one of the first colour sergeants, had served with two cavalry regiments, the Blues (Royal Horse Guards) and the 10th Light Dragoons, before joining the 30th from the Army of Reserve and then transferring to general service in 1806. At the same time, as has already been noted, trained men were coming in from the militia regiments. During the Waterloo campaign, the Old Three Tens were the most battle-hardened unit in the British brigade of the third division. The only ones who had seen service in the Peninsula, they numbered many Peninsular veterans in their ranks, recognisable by their dark complexions and a tendency to swear in Spanish or Portuguese. Nor was there a single man in the ranks who had served less than two years.

For the purposes of recruiting, which was carried out with increasing urgency as the war dragged on, the country was divided into eighteen districts by a system established in 1802. Each district had its headquarters at a specific town, and was commanded by a field officer whose duties included giving intermediate approval to recruits, unless recruiting was taking place close to regimental headquarters. He was assisted by an adjutant and a surgeon, the latter with the all-important task of establishing that the recruits were fit for service.

Some contemporary commentators opposed recruiting districts on the grounds of expense. Nevertheless, it was a means of supervising a system which might otherwise have become chaotic, so intense was the rivalry between recruiting parties from different regiments, and between the army and the navy, for a commodity that was in short supply. Although some recruiting parties stayed only briefly in a particular location, less than six months in Taunton in 1812 for example, others became almost permanent fixtures. The 30th were recruiting in Sleaford, a Lincolnshire market town, before the French Revolution, and were still there three decades later. Throughout this period they acquired a steady influx of men for the regiment.

The desperate nature of recruiting is borne out by the number of recruiting parties active throughout the British Isles. In July 1805, for instance, there were 405 recruiting parties active in the eighteen districts. Within a year the number had risen to 1,113. As for the 30th, depot returns indicate the geographical scope of the trawl for men. For example, in October 1809 there were five recruiting parties, in Glasgow, Sleaford, Cambridge, Dublin and Galway, who between them enlisted twenty-two recruits. A year later this had increased to seven recruiting parties, Edinburgh replacing Glasgow, Enniscorthy replacing Dublin, and Leicester and Tullamore being added to the list. They brought in twenty-five recruits, although a further twenty-four men volunteered from the Tipperary Militia. Although the locations changed, there were still seven parties active in October 1811, but the number of recruits was dropping, only fifteen in this month. However, a year later, when news of the 1812 victories in the Peninsula had reached England, the depot took in twenty-six recruits in one month alone.

There was a further development in the organisation of the system in 1812, when the eighteen districts were subdivided and an experienced officer was appointed to command each of the subdivisions. The first two officers of the 30th to fulfil this function were Captain James Fullerton, the Scot who fares so badly in Macready's Journal, and Lieutenant Stephen Masters. Fullerton had been involved in recruiting since he transferred into the 30th from the 2nd Ceylon Regiment in 1809. In 1812 he was appointed superintendent of Derby, a subdivision of the Nottingham recruiting district, where he remained until 1817. The following year he sailed to India with the remnants of the second battalion. Masters was appointed superintendent at Castlebar, County Mayo, in 1813. He had been with the regiment since 1807, when he exchanged from the 9th Garrison Battalion. He sailed with the 2/30th to Portugal, and on to Gibraltar in 1809, but by June of that year he had been invalided home for recovery of health. By 1810, he was engaged in recruiting, and remained a recruiting officer until he went on half-pay in 1817.

What actually qualified an officer to act in this capacity is far from clear, although Matthias Andrews' experience as adjutant in the second battalion may have given him the necessary administrative competence to superintend in Reading after reduction and before he joined the regiment in India in 1820. Macready had no doubt about Fullerton's suitability for the position, ascribing it to cowardice, but this was a quality he tended to identify in anyone he personally disliked, and his dislike for the Scotsman was particularly strong. As for Masters, a more interesting possibility suggests itself. Bannatyne gives the example of Lieutenant Michael Sparkes, who was retained as recruiting officer in Sleaford when the first battalion sailed to India because he was a married man with young children. In Sparkes' case, he had already attracted the notice of General Graham in Ireland while serving as an acting engineer. Graham requested his services in Cadiz and he remained there when the rest of the second battalion sailed back to Portugal. As a result, he fought at Barossa, and finally left the 30th to take up a captaincy in the Royal African Corps, a clear example of an officer rewarded for outstanding service. Sparkes' case may explain why Masters remained on recruiting duties after he had recovered his health, for he was also a married man with young children, eight by the time he went on half-pay, with another two to come.

With the establishment of recruiting subdivisions and the appointment of superintending officers, regimental officers were no longer attached to recruiting parties. Before 1812, every recruiting party from the 30th consisted of an officer, two sergeants (or a sergeant and a corporal), one or two drummers, and between three and six privates, men chosen for their intelligence and wit. After 1812, the officers who had been recruiting in England and Ireland, with the exception of Fullerton and Masters, joined the second battalion in the Peninsula. This was of benefit to the battalion, who had so many of their officers detached on staff duties that if one or two fell sick or went home on leave there was serious depletion, particularly among the captains. For example, in February 1813 there were only two captains, eight lieutenants and two ensigns to command the four companies which had been left in Portugal after the sickly men were sent home. As for staff, this consisted of the adjutant and one assistant surgeon.

With or without an officer in command, the members of a recruiting party could turn their activities into profit. Recruiting sergeants received sixteen shillings for each recruit added to the strength of the regiment, while the other members of the party shared 15/6d between them. If we focus on the recruiting party in Sleaford for 1810, the following picture emerges. For most of the year there were two sergeants, although for the last couple of months this reduced to one. The number of corporals varied between two and four while the number of privates, three for most of the year, temporarily increased to ten in February and March. One drummer remained with the party throughout the year. The total number of recruits for the year was thirty-eight, bringing the sergeants over thirty pounds, while the rest of the party had a slightly smaller sum to share among themselves. Obviously, these men missed out on the prize money accrued from active service, but they also escaped the attendant dangers. In addition, the 'bringer of the recruit', who was likely to be a local innkeeper, received £2.12.6d per recruit. It is no wonder, therefore, that recruiting and alcohol were so closely connected.

And strong persuasion might well be needed. The army was little respected:

Soldiers were regarded as day labourers engaged in unsavoury business; a money grant, and opportunities for adventure and plunder, an occupation where at all events food and clothing equal to that of a labourer were provided, and steady employment – these were regarded as sufficient enticement to draw men on whose devotion and courage the safety of every cottage, factory and mansion depended.[45]

It is understandable that the vast majority of the men drawn in by the recruiting sergeant's clever tongue were labourers. Nor was the national return particularly impressive. In January 1809, for example, from a total population of 15 million only 234,177 were serving in the regular army, including foreign and colonial troops. This, admittedly, was an improvement on the 104,000 men serving with the colours in June 1803, before the augmentation of regiments like the 30th. By 1813, however, with a full-scale war being fought in the Peninsula, the number had risen only to 255,876.

When the situation was really desperate, or when an officer was recruiting for rank (a means of promotion), as was permitted in 1794 and 1795, and again for a couple of years after the failure of the Peace of Amiens, a regiment might resort to the services of a crimp. This unsavoury character made it 'his business to entice others into a military life, generally by unfair means'.[46] These means might involve simple bribery, in the form of excessive bounties, which could be recouped from the regiment. Alcohol was frequently resorted to as a method of persuasion, and in the most extreme cases kidnapping was not unknown. There is no evidence that the 30th received men from the crimps, although several officers were recruiting for rank in 1804 and 1805, but several men had experience of how the crimps operated. In 1803, during an investigation into recruiting abuses, Private Richard Macready, of Captain Vaumorel's company, testified that he was crimped in Dublin for the Light Horse, put on board ship and taken to Dungannon Fort. He eventually joined the 30th. Others told a similar story, but since these events happened in 1797, when Ireland was in a convulsed state, the officer under investigation, a Mr Bradshaw who had been a captain in the 60th Foot, was cleared of imputations of fraud. Instead, the court accepted his defence that 'some errors must inevitably have arisen' and he would 'rectify all inaccuracies that may be discovered when a final settlement of his accounts shall take place'.[47]

No first-hand accounts of recruiting by the 30th exist, since the four officers whose journals survive were not involved in this activity. Similarly, if any man in the ranks recorded his experience, his account has long since disappeared. The process can only be surmised, therefore, from the accounts of those men who did record their experiences. There were several well-tried lures to draw in the gullible and the vulnerable:

> To a labouring man the attractions of the army lay in the bounty, the prospect of plunder and travel, and the distinctive dress – often in themselves enough, when placed against the long toil, the monotonous round and the weary drudgery of a working man's life.[48]

A clever sergeant would know how to exploit such feelings in his audience, as he told them tales of regimental glory, unimagined wealth and the promise that they would one day wear a sergeant's, or even an officer's, sash. There was also the enticement of the bounty, which in 1812 rose as high as £23.17.6d for unlimited service, another reason for the impressive October recruiting figures.

The bounty was essentially a bribe, with all the disadvantages associated with bribery, although it was originally introduced as the means by which a man could equip himself with the necessaries which were not supplied by the army. There was also competition between army and navy recruiting parties, and between the regulars and the militia, with recruiting officers putting their commissions at risk by offering sums above the stipulated amount. This amount also varied greatly, depending upon the present needs of the army. By 1814, when Napoleon was on Elba, the amount decreased to £5 for unlimited service, only to rise to £7.7.0d when he returned to France.

Whatever a man's reasons for enlisting, as soon as he accepted the king's shilling he became part of the process which transformed raw recruits into rough soldiers, a process best illustrated by examining what might happen to such an individual. Edward Keys was a labourer from Billingborough, a small Lincolnshire village 10 miles from Sleaford, where a recruiting party for the 30th had been operating for over twenty years. The area of the large, rural county of Lincolnshire, the 'part' of Kesteven, was fertile recruiting ground, drawing men from the villages all around, from the towns of Bourne and Grantham (which later had its own recruiting party), and even from the city of Lincoln. The draining of the Fens and the building of a canal had been attracting Irish navvies to the area for some time and Keys himself may have been of Irish extraction. Wages for agricultural workers were relatively high here because of the competition for labour, which makes the attraction of army service somewhat surprising.

The officer in charge of the two sergeants, four corporals, two drummers and twelve privates who constituted the recruiting party was Captain James Fullerton, of whom Macready wrote: 'This man systematically avoids service – glory has no charms for him – like Falstaff he sees honor [sic] as a mere escutcheon and he'll none of it.' It is impossible to know whether Macready's evaluation is justified, although another story he tells about Fullerton insulting a man and then refusing to fight a duel does suggest a somewhat devious and possibly craven nature.[49] Whatever the truth, however, he would certainly have enjoyed a more leisurely and relatively comfortable existence than his fellow officers in the Peninsula and India. He had probably been in Sleaford long enough to establish his position in the social hierarchy. Like John Shipp, he may have lived a life where 'nothing but gaiety prevailed, and as [he] was the only officer at the place for a considerable time, [he] received invitation after invitation to dinners, balls and suppers'.[50] Shipp was writing about Wakefield, but the social scene in Sleaford was likely to be very similar.

February 1812, and in Spain, a faraway country of which most Lincolnshire folk knew little, Wellington's carefully nurtured army had recently taken the French-held town of Ciudad Rodrigo and were about to advance on the bigger prize of Badajoz. As the 2/30th were part of that army, a silver-tongued recruiting sergeant could easily spin his tales of the glory awaiting any man willing to join this fighting regiment. He could also resurrect and embellish stories from Toulon, Corsica, Malta and Egypt. He was unlikely to mention India; not much glory there – a harsh climate, tedium, disease, although arrack and native women were some consolation. Nor did he have the famous havercakes (oat cakes) of the 33rd to tempt his listeners.

Billingborough was profitable territory and men who were initially reluctant could be persuaded to change their mind. This part of Lincolnshire was sparsely populated. Outside the city of Lincoln and a few market towns, small villages dotted a landscape rolling east to the flatness of the Fens and the towns of Boston and Spalding, which were not in the party's recruiting area. Billingborough itself was a hamlet of about 550 inhabitants, most of the men farm labourers with the odd agricultural craftsmen like blacksmiths and wheelwrights. There was little time to waste. Like most sporting activities (and there was an element of the chase in this business of calling men to the colours) recruiting had its close season. The desperate need for men in an army where too many were succumbing to the Iberian climate and its attendant diseases meant that the government had extended the season from winter into summer and autumn, but spring was still officially off-limits, presumably because in a largely rural country the needs of agriculture had to take precedence. It might have been a rest time, but it was also a time when the recruiting party had no extra income to share among themselves.

A good place to begin the business of recruiting was one of the village inns, The Fortescue Arms, for example. Not only would drink befuddle the thought processes of the listeners, but it was safe to assume that the men who frequented it were their most likely prey.

One such man might well have been Edward Keys, a labourer. (Whatever his agricultural skills, that is how he was returned in military records.) At this dead time of the year there could be no better place to pass the hours than at the inn. The hard labour of working the land would start again all too soon. For the moment he could listen to the tales of the recruiting sergeant, tales of loot and prize money, enough to turn a mere labourer into a nabob. He would be tempted with the teeming riches of Spain, which many had laid their hands on only weeks before in Ciudad Rodrigo. (The reality for the 30th had been the backbreaking work of digging trenches, but that was another story.) Money, women and adventure were dangled as temptations – although there might also be some mention of honour and duty.

It is doubtful if Keys himself knew why he responded. Life in Billingborough was not exciting. Perhaps he glimpsed the possibility of a different life beyond the narrow confines of rural Lincolnshire? Perhaps he was seduced by the promise of riches beyond his dreams? On the other hand, was there some local problem he wished to escape? Whatever his motive, Keys accepted the sixteen guineas, or some part of it, that the recruiting sergeant was offering to all who would fight for King and Country.

Although a recruit was allowed a period of grace of at least twenty-four hours to reconsider his decision to enlist, in practice considered reflection would have proved impossible. In all probability, he would have been drinking the hours away. Even after he had sworn the oath that would make him part of His Britannic Majesty's army, subject to its strict rules and regulations, he could still have changed his mind but only on return of the bounty (too much of which would probably have disappeared down the throats of the recruiting party), as well as another twenty shillings to defray expenses.

The process of attestation was completed before a magistrate to produce documentary evidence of enlistment. The recruit had to testify on oath his name, trade, place and date of birth. He also had to swear that he did not belong to the militia, another regular regiment, the navy or the marines. He then undertook to serve either for life (unlimited service with promise of a pension) or for seven years (without a pension), assuming the king required his services that long. The magistrate attested to the apparent age, the height and appearance (complexion, hair and eye colour) of the recruit, and the date of enlistment. The document stated that the recruit himself had stated his age and that he had no Rupture, and was not troubled with Fits, and was no way disabled by Lameness, Deafness, or otherwise, but had the perfect use of his Limbs and Hearing, and was not an Apprentice; and acknowledged that he had voluntarily enlisted himself to serve His Majesty King George the Third, in the [30th Regiment of Foot, commanded by Lieut. General Robert Manners].

The magistrate also attested that certain of the Articles of War had been read to the recruit.

These were the third and fourth articles of the second section and the first article of the sixth section, concerning mutiny and desertion. The first of them made explicit that

> Any Officer, or Soldier, who shall begin, excite, cause, or join in any Mutiny or Sedition in the Troop, Company, or Regiment, to which he belongs, or in any other Troop or Company in His Majesty's Service, or any Party, Post, Detachment or Guard, on any pretence whatsoever, shall suffer Death, or such other punishment as by a Court Martial shall be inflicted.

The second extended the scope of mutiny:

> Any Officer, Non-Commissioned Officer, or Soldier, who, being present at any Mutiny or Sedition, does not use his utmost endeavours to suppress the same, or coming to the Knowledge of any Mutiny or intended Mutiny, does not, without delay, give Information thereof, to his Commanding Officer, shall be punished by a Court Martial with Death, or otherwise, according to the nature of the offence.

As for desertion, the third of these articles stated that

> All Officers and Soldiers, who, having received Pay, or having been duly enlisted in His Majesty's Service, shall be convicted of having deserted the same, shall suffer Death, or other such Punishment as by a Court Martial shall be inflicted.

Next a surgeon signed and dated a statement that he had 'examined the above named [Edward Keys] and find that he is fit for His Majesty's Service'. This would probably be the duty of a local doctor since it was unlikely that a district surgeon was stationed in an area like Sleaford.

Finally the recruit himself swore

> to be true to our Sovereign Lord King George, and to serve him honestly and faithfully in Defence of his Person, Crown, and Dignity, against all his Enemies and Opposers whatsoever, and to observe and obey His Majesty's Orders, and the Orders of the Generals and Officers set over me by His Majesty.

If the recruit had received the bounty in full, that would be the end of the attestation process. Should he have received it only in part, however, the balance due was noted on the document and countersigned by a witness who certified himself accountable for the balance as soon as the enlisted man was approved at the headquarters of the regiment.

From this point Keys, like all recruits, was closely watched until he had been brought safely to the regimental depot which, for the 30th in 1812, was at Hull. He represented money to the recruiting party, and they knew that on average one in ten recruits subsequently absconded, even though this was not the case in their regiment and particularly not for recruits raised in England. If they were thinking more altruistically, they also recognised how desperately the second battalion in Portugal needed reinforcements. Keys, however, was not one to run away. Whatever his motive for enlisting, he was to prove a good soldier.

So far he had experienced only the periphery of military life. When he arrived in Hull, however, he discovered a depot bustling with the business of turning recruits into useful soldiers. In command was Captain (Brevet Major) James Spawforth, supported by Captain Robert Douglas, who had exchanged into the 30th from the 36th the year before. The senior subalterns were Lieutenants James Skirrow and Richard Elliott, both of whom had been recruiting for several years. The former subsequently joined the first battalion in India, while the latter remained with the second battalion and saw active service in Flanders, culminating at Waterloo. The juniors were Ensigns Samuel Robert Poyntz, George Darling, George Madden and Thomas Kelly. If Keys was not too overawed by his new experiences he might have noticed that three of the ensigns, all of them little more than boys, were as green as he was. The exception was Ensign Poyntz. Samuel Robert was the middle of the three brothers who had all served as volunteers with the 30th; a son of the regiment, he was as familiar with the niceties of regimental life as any superannuated captain. Indeed, Samuel Robert, although still only 18, had six years of military experience behind him.

Under the command of these officers were five sergeants, two drummers, eight corporals and forty-seven private soldiers, including five boys. They constituted a mixed bunch: men from the recruiting parties, invalids from Spain and Portugal or from India, volunteers from the militia, four of whom joined in February 1812, and the thirty-one recruits, eight of them from Sleaford, who had also joined in February. They had one thing in common, however; they were all members of that family known formally as the Thirtieth Regiment of the Line, the Cambridgeshire Regiment.

Keys may well have been dismayed to discover that some of his bounty was immediately claimed back to pay for necessaries. Indeed, one must hope that he did not share the experience of too many recruits and find himself in debt as he paid for his three shirts, three pairs of socks, one pair of mitts (much appreciated in windswept Hull), black stock (for which he would never be grateful), foraging cap, clothes and shoe brushes, combs, blackball and greatcoat, along with the straps for carrying it. Too many recruits shared the experience of Joseph Donaldson who, overwhelmed by the mistake he felt he had made in enlisting, fell victim to his new companions' assurance that he would not want for friends while his bounty lasted,

> So I found; for every little attention was paid me that they could devise. One brushed my shoes, another my coat; and nothing could equal the many professions of good-will and offers of service I received. There was a competition amongst them who should be my comrade, each supporting his offer by what service he would render me, such as cleaning my accoutrements, teaching me my exercises, etc. It appeared to me that I was set up at auction to be knocked down to the highest bidder. But I paid little attention to them. My mind was taken up, thinking of my folly, and ruminating on its consequences.
>
> After holding a private consultation amongst themselves, one of them took me aside, and told me it was the usual custom for each recruit, when he joined the company, to give the men of the room he belonged to 'a treat'.[51]

When it had been established that the going rate was a guinea, Donaldson then found himself treating an increasing number of soldiers to whisky.

Drill quickly became the focus of Keys' daily existence as the army sought 'to banish the air of the rustic', 'ensure precision and correctness', and 'inculcate and enforce the necessity of military dependence, and of mutual support in action'. In other words, the purpose was to turn him into the kind of soldier required by the tactics of the time, one who was proficient in 'an equal and cadenced march, acquired and confirmed by habit, independent of music or sound', so that he was capable of 'that precision of movement, which is so essential, and without which valour will not avail'.[52] Before he could learn to march, however, he had first to learn how to stand as a soldier.

The regulations were precise about the position a soldier should adopt. There were only two, *to attention* or *at ease*. During his first days at Hull Keys, wearing a white canvas working tunic, spent a lot of his time banishing the rustic. The correct positions were demonstrated by a fugelman (or more correctly, a flugelman), whom James described as

> a well drilled intelligent soldier advanced in front of the line, to give the time in the manual and platoon exercises. The word flugel is derived from the German, and signifies a wing; the man having been originally posted in front of the right wing.[53]

Keys could only hope that the drill sergeant had taken War Office instructions to heart and, as well as showing 'unremitting perseverance and accurate knowledge of the part [he] has to teach, and a clear concise manner of conveying his instructions, with a firmness that will command from men a perfect attention to the directions he is giving them', would also 'allow for the weak capacity of the Recruit'.[54] He was required to demonstrate patience with willing recruits, since quickness only came with practice.

To attention required the recruit to stand with shoulders square, and body to the front; heels and knees together, but not too stiffly, feet slightly splayed, arms to the side, again not too stiffly, elbows and shoulders back, belly drawn in and chest advanced, again without too much constraint. With his body upright, his weight on the forepart of his feet, and head erect, he would begin to look like a soldier. In contrast, *at ease* required him to draw back his right foot about 6 inches, bend his left knee slightly and bring his hands together to the front of his body. He was still required to face to the front and hold his shoulders back, slouching not being allowed. In cold weather, however, soldiers standing at ease were permitted to move their arms and legs for comfort and warmth, although without quitting their ground.

Once the two basic positions had been mastered, the recruit learnt to respond to simple commands like eyes right, left and to the front, and perform the turning movements known as facings. Marching followed, starting with the ordinary step of 30 inches from heel to heel and seventy-five paces to a minute which was used in all but the most extraordinary circumstances and might have to be maintained over long periods of time and all kinds of terrain. Not that marching over rough ground would be as much a problem for a rural labourer like Keys as it would for town-bred recruits.

Once the ordinary step had been mastered, recruits could move on to the oblique, which, as its name suggests, required the men to describe an oblique angle of 25 degrees. And once they could manage this they were ready to form rank in open file, which led to a further sequence of manoeuvres: the extended 'step out', marking time, stepping short, changing the feet, the side step, the back step and the quick step. This last, at 108 steps a minute, was appreciably slower than the pace of continental infantry but was crucial when changing from column to line. Finally, there was the quickest step of all, the wheeling march at 120 steps a minute.

Initially the open file practice happened in ranks of five. The next stage was file marching in ranks of seven, plus a well-drilled soldier as a flanker, leading on to wheeling in rank. At this point it must be assumed that Keys had attained reasonable competence. As a countryman he had a definite advantage which probably enabled him to progress more easily than the poor weaver, unused to rigorous exercise and fresh air, or the truculent townsman, reluctant to take orders. At the same time, he may well have recognised that he had left one family and found another where the exasperation of a drill sergeant was a minor irritant compared with the easy camaraderie of the men in the ranks. Nor was marching the sum total of his training. The regulations were specific. 'Recruits should not be kept too long at any part of their exercise, so as to fatigue or make them uneasy, and marching without arms should be much intermixed with the firelock instructions.'[55]

The firelock, the musket popularly known as *Brown Bess* which had been the mainstay of the army since the 1720s, was first given to Keys when he was being drilled in the proper positions of a soldier, and practice in its use subsequently punctuated his other training. Since 1797 the India Pattern musket, developed by the East India Company two years earlier, had been standard issue to British infantry. Slightly lighter at 9lb and slightly shorter at 39 inches than earlier versions, it was easier for the soldier to carry. In addition, the weapon had a 14-inch bayonet which, upon occasion, was the deciding factor in settling a fire-fight. Correct use of the bayonet was also an essential part of an inspection.

The 'Different Motions of the Firelock', as they are identified in *The Rules and Regulations*, were supporting arms, carrying arms, ordering arms, standing at ease, attention, and shouldering from the order. To this list was added the instruction that

> The recruit must be accustomed to *carry* his arms for a considerable time together; it is most essential he should do so, and not be allowed to support *them* so often as is practised, under the idea of *carrying* them is a position of too much constraint.[56]

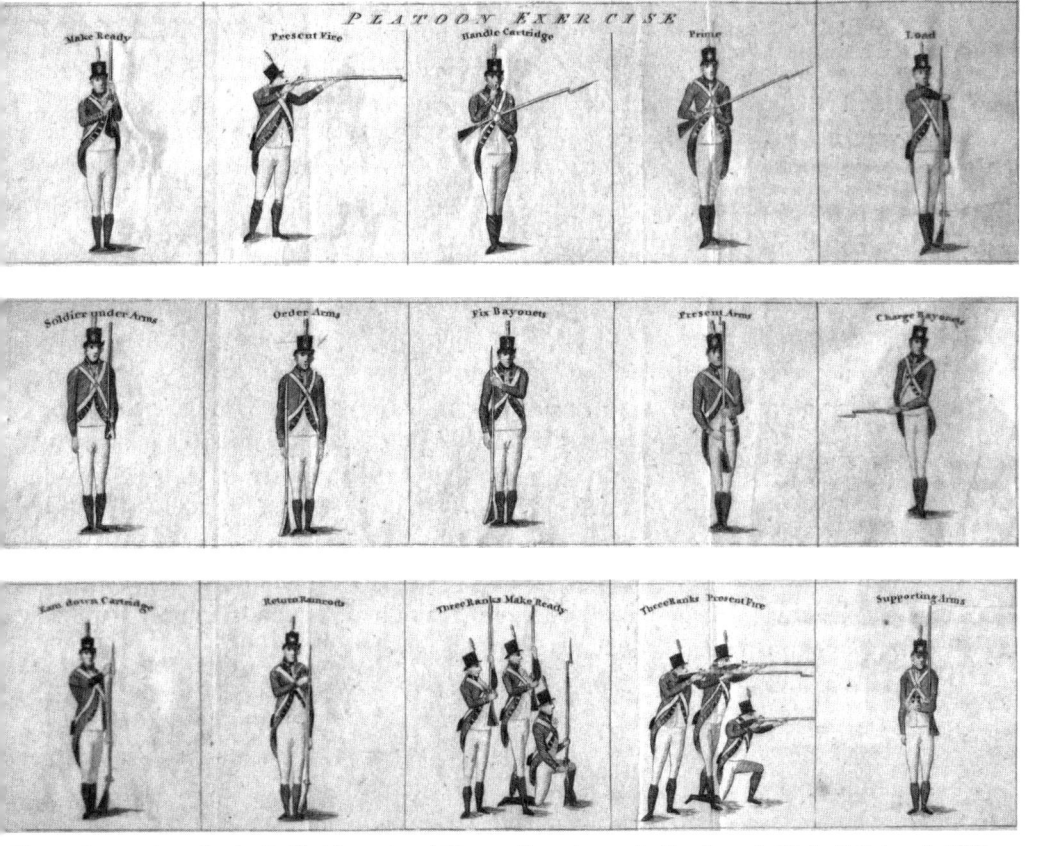

Military Instructions for the Drill, Manual and Platoon Exercises, pub. Denham & Dick, Edinburgh 1803

Carrying arms, of course, was more onerous than supporting arms, and there seems little doubt that most units used the latter position when off the parade ground.

The proper drill for the musket was undertaken in closed files, with the men standing one pace or 30 inches apart. This regulation might be waived in the training of recruits, however. The manual exercises consisted of fourteen commands and the platoon, ten. Together they took the soldier through the whole process of handling, loading and firing his musket and thus were crucial to the unthinking efficiency of the infantryman.

There follow in *The Rules and Regulations* an explanation of priming and loading, as well as a further section on firing which relates to firing by battalion, wing or grand division. For the recruit in the initial stages of his training, however, such matters did not concern him. When he moved from the manual to the platoon exercises, though, it is possible that the reality of soldiering came home to him. The thought of using the bayonet might stir his imagination somewhat unpleasantly, even though old-timers would have told a recruit like Keys that a bayonet charge was a rare event, although firing salvoes was all in a day's work – even though such days came rarely in a soldier's career. What would have been impressed upon him was the importance of removing the ramrod before firing. In the heat of battle too many raw soldiers disabled themselves by forgetting this simple detail and thus losing their capacity to re-load.

By this time, the recruits had been drilling in platoon formation, three ranks and as many as twenty files, closely ordered, muskets shouldered, so that each man occupied a space slightly under 2 feet. There were enough officers and sergeants at the depot for the officer in command (young Mr Poyntz, perhaps, the lad who knew a thing or two about soldiering) to take position to the right of the front rank, covered by a sergeant in the rear rank. Two other sergeants formed a fourth rank, three paces from the third rank. The men within the platoon were then told off into subdivisions, which probably meant little to the recruits, but ensured that four experienced soldiers, recovered invalids perhaps, were prominent in the front rank, on the right and left of each subdivision. Assembled thus, they were put through the motions of opening and closing ranks, and dressing to the front, to the rear, and obliquely. They could then be exercised in the movements of the firelock in this more formal configuration.

The recruits were then put through the various marching procedures, a somewhat confusing experience when some of the commands came from Mr Poyntz, as commander of the platoon, while others were delivered by the drill sergeant, playing the role of commander of the battalion. Consequently, while the ensign delivered orders to step out, mark time, step short and so on, the drill sergeant set the exercises in motion with the commands, 'eyes right' and 'march'. Nor did they merely march forward. They also practised the side step ('to the right close'), the back step ('step back – march'), file marching ('the left face – quick march') and wheeling. Then there were the equally complex movements on

```
  3             5      5              1
  4                                    4
   4    2       7      6    2         4
```

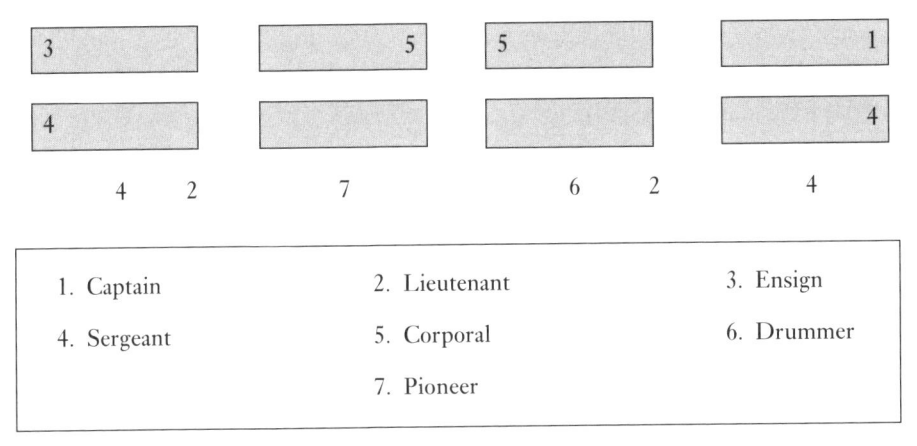

1. Captain	2. Lieutenant	3. Ensign
4. Sergeant	5. Corporal	6. Drummer
	7. Pioneer	

British Infantry Company on Parade

alignment, in open column, of subdivision, and wheeling in alignment. So it would go on: countermarch by files, wheeling on the centre of the platoon, oblique marching, increasing and diminishing the front of an open column while on the march, breaking off files to pass a short defile, marching in quick time. Different formations were learnt and practised: from front to file, from file to either flank, marching in echelon, to instance but a few. And the drill sergeant warned them that such practice would continue throughout their military careers, never more crucially than when the battalion came under the scrutiny of an inspecting general.

Of course, all this learning and practice was not the business of just a few days, either for the recruits or for the young officers. The platoon would soon have realised that the subalterns at the depot (except Lieutenant O'Halloran, newly transferred from the 54th) were learning the business of soldiering just as they were. There would have been a significant difference, however. While the officers' mistakes were politely pointed out to them by the drill sergeant, no such courtesy was afforded to the men in the ranks. They were simply bawled out for their blunders.

The next step for Keys was to learn and practise battalion manoeuvres, but the second battalion was far away in Spain. By the time he joined them, they were retreating from Burgos. On the 25th October he fired his musket in anger for the first time when he faced the French across the River Carrion at Villamuriel. There he quickly learnt the realities of being in action, a hard struggle to hold and finally drive back the French. Then there was the long, difficult march back to Portugal, an experience which taught him the miseries of soldiering and put all the months of training into harsh perspective. Among those who did not survive the retreat was young Mr Kelly, who died of exhaustion in a hospital cart.

As for the battalion manoeuvres, he finally experienced them during the winter months when the battalion was quartered at Vila Nova del Rey. On the 16th January 1813 General Hay inspected the battalion and made the following comment:

78 *Inside the Regiment*

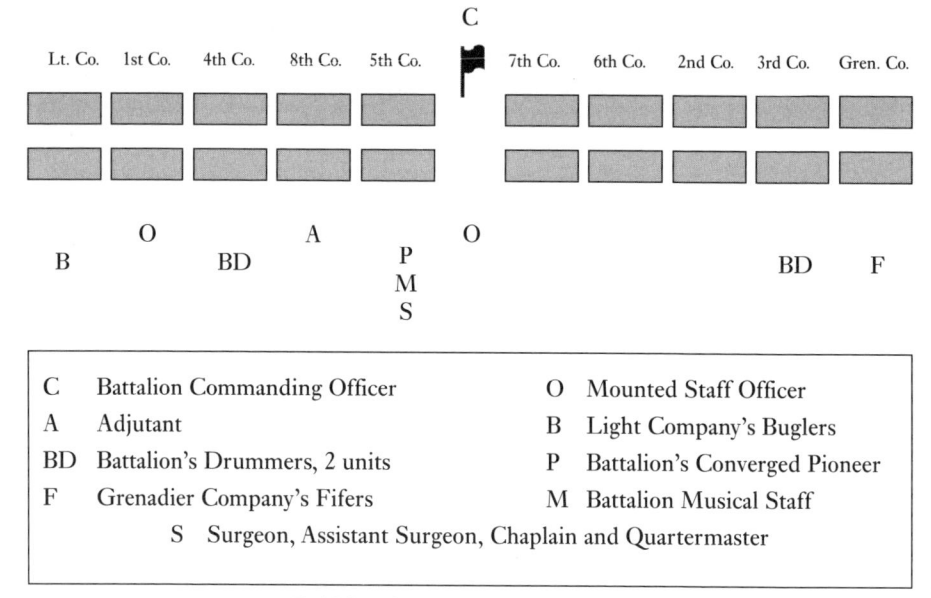

| | | | | C | | | | | |
|Lt. Co.|1st Co.|4th Co.|8th Co.|5th Co.|7th Co.|6th Co.|2nd Co.|3rd Co.|Gren. Co.|

                O   A   O
    B   F
              BD   P   BD
                                 M
                                 S

C	Battalion Commanding Officer	O	Mounted Staff Officer
A	Adjutant	B	Light Company's Buglers
BD	Battalion's Drummers, 2 units	P	Battalion's Converged Pioneer
F	Grenadier Company's Fifers	M	Battalion Musical Staff
	S Surgeon, Assistant Surgeon, Chaplain and Quartermaster		

British Infantry Battalion on Parade

Privates: The body of men pretty good mostly young & have a clean & healthy appearance – the men are drilled & drilling according to the King's Regulations. Their numbers actually in the ranks correspond exactly with the returns – every man present does his duty as a soldier.

As for the field exercises and movements, 'Formations [were] according to the established regulations, their movements & formations as far as I have had an opportunity of seeing are made with precision & a proper degree of celerity.'[57] It must have been difficult for the battalion to perform, and Hay to assess, the required manoeuvres in an area where everything was on a steep gradient, but the men in the ranks obviously gave a clear impression of competence.

As a young, fit man Keys stayed with the four companies in Portugal until the summer of 1813. He was also part of the Flanders expedition in 1814. He missed the actions at Quatre Bras and Waterloo, however, being returned as in the general hospital. Three weeks later he was dead. Nevertheless, in his short career with the 30th he had proved himself a well-conducted soldier.

Chapter 6

The Backbone of the Regiment

There can be little doubt that the efficiency of any regiment depended upon the quality of its non-commissioned officers, particularly its sergeants. As the lynchpin between its officers, particularly the inexperienced and often untrained subalterns, and the men in the ranks, good sergeants could ensure efficiency and discipline, a fact recognised by Wellington. The honorary rank of colour sergeant, nominally instituted by the Prince Regent in 1813, was Wellington's suggestion as a fitting reward for men who had given particularly distinguished service.

James defined a sergeant (or *serjeant* to use the more common contemporary spelling) as 'a non-commissioned officer or inferior officer in a company or troop, armed with a pike, and appointed to see discipline observed' both in and out of action. Good sergeants meant well-disciplined troops who would be kept under control, particularly during those long periods when the men were not under arms, and consequently, more likely to succumb to the temptations which made for disorder. As the career of Samuel Bircham demonstrates, the best of them could take command in a crisis as Bircham did at Toulon.

Sergeants were also required

> to teach the private men their exercises; and to order, straighten, and form rank, files etc. He receives the orders from the serjeant-major, which he communicates to his officers. Each company has generally three serjeants in the British service.[58]

In his *Regimental Companion*, James elaborated on the role of the sergeant within the daily life of the regiment:

> A non-commissioned officer is to attend strictly to every circumstance of a soldier's conduct and behaviour in his quarters, and to make it his business to discover the different shades of character, so as to satisfy his commanding officer on every point of enquiry.
>
> Every non-commissioned officer must be perfectly acquainted with the duties of a battalion, be master of the manual and platoon exercises, etc and know how to write in a clear and expeditious manner…

> Non-commissioned officers enforcing the orders they have received, must avoid all kinds of altercation. They must be firm, collected, and concise in their communications, and by no means peevish, brutal, or impatient.[59]

In the hierarchy of non-commissioned officers, the highest position was occupied by the sergeant-major, one to a battalion. The 30th, therefore, always had two sergeant-majors during the two-battalion period, 1803–1817. The first to hold the post was David Glass, a long-serving soldier who was already RSM in 1803. This experience was most useful in the junior battalion, with its function as a training ground and feeder unit for the senior battalion. Consequently, George Stephenson was appointed RSM in the first battalion. Interestingly, both Glass and Stephenson were commissioned in 1810, in acknowledgement of their service, Glass as ensign in the 4th Royal Veteran Battalion and Stephenson as ensign and adjutant with the first battalion in India. Glass was succeeded by James Woods, who was already an acting sergeant-major in Gibraltar in 1809 and who remained with the second battalion until reduction in 1817. He had joined from the militia in September 1808, and within a month had advanced to corporal and then to sergeant. In India William Ledge, the long-serving soldier who was later to be commissioned and appointed adjutant, replaced Stephenson. All these men seem to have fulfilled the position of RSM with distinction, as their subsequent commissions demonstrate.

According to James:

> The serjeant-major is the first non-commissioned officer in the regiment after the quartermaster. He is, in fact, an assistant to the adjutant. It is his peculiar duty to be perfect master of everything that relates to drills; and it is always expected, that he should set an example, to the rest of the non-commissioned officers, of manly, soldier-like, and zealous activity. He must be thoroughly acquainted with all the details which regard the interior management and the discipline of a regiment. For this purpose he must be a good penman, and must keep regular lists of the serjeants and corporals

as well as the duty rosters for the battalion, being solely responsible for their accuracy. He had to

> look well to the appearance of the men, and order such to drill as he sees awkward, slovenly, or in any way irregular. If it be meant as a punishment, he specifies the time for which they are sent for drill; if only for awkwardness, they remain there until their faults are removed.[60]

It follows, therefore, that when a battalion was complimented on its drill during an inspection, the sergeant-major could take much of the credit, even though the initiative for extra drill came from the commanding officer.[61]

When a battalion was found lacking, as the first were in April 1809 at Trichinopoly and the second at Cadiz in June 1810, the sergeant-major had to accept some responsibility. General Wilkinson, who inspected the first battalion, made excuses for a corps in which he had served for so many years, detailing the numbers of men who had been at sea and the time they had spent on board ship.[62]

This is perhaps a little disingenuous when compared with the second battalion in November 1813. They had been reunited as a single unit for only two months, after the four companies returned from the Peninsula; at this point the six companies included in the ranks a large number of recovering invalids and recruits. Nevertheless, they were praised for their field exercises and movements which again 'were performed with precision, and the formations made with correctness, and a proper degree of celerity'. This was very different from 1810, when 'sufficient attention however [had] not been paid to the drill of the regiment, and the field movements were by no means accurate', and reflected credit on RSM Woods, but also on Lieutenant-Colonel Hamilton, who had a particular talent for bringing units up to scratch and on this occasion was complimented for bestowing great attention on the battalion, which had made 'the progress in Discipline, in its Field Exercises, and is fairly versed in the manoeuvres prescribed by His Majetsy's Command'.[63]

To return to the responsibilities of the RSM, he had a further duty to put non-commissioned officers under arrest before reporting to the adjutant what he had done. This was a duty which he might be required to carry out with unfortunate regularity since even some of the best NCOs were unable to resist the temptation which was so often the downfall of the private soldier, the lure of alcohol. Other offences which required the RSM to exercise his power were 'confining and releasing a prisoner without orders', acting against an officer's orders, 'striking and ill-treating a private', 'breach of regimental orders by associating and drinking with private soldiers' (a reminder of the strict hierarchy of the army), sitting with a drunk soldier, 'absent from quarters after hours', insolence and disrespect, and the catch-all 'unsoldierlike conduct'. Except for drunkenness, the acquittal rate and the chance of being pardoned was much higher for NCOs than men in the ranks and even those found guilty and demoted could still regain their former position.

In addition to his responsibility for the discipline and general behaviour of the non-commissioned officers, the RSM, in his role as drill-master, was required to oversee the drill of all the young officers who came into the battalion, a duty which devolved on him from the adjutant. He instructed them in manual and platoon exercises, slow and quick marching, and all the other manoeuvres which made up early nineteenth-century drill. This could prove lucrative since each officer who received instruction was obliged to pay him for the privilege.

James concluded his observations by remarking 'that the good and bad appearance of a regiment, with or without arms, depends greatly upon the skill and activity of a serjeant-major; and that he has every inducement to look forward to promotion'.[64] In James' opinion, therefore, all four RSMs of the two-battalion period received their just reward.

In the muster rolls, the name of the RSM is followed by a list of staff sergeants who were equally important to the interior management and economy of the battalion. Taken in alphabetical order, the first was the armourer sergeant, who had responsibility for the battalion's arms under the command of the quartermaster. William Scott, promoted from private in July 1803, initially held the position in the first battalion and Joseph Peale (reduced to private in August 1805) and Nathaniel Artis, in the second battalion. Unfortunately, the records give no indication of why Peale was reduced during the annual encampment on the Curragh. Artis joined the regiment on the 3rd September, served one day as a corporal (without any previous military experience) and was then promoted to armourer sergeant. This would normally be a somewhat puzzling promotion because of its rapidity and specific nature, but Artis was a gunsmith, 28 years of age, so his arrival in the second battalion must have seemed like the most fortuitous of coincidences. He remained with the second battalion until reduction, when his conduct was described as good, spent a further year with the Royal Veteran Battalion, again as armourer sergeant, and finally retired to Stilton, in Huntingdon where he may well have taken up his previous trade as a gunsmith. Peale, meanwhile, was transferred to the first battalion, where he quickly redeemed himself. Scott was reduced in June 1805 and the first battalion functioned without an armourer sergeant until April 1807, when Peale was promoted. A year later, Peale was dead and Scott returned to his former position, which he held for four years, until a second reduction in June 1812. After this there is no further reference to an armourer sergeant.

The paymaster sergeant (or paymaster's clerk as he was known), needed to be 'an honest, steady non-commissioned officer, (who is a good accountant and writes well)'.[65] Each company had a pay sergeant, but the staff sergeant had overall responsibility for ensuring the men actually received their money. He also checked the state of their necessaries, which had a strange habit of 'disappearing', and making up the monthly abstract for everything relating to pay. In order to do this, he collated the returns of the company pay-sergeants, who in turn were responsible for paying the men twice a week and accounting weekly to the commanding officer of their company for all disbursements.

The first battalion definitely had problems with their staff sergeants. In 1803 the paymaster sergeant was Robert Cummins. He was reduced in March 1804, and six months later William Grellis, a weaver from Galway who had enlisted in 1798 and fought in the Egypt campaign, was promoted from private. He had been a corporal and, briefly, a sergeant, before being demoted. Grellis initially lasted eighteen months before also being reduced. The position was left vacant for over a year, but in July 1807 Grellis was promoted for the second time, this time holding the position until he was discharged in 1821. The comment on his discharge papers that he was 'generally well conducted' acknowledges that there had been some bad patches in his career. Thomas Cuthbert held the position in the second battalion from 1805 (the point at which the battalion acquired a paymaster) to 1817 and reduction. He was a trimmer from Leicestershire who enlisted in September 1804, served six days as corporal and nearly twelve years as a sergeant. On discharge, his conduct was described as excellent, and he was commended for his service as paymaster clerk.

Judging from what happened in the 30th, the quartermaster sergeant, like the RSM, was likely to gain a commission. Three quartermaster sergeants, Ninian and Henry Craig, and Robert Daniell were commissioned as company officers. Other quartermaster sergeants like Arthur Poyntz and Nicholas Wilson in the first battalion became quartermasters, perhaps a more predictable step. John Forster Kingsley, who joined the second battalion as quartermaster, had made the same progression in his previous regiment. The quartermaster sergeant was required to work under the direction of the quartermaster. Since the quartermaster, unlike the paymaster, did not have to support his commission with a large sum of money, his sergeant would be an obvious candidate for promotion when there was a vacancy. According to James, he needed to be 'a steady man, a good accountant, and be well acquainted with the resources of a country – town or village'.

The last of the staff sergeants listed in the muster rolls was the schoolmaster sergeant, whose duty was to instruct the children of a battalion where, with the support of the commanding officer, a school had been set up. An inspection return of the first battalion for 1815 makes clear that not only children attended. The school was

> in very good order, it is attended by a number of non-commissioned officers but by few privates, the whole of the boys and girls of a sufficient age attend, many of them made good progress in arithmetic. The sergeant attached to the school is of a good character and perfectly competent to the duties.[66]

A later inspection report from 1820 noted that the schoolmaster sergeant was 'vigilant and correct' and 'the children under his tuition make great progress in the different sciences'. In other words, the army was giving an education to both men and children which they would have been unlikely to receive in a similar civilian situation.

The position of schoolmaster sergeant was instituted in 1811. The first schoolmaster sergeant with the first battalion was Luke Berry, appointed in January 1812, but (following the pattern of the battalion's staff sergeants) was then reduced in July 1813. No replacement is named in the musters but the comments in the 1815 inspection report suggest that there was an acting schoolmaster sergeant. The schoolmaster sergeant of the second battalion was Luke Lydon, a labourer from Galway. This seems an unlikely background, but as we have seen, *labourer* was an indeterminate label which had no connection with natural intelligence and talent. Lydon was a man of exemplary long service who enlisted into the second battalion in 1808, aged 24, and remained with the regiment until 1830. He was a sergeant within two years of joining, and two years later was sent to Chelsea for training as schoolmaster sergeant. He remained with the depot, where the children were, until the battalion returned from France at the end of 1815. He accompanied them to Ireland and, in 1817, sailed with the remnants to India, where he continued to serve as schoolmaster sergeant. Sadly, his career came to a melancholy conclusion. His discharge papers noted that 'his conduct has been that of a very good, efficient NCO'. His constitution was broken, however, and this, according to the regimental surgeon, had affected his mind. Nevertheless, he survived to claim the GSM for his Peninsular service.[67]

In his dictionary James mentions three other distinctions of sergeant. The drill sergeant was

> an expert and active non-commissioned officer, who, under the immediate direction of the serjeant-major, instructs the raw recruits of a regiment in the first principles of military exercise. When awkward, or ill-behaved men are sent to drill, they are usually placed under the care of the drill-serjeant.[68]

There is no record of who performed this function in either battalion, but it must be hoped they shared James' view that they should not put their charges under so much pressure that they became antagonistic to the exercise.

A lance-sergeant was merely a corporal who acted as a sergeant in a company while still receiving a corporal's pay. Covering-sergeants had a function to perform during exercise, when they were required to stand and move behind each officer commanding a company or platoon. When the ranks were in open order, which required the officers to move forward, the covering-sergeants would take their place, returning to their former positions when the order to close ranks was given. In a more light-hearted vein, James also mentions *white-sergeants*, ladies who were able through the weakness of their husbands to interfere in military matters. Not surprisingly, none of this last category found her way into regimental records.

A further distinction which James did not include in his dictionary, even in the 1816 edition, was the newly-instituted rank of colour sergeant. This honorary rank was established in May, 1813 and a memorandum from Horse Guards set out the particulars of the new appointment:

> With a view to meliorate the situation of the non-commissioned officers of the infantry, and to hold out to the most deserving of them a station somewhat raised above their comrades, but in no respect interfering with their present duties, or in the slightest degree lessening their liability to reduction or other punishment on subsequent misconduct; it is proposed that one of the sergeants on the establishment of each company shall hereafter be denominated the *colour sergeant*; that it shall be the province of these sergeants exclusively to be orderly over the colours when in the field, two, four, or more being appointed to that duty, according to the circumstances of the case; that they shall receive, in addition to their pay, each the sum of four pence per diem; and that they shall be distinguished by wearing a crown over their chevrons.

The news of the new rank took time to reach India and it was March 1814 before Vaumorel appointed the first colour sergeants to the senior battalion. Although the number per battalion was ten, he initially appointed five, all long-serving NCOs of exemplary character and conduct. A month later he added one more, and then in October two men who had served with distinction in responsible posts. Thomas Harris was acting sergeant-major at Poonamallee, which was a staging post for invalids returning to Europe and newcomers from Europe. Henry Murphy was initially store sergeant at Madras, and then at Poonamallee.

Hamilton's choices deserve consideration because they tell us a lot about the kind of men who initially filled the new rank, particularly the variety of their background and the similarity of their military experience. As we have seen, Hamilton's words of highest approval were 'zealous', 'gallant', 'honest' and 'trustworthy'. Presumably, he found all these qualities in the men he singled out for the new honour.

Two of his chosen men were already sergeants before augmentation and were among the senior NCOs transferred to bring experience to the new unit. Taken together, William Brien (or Bryan) and Matthew Donnellan had forty-three years of service when they were rewarded with the rank of colour sergeant. Brien was a labourer from Cashel, Tipperary, who enlisted in 1795, aged about 18, according to his discharge papers. He served six years as private and three years as corporal before being promoted to sergeant. Hamilton stated in his discharge papers that 'he has served faithfully and honestly… [and] always conducted himself as a good and faithful soldier'. He was about 5 feet 9 inches tall, above the average height of the battalion, as were many of the sergeants.

Matthew Donnellan was also an Irish labourer from Roscommon who enlisted in the same year as Brien, when he was 23. His promotion was rapid. He served only a year as a private before being promoted to corporal; two and half years later he was made sergeant. Both Brien and Donnellan saw extensive active service with the second battalion. Although neither of them claimed the GSM, in all probability having died by the time it was belatedly awarded, they both served in the Peninsula. Donnellan was also the battalion clerk during this period, working under the adjutant, and completed official returns with exemplary neatness.

Hamilton's next two nominees, both labourers, came into the regiment in 1803, at the time of augmentation; John Ward on the 18th August and Joseph Berridge on the 15th October. Some complication is caused by Berridge being variously recorded as Burridge, Burrage and even Burmage, but evidence from the muster rolls makes clear that the colour sergeant of 1813 is the recruit from the Army of Reserve of 1803. Berridge was 18 when he enlisted, a labourer from Wigston, Leicestershire. It was some years before he attracted attention, but having been promoted to corporal in March 1808 he was made sergeant five months later. During 1812 he was acting RSM. So his appointment to colour sergeant was no surprise.

John Ward, from Dunton in Buckinghamshire was 22 when he joined the 30th, like Berridge from the Army of Reserve. His promotion was rapid, corporal in 1804 and sergeant in 1805. When he claimed the GSM, he received bars for Fuentes de Oñoro, Badajoz and Salamanca, although an earlier statement of service had omitted the last action. There is nothing in the muster roll for July 1812 to suggest that he missed the battle and its omission from the statement of service for 1827 was probably an oversight.

George McCann, a labourer from New Brunswick, enlisted into the second battalion at Athlone in May 1805, aged 25. A month later he was made corporal, and ten months after that he was promoted to sergeant. He, like Ward, survived to claim the GMS, with bars for Fuentes de Oñoro, Badajoz and Salamanca. He also served as drum major from May 1811 until September 1812.

So far all the colour sergeants were men who served only with the regiment into which they enlisted. The next of Hamilton's choices was a man who moved between regiments. Joseph Scotton, whose career has already been referred to, was a Leicestershire man, born in the parish of Claybrook, near Lutterworth. He was a hosier which was probably a family occupation. His discharge papers give his date of enlistment into the 30th as the 5th August 1806, when he was 30. This was the point when many of the men who had come from the Army of Reserve in 1803 transferred to general service, or transferred out of the regiment into garrison battalions. Scotton first appears in the muster rolls in 1803; after more than two years with the second battalion he was obviously happy to continue his military career.

What makes Scotton interesting are his two earlier periods of service as a cavalryman, two and a half years with the Royal Horse Guards and seven years with the 10th Light Dragoons. The transfer from cavalry to infantry is unusual, but the Army of Reserve was an infantry corps and as a still young, retired soldier he would have been an obvious choice for this force. Whether Scotton volunteered or was impressed is impossible to establish but he may have found that peacetime life as a hosier did not suit him. Possibly, after an absence of ten years, he resented the increased mechanisation that was replacing the cottage industry.

As a cavalryman he never rose above the rank of trooper, whereas with the 30th he was made corporal within five months of volunteering for general service, and sergeant eighteen months later. He also provides evidence, as does Donnellan, that Minet and Hamilton could overlook a minor failing in an NCO, although for a serious offence demotion would prove permanent. Donnellan's fall from grace occurred in August 1810, while the battalion was in Cadiz. He was demoted to the ranks, where he served for five months before being promoted to corporal. By May 1811 he was once more a sergeant. Scotton's experience was similar, if somewhat speedier. He was demoted on the 18th January, made corporal a week later, and restored to the rank of sergeant in August of the same year. No doubt a valuable lesson had been learnt.

Like the other colour sergeants so far considered, Scotton was present at all the actions in the Peninsula, having enjoyed excellent health throughout.

The last of the original seven colour sergeants was Thomas Connolly, another Irish labourer, from Leaney, County Antrim, who had joined the regiment in July

1803. He was promoted to corporal in October 1809, and to sergeant two years later. Although he was in the general hospital for the second half of 1812, he was present at all the actions in Spain except Villamuriel.

The original colour sergeants first appear in the muster roll for September to December 1813, three of them English and four Irish. In the next muster roll (December 1813 to March 1814) two more were added. Christopher Barnwell was an Irish labourer who enlisted in September 1805. Six months later he was promoted to corporal, but then waited another three years before being made up to sergeant. Like Brien and Ward, he spent much of the first period in Ireland on recruiting duties, but sailed with the rest of the battalion to Lisbon in March 1809. He probably missed Fuentes de Oñoro because of sickness but was present at all the actions of 1812.

Joseph (or Josiah) Harrison was the tenth of the original colour sergeants, a labourer from Bottesham in Cambridgeshire who enlisted in 1806, aged 19. Within three years he was a young corporal, and two years later he was promoted to sergeant. Interestingly, his discharge papers say that he served as corporal for only a year, but the muster rolls contradict this and are probably more reliable. He was the third of the original colour sergeants to claim the GMS, having seen action at Fuentes de Oñoro, Badajoz and Salamanca.

Considered as a group, it is significant that all but one had come into the army as *labourers*, a reminder that the army did indeed offer opportunity to men of talent, whatever their background. Their service records also suggest that they were the kind of men Wellington had in mind when he persuaded the Prince Regent to institute this new rank. Although there were longer-serving sergeants than all of them except Brien and Donnellan, Hamilton was presumably looking for something more than years of service. All of them had taken the chance over the years to reveal qualities of leadership, those qualities of zeal, gallantry, honesty and trust which Hamilton valued so highly. Furthermore, it is heartening that he could accommodate the occasional minor lapse within the wider concept of meritorious conduct. Yet for some of them the Peninsula and the appointment to colour sergeant was the high point of their military career.

By Waterloo only four of the original colour sergeants still held that rank. George McCann had been reduced two months previously for unsoldierlike conduct and although he was re-appointed sergeant a month later he never regained the higher honour. He retired, 'worn out', when the second battalion was disbanded with the comment that his conduct had been good. A colour sergeant, though, needed to sustain exemplary conduct. John Ward had also returned to the rank of sergeant early in 1815, but for a different reason. He was appointed Assistant Provost Marshal, a position of considerable responsibility in maintaining discipline, which he held for the rest of the year until the battalion left France. Once he was back with his unit, however, he was restored to the rank of colour sergeant. Transferred to the first battalion upon reduction he retained this rank until December 1821 when he was QMS. Three years later he became the regiment's quartermaster, finally retiring in 1847 after forty-three years' service.

A commission came much earlier for Joseph Berridge. Having served in Flanders, he was made ensign without purchase in March 1815. He missed Quatre Bras and Waterloo because he was at the regimental depot in England. After Napoleon's final defeat, and the general reduction of the army, the rate of promotion slowed down. Berridge remained an ensign until 1820, when he was promoted to lieutenant, again without purchase. This remained his rank until his death at Castlebar in 1833. Nevertheless, like other promoted sergeants, the young labourer from Wigston, who found himself in the Army of Reserve, and then in the ranks of the 30th in 1803, had demonstrated that the early nineteenth-century army, caste-ridden though it was, still offered rewards for exceptional talent.

Neither Thomas Connolly nor Joseph Harrison was still a colour sergeant when Waterloo was fought. After he returned from the Peninsula, Connolly spent the period from September 1813 until October 1814 on furlough, and then at the regimental depot. When he finally rejoined the battalion he was returned in the muster roll as sergeant, with no explanation as to why he no longer held the higher position. It might be surmised, however, that his protracted absence had persuaded Hamilton to replace him with another equally deserving man, probably Edward Lane, who was appointed colour sergeant in the same month that Connolly arrived in Flanders. Connolly is subsequently returned as in the general hospital, where he seems to have been the hospital sergeant. This was at the time of Waterloo so, like Ward, he was entrusted with a position of considerable responsibility. Again like Ward, he remained in this position until the end of the year. He also survived reduction, transferring to the first battalion in 1817. He died in India four years later, still with the rank of sergeant.

Harrison moved in a different direction, being appointed quartermaster sergeant in 1814, a position he held at Waterloo, where he received a wound in his foot. In October of the same year he was reduced. There is no explanation in the muster roll why he was demoted to the ranks, but it is possible that the temptations of a quartermaster's resources proved irresistible. A further mystery is contained in his discharge papers, which list him as serving as QMS for three years, although the muster rolls make clear that the position was held by Robert White from October 1815 until reduction, by which point Harrison had left the regiment, having been discharged in 1816 on account of his Waterloo wound. Significantly perhaps, there is no comment on Harrison's conduct.

William Brien missed the Flanders campaign of 1814. He remained at the depot until February 1815, when he joined the battalion along with Sergeants Charles Kilmartin and Francis Brady, the two of them, somewhat unusually, having travelled without a detachment. He fought at Quatre Bras and Waterloo, but after this the deterioration in his health must have been fairly rapid, and he was discharged a year later, either suffering from asthma, a condition that had developed in the Peninsula, or for 'general debility'. Hamilton wrote on his discharge papers:

I do hereby certify that Serjt Wm Brien has served faithfully and honestly in said Regiment for the space of twenty three years two hundred and twenty four days during which period he always conducted himself as a good and faithful soldier.

In 1830 the War Office began a thorough check of pension records, and discovered that Brien's discharge details claimed two years' service to which he was not entitled. He had actually enlisted in 1797 rather than 1795 and was called upon to explain the discrepancy.

He wrote in his defence that he was

> entirely unconscious of any Error having been made in my Statement of Service and as it appears from the Report of the Court of Enquiry that I have rec'd credit for two years service more than I was legally entitled to, I must beg leave to state that the Error was not in any way occasioned by me, as I never was a Clerk in the Orderly Room of the Regt and never had the smallest influence over any person in that situation, and I here most solemnly aver that I had no act or part either directly or indirectly in causing any erasure to be made in the Record Book of the Regiment. I further beg leave to state that I am perfectly willing to refund in any way which your honor may consider most eligible the amount overdrawn in consequence of the Error in the statement of my service, but I most earnestly beseech your honor not to deprive me of my pension and consign me to beggary in my old age after having spent the best years of my life in the service of my Country, and when I state that I have spent the best of my life in the service of my Country, I do not make a vain Boast as the following simple statement will show – I was at the taking of Malta in 1800, through the whole Campaign in Egypt and present in every action, in the Peninsula from April 1809 to June 1813 and fought at the battle of Almaida [Fuentes de Oñoro], Badajoz (where I was wounded) and Salamanca, besides several actions of lesser note, I had likewise a share in the memorable Battle of Waterloo. I have only further to state that I am now an old man and totally unfit to provide for myself in any way and I most humbly beg that your honor will be graciously pleased to take my case into consideration, and not by stopping my pension throw me destitute upon the World.

One hopes that he was allowed to keep his well-deserved pension, but there is no official confirmation.

Like Brien, Matthew Donnellan had also retained the rank of colour sergeant, but he was not present at Waterloo. He had sailed with the battalion from Jersey to Flanders at the beginning of 1814, experiencing the bitter cold and harsh conditions of Graham's expedition to drive the French out of Antwerp. However, in October of that year he was sent to the depot, and then to a recruiting party. He was by this time 43, and was probably feeling the effects of many years of active service, from Malta and Egypt to Spain, Portugal and Flanders. When he was discharged upon reduction in 1817, he had served with the regiment for twenty-two years. The rigours of India were not ideal for a man of his age who was described on his discharge papers as 'worn out'. Hamilton, who had a long memory, wrote that his conduct was 'most excellent and [he] behaved most gallantly in Egypt'.

It is something of a surprise that Joseph Scotton was still a colour sergeant at Waterloo. In July 1814 he was reduced to sergeant, although he does not appear in the list of regimental courts martial. Nevertheless, his offence must have required some punishment because he was not restored to his meritorious rank until February 1815. He fought at Waterloo, where he received the leg wound which brought his career to an end. Having spent three months in the general hospital, and another three months invalided in Brussels, which suggests the seriousness of the wound, he was able to join the battalion as they left France. He remained at Dover when the rest of the battalion sailed to Ireland, and then reported to Chelsea, where he was discharged with a pension on the 6th September 1816. Hamilton endorsed him as 'a most deserving soldier, having been appointed colour sergeant'.

Christopher Barnwell, still a colour sergeant on the 18th June 1815, was the third of the original appointees to receive a wound at Waterloo which in his case proved fatal. The muster roll for the 24th June records that he died that very day at the hospital of the 81st Regiment in Brussels, still owed the prize money due to him for his service in the Peninsula.

It is beyond the scope of this work to discuss all the colour sergeants appointed from 1813 to 1829, when the regiment returned to Britain from India, but the ones instanced above may be taken as typical of the men Vaumorel and Hamilton appointed. Similarly, to consider all the sergeants individually who served with the regiment in the period under consideration would prove self-defeating, particularly since so many of them followed similar careers. Even by confining our attention to the second battalion, which existed for only fourteen years, we would be considering 199 individuals. By focusing on this battalion in general terms, however, it is possible to draw conclusions which would be equally applicable to the first battalion, and to the regiment in its single-battalion state.

Perhaps one of the most surprising aspects of their careers is the frequency with which sergeants were demoted. In the second battalion alone there were sixty-four demotions, and even more in the first. As we have seen, reduction to the ranks might not be the end of the story. Indeed, so brief were some of the periods of reduction that it may have been regarded as the most appropriate punishment for a sergeant who had committed a forgivable misdemeanour. Twenty-three men were eventually reinstated to sergeant, while others were given a second chance as corporal, as if this rank was more appropriate to their talents. Reinstatement might not prove permanent, however. Five of the twenty-three who were reinstated were subsequently demoted for a second time. Somewhat surprisingly, one of them, Thomas Davison, was then made sergeant for a third time. He had first been promoted from corporal in September 1805, only to be reduced in October 1806.

Promoted for a second time in October 1808, he was then reduced to the ranks in August 1810. His final promotion to sergeant came in September 1812, preceded by five months as corporal during which he had presumably proved himself a reformed character. He was appointed corporal the day after the assault at Badajoz, so it is possible that his conduct there attracted favourable attention. He was one of the NCOs who did not return from the Peninsula, dying in June 1813 at the point when the four companies were about to sail back to England.

Whether or not a man was re-promoted depended very much upon the offence he had committed which led to his demotion. Later inspection returns contain details of regimental courts martial, and from these it is possible to identify the offences which led to permanent reduction. Of the eight sergeants for whom there is a record the most common offence was unsoldierlike conduct, sometimes amplified by further detail. For example, Sergeant John Carroll was convicted of unsoldierlike conduct and disobedience to orders for which he was reduced, but he was re-appointed six months later. Sergeant Michael Jacob, however, who was reduced for unsoldierlike conduct while recruiting remained in the ranks. Sergeant George McCann's unsoldierlike conduct, as we have seen, led to his demotion from colour sergeant to sergeant, while Sergeant William Haydon, found guilty of unsoldierlike conduct and neglect of duty, although sentenced to reduction was restored on account of his good character. Sergeant Edward Costello, who was found guilty of unsoldierlike conduct and neglect of duty, had to wait four months for re-appointment but Sergeant Brien Cline, reduced for disobedience to orders and disrespect to the QMS on the 5th May 1815, was restored on the very day of his court martial.

Only one sergeant whose offence is known was not reappointed. John Surety was found guilty of sitting with a drunk soldier in May 1814, thus undermining the hierarchy and the discipline of the battalion. A year later he was a casualty at Waterloo.

Just what unsoldierlike conduct might encompass is made clearer by the records of the first battalion, where offences such as confining and releasing a private without orders, using improper language to the QMS, being drunk and late for inspection or drunk and unfit for duty appear in the records. Even in the first battalion, where punishments tended to be harsher, no sergeant was sent to the halberds. Where a flogging was added to reduction, as happened several times in India, the physical punishment was always altered to a period of solitary confinement, sometimes in irons. The first battalion also practised suspension from rank and pay for periods varying between fourteen days and a month. There was clearly a recognition that to send a senior NCO to the halberds might well undermine the overall discipline of the battalion.

What ultimately happened to sergeants, apart from demotion, is surprisingly varied. Forty-three of the second battalion sergeants survived to receive an honourable discharge, a considerable number of them men who had been reduced and re-appointed. They tended to be described in their discharge papers as 'worn out' or suffering 'general debility', although some, like Brien, had specific medical conditions. Even a worn-out soldier might find his service extended in a defensive unit. Two sergeants transferred into a Royal Veteran Battalion (Lisbon) before the departure from the Peninsula, while earlier in 1806 three sergeants went into garrison battalions along with the men from the Army of Reserve who chose not to volunteer for general service.

The introduction of short service meant that men could serve for seven years, after which they could re-enlist, whereupon their earlier period of service would count towards a pension. A steady stream of men came into the battalion under this arrangement and some of them rose to the rank of sergeant. What they chose to do after their seven years' service varied. Brien Cline and Charles Dewar both left at that point, but Charles Haughey and John Carroll re-enlisted, the former to rise to the rank of QMS with the first battalion in India, the latter to become a colour sergeant. In total fourteen sergeants transferred from the second to the first battalion during the two-battalion period, while a further fifteen went to India after reduction, including five colour sergeants. Most of the transfers happened while both battalions were in Ireland, or at least while the second battalion was on home service. Two sergeants, however, are returned as transferred to the first battalion while serving in the Peninsula and both sailed back to Britain, but one of them, Charles Stradling, instead of going to India, was sent on recruiting duties. A woolcomber from Wellington, Somerset (not the usual recruiting ground of the 30th) he had served with the Marines for ten years in the last decade of the eighteenth century and was 40 when he joined the 30th at the end of 1804, having served 'elsewhere' between 1800 and 1803. He arrived with a detachment from the fourth battalion of the Army of Reserve, in which unit he was already serving as sergeant and retained this rank in the 30th without interruption until his discharge in 1815 for 'chronic rheumatism and debility'. It was normal practice, in fact, for a sergeant (or corporal) in either a militia unit or a battalion of the Army of Reserve (later the Army of Defence) who came into the regiment with a detachment of volunteers to retain his NCO rank. Similarly, NCOs who transferred between regiments remained at the same rank. In the spring of 1812 a detachment arrived from the 33rd, including four corporals. Unfortunately, two of them quickly lost their rank, although one of the others was subsequently promoted to sergeant.

To return to transfers between the two battalions, only six sergeants made the journey in the opposite direction, from the first to the second battalion, and they were generally superannuated men. Robert Smith, transferred early in 1805, was discharged in December of that year. There is no record of his service, but it was probably similar to that of Dennis Farrell and George Dawson. The former had served with the 69th for a year before transferring into the 30th in 1778. He was discharged in 1809, as the second battalion were preparing for active service, having moved from the first to the second battalion in 1805, when the first battalion was nominated for active service. George Dawson spent five years with the 79th before joining the 30th in 1783. He transferred from the first to the second battalion in

1806, as the first battalion sailed to India. Like Farrell he was discharged in 1809, having served as a sergeant for seven years, a position Farrell held for sixteen years. Both men were described on their discharge papers as worn out. They had been well-conducted and brave, and they were praised for their fidelity and zeal. Particular mention was made of their participation in the taking of Malta and in the Egypt campaign.

Of the remaining three sergeants, William Burke died in 1808, soon after he was transferred from the first battalion to the second, John Wilson only made the transfer on paper, and John Gould disappears from the records without explanation in 1811. He had been reduced in July 1809, promoted five months later after a month as hospital sergeant, and then sent to England to recruit.

Scotton was the only sergeant to be discharged specifically on account of wounds received in action, but other sergeants received wounds and seven sergeants were actually killed in action, two at Badajoz, one at Villamuriel, and four at Waterloo. A further five died of wounds, one after Salamanca, one after Villamuriel and three after Waterloo. Two of the casualties in the Peninsula were long-serving sergeants who had joined the second battalion upon its formation (John Tully at Badajoz and Francis Keith at Villamuriel). Perhaps the most unfortunate of these casualties was Patrick Gunning. Until the 17th June 1815 he was hospital sergeant in Brussels. He joined the second battalion that evening and was killed the next day at Waterloo.

Spain and Portugal exacted a heavy toll because as well as the battle casualties a further fifteen sergeants died of natural causes, where *natural* implied Iberian fevers or the effects of hard campaigning, in the three and a half years the battalion were part of Wellington's Peninsular army. This can be set against the total of twenty sergeants who died of natural causes in the fourteen years of the battalion's existence.

There were two other non-natural deaths in distinctly unusual circumstances. In 1805 Edward Laughron was hanged for the murder of his wife, and Charles Watson was murdered in November 1811, while the second battalion was behind the Lines of Torres Vedras. The adjutant, William Stewart recorded in his journal that Watson died after an evening spent drinking with some Portuguese at the Great Redoubt, although the muster rolls record him merely as having died. As the result of his death a detachment was sent out every evening to bring the soldiers back from the drinking booths at sunset.

Perhaps the most unexpected reason for departure from the regiment, given the status a sergeant enjoyed, would be desertion. Nevertheless, seven sergeants deserted, for reasons which are impossible to surmise from the records. Four of them, all long-serving, deserted in 1807, but it is impossible to find any circumstance which might explain this. One had already disappeared in 1805, less than a year after he was made sergeant. The last one went on the 30th December 1815, days after the battalion returned from France. It might be surmised that after the rigours of the Flanders and Waterloo campaigns he decided that he had had enough of soldiering, but he had only joined the battalion in September.

Significantly, there were no desertions during periods when the battalion was on active service.

One notable difference between the two battalions was the number of NCOs who resigned in the first, on average three a year. There is no indication in the muster rolls of their reasons, although in some cases there were clear indications of poor health. Furthermore, some of the men who resigned were later returned to their previous rank. There is only one example in the second battalion of an NCO returning to the ranks without being reduced, although the term *resigned* is not used.

Although, as we have seen, it was possible for a man to be promoted from the ranks to armourer or paymaster sergeant, or to retain his rank when he transferred from another regiment or from a unit outside the regular army, it was very unusual for promotion directly from the ranks to sergeant. There are no examples from the two-battalion period, although George Flowers, who enlisted in about 1795, was immediately promoted to sergeant and sent on recruiting duties. The normal course was promotion to corporal and, after some time at this rank, further promotion to sergeant. The rapid promotion of men like Joseph Berridge and James Woods was unusual. Most men spent at least a year as corporal before being promoted to sergeant, although many never reached the higher rank.

Demotion was actually even more common among corporals than sergeants, and a second promotion much rarer. In the surviving records there are twenty-seven cases of a corporal standing a court martial in the first battalion, and seven in the second. The most common offence was drunkenness. Indeed only three cases in the first battalion did not involve drunkenness, one instance of neglect of duty, one of gambling and one of giving false orders. Drunkenness might be compounded by occurring when a man was orderly corporal. Even more seriously, some of the company's mess money might be used to finance some deep drinking. In the second battalion there were four cases of drunkenness, two when the men were absent without leave. Disrespect to an officer, unsoldierlike conduct, and extortion and disobedience were the other three offences.

The career of Terence O'Neil, a labourer from Leitrim demonstrates the typical career of a corporal. He appears memorably in Macready's journal as the man who roared as the light company went into action at Quatre Bras, 'Close your files, and hould up your heads, my lads!' O'Neil served with the second battalion until reduction, when he was invalided out as asthmatic. Having joined the regiment in April 1808 from a militia regiment, he was promoted to corporal four months later, only to be reduced in July 1810. He spent two years in the ranks before again being promoted to corporal. There was another demotion in September 1812, although there is no reference to him in the list of regimental courts martial in the relevant inspection return. His seesaw career continued when he was once more made corporal in March 1814. It would seem that September was a bad month for him because just six months later, as lance sergeant, he was 'found drunk' and reduced. There is no date given for his reinstatement, but he appears in the September muster roll as corporal, and successfully retained his position until he was discharged. His discharge papers state that he was a corporal for eight years, which is true if the periods of demotion are ignored, and that his conduct was good.

James defined a corporal as 'a rank and file man with superior pay to that of common soldiers, and with nominal rank under a sergeant. He has charge of one of the squads, places and relieves sentinels, and keeps good order in the guard.'[69] To elaborate, a corporal enjoyed a relationship with his squad similar in some ways to that between a captain and his company. He assembled the squad for inspection and prepared lists for the orderly sergeant so that the roll could be completed. The orderly corporal inspected the men for guard, while the corporal of the guard was responsible for the good order of the guard room, including its furniture and utensils. He also inspected the sentry books and had to be present when one sentry relieved another, checking everything was in order before allowing the changeover. A corporal (sometimes a sergeant) kept the company size and duty rolls, and visited barracks or quarters at tattoo to report any absences or irregularities. In the morning he reported any cases of sickness, and ensured cleanliness. A corporal from each company, as well as a sergeant, attended the orderly room for daily orders, and he was expected to deliver these orders accurately. Like sergeants, corporals were responsible for the behaviour of the soldiers at all times. Any misconduct had to be reported, while conniving in misconduct was a serious offence.

It is tempting, when considering the frequency of demotion, of both sergeants and corporals, to conclude that the appointment of NCOs was a random process that produced disappointing results. This would be to overlook the outstanding service of the vast majority who held their position from appointment to discharge, and the excellent conduct of the many who were given a second chance. They were indeed the backbone of the regiment, particularly complimented in every inspection report for their efficiency and sense of duty.

Chapter 7

Officers and Gentlemen

The history of any regiment of the Revolutionary and Napoleonic period tends to be the history of its officers, for no better reason than the relative social standing and literacy rates of the officers and men. There are exceptions, of course; collections of letters like those of Private Wheeler of the 51st, and the many memoirs subsequently written (or written for) and published by men in the ranks. Overall, though, the imbalance of voice bears no relation to the respective numbers of officers and men.

The career of an officer can be traced month by month in the returns, and often elaborated through statements of service while on full or half-pay. Furthermore, their voices predominate in the wealth of letters and journals from the period. For the 30th we have the journals of William Stewart, John Carter, Edward Neville Macready and James Goodall Elkington, as well as various letters, many of them to William Siborne. Then there are the obituaries of the most celebrated, like General Wilkinson and Lieutenant-Colonel Hamilton. Major Bailey even figured in the rare event of a divorce by Act of Parliament, while Surgeon John Hennen wrote a distinguished treatise on the principles of military surgery and Arthur Gore translated Craan's commentary to his map of the Battle of Waterloo, adding further comments of his own. All this information means that a fairly detailed impression can be gained of the men who officered the regiment.

Length of service is an interesting aspect of an officer's career. This could mean anything from several decades in just one regiment, as the careers of Wilkinson and Hamilton demonstrate, to a matter of months, weeks, or no time at all. More officers were appointed to the 30th than actually served; at least sixty of the 249 who served in the period 1803 to 1817 never actually joined either battalion. There were various reasons for this. In 1803, for example, a large number of officers came into the regiment from half-pay upon augmentation. Because the needs of the time were desperate, the collapse of the Peace of Amiens making a renewal of war inevitable, they were invited to return to full-time service without having to pay the difference between their half-pay commission and a full commission. Some of them, however, then exchanged back onto half-pay, keeping the difference. This was business dealing which could be conducted away from the regiment, so there was no need to join. Several young men, students at the Royal Military College were commissioned into the 30th before the completion of their studies. Some, like James Poyntz, who had strong links with the regiment, and Jonathan Flude, eventually joined the second battalion. Others, however, eventually went elsewhere. Edward Boyd, appointed ensign in August 1811 while still a student, was then appointed to the Staff Corps in December of that year. Staff duties might also be a reason why an officer never physically joined the regiment, but this could be complicated by other circumstances. The Honourable Philip Stanhope was appointed to the first battalion by the Commander-in-Chief, India. He was an aide-de-camp to General Lord Moira, but he was still named for several months in the returns. Then his commission with the 30th was cancelled, presumably on the orders of Horse Guards.[70]

Half-pay statements make clear how a man might function as a *paper* officer. Lieutenant J.W. Brydges exchanged from half-pay into the 30th with Lieutenant Fettes in July 1814 but before he could join the regiment in either India or Flanders he was appointed to the staff in Portugal. At this point his memory was somewhat confused (he was writing in 1835) because he claimed he was promoted to captain in the Portuguese service following the reduction of the 30th. In fact, he received this promotion in February 1815, only seven months after the exchange with Fettes, and two years before the reduction of the second battalion. The following year he was a half-pay staff captain. This example reminds us that memories are fallible, and records are not always totally reliable.

If the further fifty-two officers who served for less than two years are added to the sixty who never actually joined, then it might be assumed that many officers had little loyalty to their regiment, using it merely as a means to further promotion. In some cases this was undoubtedly true, but it must also be noted that a large proportion of the short-stay officers actually died while serving with the 30th. Of the six officers killed at Waterloo only two, Chambers and McNabb, had been with the regiment for more than ten years. James and Bullen, the two ensigns, were appointed in September 1813 and November 1814 respectively. (Even Lieutenants Beere and Prendergast had served for only three years.) Similarly, eleven officers died of natural causes within their first two years with the regiment. Three young ensigns were lost in the Peninsula, all in 1812. John Brooke died in March, after a fall from a horse, John Carter died of sunstroke in August, and Thomas Kelly, who had only joined the battalion from England in October, collapsed and died of exhaustion in November after the retreat from Burgos. Another group were the thirteen mainly young officers appointed in 1815 who were forced to go on half-pay upon reduction. A further two exchanged out of the regiment late in 1816, when reduction was known to be imminent.

Against the 112 officers who served with the 30th for less than two years (for whatever reason) in the two-battalion period, we need to consider 125 who stayed for at least five years. Excluding the officers who left the regiment in 1803, fifty-one served between five and ten years, and seventy-four over ten years, including twenty-three who stayed for more than twenty years. The two longest serving were undoubtedly the two lieutenant-colonels, Wilkinson and Hamilton, both of whom were with the regiment for forty-three years.

As we shall see, these impressive records may owe something to the financial conditions of these officers, but there can be little doubt that loyalty was often the principal motive. When Captain Chambers returned to England in 1810, after a period of unpleasantness in the first battalion in India, he had already signed a resignation and also had a recommendation to help him transfer into a new regiment. The geographical distance between the two battalions at this point had caused some confusion in the seniority of the officers (the most senior should have been with the first battalion), and Chambers properly belonged to the second battalion. He sailed from India in April 1810, but by September 1810 he had arrived in Cadiz, where the second battalion were stationed, in command of a detachment from England. There is no record of his having joined the depot at Wakefield, which the detachment had left early in July under the command of Lieutenant Neville, and it can only be surmised that after a fast sail from India, Chambers had attached himself to this detachment and travelled with them to Spain, where no questions appear to have been asked. He may have been motivated by loyalty, or possibly by aggrieved bloody-mindedness at the treatment he had received from his fellow officers in the senior battalion.

One further significant set of figures comprises their reasons for leaving the regiment. Obviously the eight killed in action, the forty-one who died natural deaths, the five who drowned (all in or travelling from India) and two fatal riding accidents do not constitute choice. There is also a sizeable group who simply disappear from the records, including the Army List, without explanation. Of the remainder, forty-one transferred to another regiment, twenty-five resigned or retired and sixty-four went on half-pay.

As well as the officers who transferred out of the regiment, there were those who moved in the opposite direction. On active service the 30th promised the chance of accelerated promotion without purchase, which may explain why so many officers transferred into the regiment on equal rank, while others came in from half-pay. However, promotion is a subject which needs to be considered in its own right.

The question which naturally arises when considering the officers of any regiment during the Revolutionary and Napoleonic Wars is their origin, both social and geographical. The answer, as far as it can be ascertained, varies from regiment to regiment. The background of most Guards officers tended to be socially higher than in other infantry units; and even between the regiments of the line there was considerable variation. The 30th was not a particularly fashionable regiment nor, as Macready lamented after the first, expensive Waterloo celebrations in Limerick, was it a rich corps. As he wrote, having discovered that the total cost was 1,000 pounds, of which he had to pay twenty-five:

> Nothing is more dangerous for an unmarried Corps than to possess a few dashing fellows within it – they mislead young fellows of high spirits and thoughtless good nature by the specious arguments of the credit of the Regt – the honor of the old and bold.[71]

Nevertheless, the 30th was a regiment with history, enjoying a more respected status than many of the higher-numbered line regiments which had been added to the establishment at the end of the eighteenth century, or even during the wars with France.

Geographical origin is fairly easy to establish. After 1814 every monthly return had to include the country of origin of both officers and men, information which had been included in the inspection returns for some years. The categories were English, Scottish, Irish and Other. The returns demonstrate that during the two-battalion period the 30th was essentially an Anglo-Irish regiment, with a minority of Scots, both in the ranks and among the officers. The most interesting category, however, is 'other', which applied to only one officer in the 30th, the Anglo-Indian William Stanhope, son of a commissary general. His father belonged to the generation that accepted intermarriage, later regarded as taboo. He also possessed the influence to obtain a commission for his son in the 30th. Macready referred to him as: 'a well meaning uneducated half-caste whose friends had sent him into a profession for which he had no one qualification.'[72] He served with the regiment for five years up to his death in 1819. His presence in the regiment, however, was never acknowledged in the official Army List.

Among the officers categorised as Scottish is one who might properly be identified as 'other'. Alexander McNabb, obviously of Scottish ancestry, was born in Virginia in 1773. He was the son of an American Loyalist who served as assistant surgeon with Major McAlpine's Corps of Loyalists during the War of American Independence and who was obliged to move north at the end of the war. Alexander first worked as confidential clerk to the Executive Council of Upper Canada and also owned considerable property in Toronto. Nevertheless, in 1800 he was motivated to join the Queen's Rangers as an ensign. Three years later he was on half-pay but in 1804 he transferred to the 30th as lieutenant, serving in addition as the second battalion's paymaster. He was promoted to captain two years later and about the same time took up his first staff appointment, as town major, Gibraltar, where the second battalion was stationed. He then saw service in Cadiz and behind the Lines of Torres Vedras. Like many other officers and men he suffered a period of sickness in Portugal and was sent to Lisbon to recover. He was given further staff appointments, including commandant at Coimbra and Figuera. Thus he remained in Portugal when the second battalion returned to England but by December 1814 he had joined them in Flanders, and six months later fought with them at Quatre Bras and Waterloo. There is some doubt about the circumstances of his death. According to one version, the source of which is obscure, he was an extra aide-de-camp with General Picton and was killed fighting with Picton's division. Macready, however, recorded that McNabb was one of the four officers killed during the French cannonade which caused so many casualties in the square of the 30th and 73rd late in the battle. He even recalled that McNabb fell victim to grapeshot, a detail which invites credence.

The social background of the officers of any line regiment, including the 30th, is rather more difficult to ascertain. Although they may popularly be thought to have come from the nobility and the gentry, the reality was rather different. At the very least, the rapid expansion of the army in response to the French threat meant that such a narrow social stratum could not have provided the manpower required to officer over 100 line regiments, to say nothing of the Guards, the cavalry and the artillery.

Despite the popular perception already noted, peers or their close relatives always constituted a small minority, since there were fewer than 500 peerages at this time. The country-based gentry provided a larger number of officers, but even here not as many as might be expected. Increasingly, officers came from the next level of society, what may best be described as the middle class, although the connotations this term has subsequently accrued need to be forgotten. Sons of vicars, for example, were plentiful in the officer ranks, as were the offspring of men who had made money in trade (and could, therefore, buy a commission for their sons). Not surprisingly, a large number of officers, whatever their social class, were the sons of officers.

Not every officer of the 30th can be placed socially, but some observations can be made which would undoubtedly apply to other regiments of the line. As has already been noted, no line regiment enjoyed the social kudos of the Guards, which explains why only two peers and one baronet served with the 30th. Furthermore, both Lord Forbes, later Viscount Granard (1804–1809), who was with the Brazilian Legation, and Lord Ashbrooke (1803–1804) were of the rather less respected Irish peerage. Nor did either of them actually spend any time with the regiment. Captain Sir Charles Wyndham Burdett transferred into the 30th in 1803 from the 37th Foot and quickly won the respect of Lieutenant-Colonel Wilkinson, who described him as 'intelligent, active & zealous in the performance of his military duties, and that few officers can be better entitled to promotion than he is, nor any more likely to do credit to whatever rank he is preferred to'. This testimonial, written in March 1810 at Burdett's request, seems to have achieved the desired effect because ten months later Burdett was promoted into the 56th Foot with the rank of major.

Arthur Gore (1814–1817) was described in the monthly returns as 'the honourable', as was Philip Stanhope in India, while Alexander Hamilton was the great-grandson of the Marquis of Lothian. There is little doubt that other officers could trace their ancestry back through several generations to the nobility, but this was not the level of society that most of them occupied when they received their commissions.

Obituaries are a valuable means of identifying an officer's social status. For example, William Wilkinson was described as 'the third son of a gentleman of large property in Northumberland and Durham'. A note in the front of William Stewart's journal describes him as 'of Drumnagesson House', which again indicates that he was born a gentleman.

When we consider the officers who were the sons of officers, the obvious starting point is that all the young men who came into the regiment from the Royal Military College had military connections. Jonathan Flude (1811–1814), for example, was the son of the late town major of Berwick. The only officers for whom it is possible to trace a father-son succession within the regiment, however, are Arthur Poyntz, who rose from the ranks to be appointed quartermaster, and his three sons, Arthur (1807), Samuel Robert (1811–1817) and James (1814–1844). The eldest son accompanied his father to India as a very young volunteer. This did not prevent him from receiving an ensigncy in March 1807, and he was still only 14 when he was promoted into the 17th Foot. Samuel Robert, who may also have been in India initially, joined the second battalion as a volunteer in January 1811, and was then commissioned in the same year, presumably just old enough under regulations introduced by the Duke of York to prevent the commissioning of children. He was one of the officers who went on half-pay in 1817. Despite having been in India with the first battalion since 1814, he properly belonged to the second battalion. The youngest brother, James, accompanied Samuel Robert to Portugal in 1811, subsequently claiming a General Service Medal for Fuentes de Oñoro, where he had fought as a volunteer, aged 11. He was then sent to the Royal Military College and was finally commissioned into the 30th in 1814. He survived the disbandment of 1817, and eventually retired with the army rank of major in 1844.[73]

The Maxwells' association with the 30th spans a longer period than this study but constitutes the strongest link with the regiment, five members across two generations. Christopher Maxwell joined the regiment in 1755, and remained until 1794, rising to the rank of lieutenant-colonel. His elder brother, David, followed him in 1759 but remained only three years. In the next generation, three nephews of Christopher and David, themselves brothers, served with the regiment. The eldest, William, joined in 1792 but was quickly promoted elsewhere. A second David joined in 1793 and stayed ten years, only leaving on the death of William, which made him heir to the family property. Finally, a second Christopher joined in 1794, staying twenty-three years and, like his namesake, rising to the rank of lieutenant-colonel, although not to command of the regiment.

Another family link was established when Augustus Lockwood joined the regiment in 1841 as assistant surgeon. He was the son of Purefoy Lockwood (1811–1816), known as 'Bombproof' Lockwood after surviving a near fatal wound at Quatre Bras. Two brothers who served during the two-battalion period were George (1807–1811) and John Rumley (1809–1819). The elder brother suffered the effects of the Portuguese climate and died in Lisbon. The younger, seriously wounded at Villamuriel and again at Waterloo, was killed by the climate of India. Two other officers with family connections were the cousins, George Grey (1804–1812), killed at Badajoz, and Owen Wynne Grey (1804–1829).

More commonly, brothers served in different regiments, and one of the saddest such situations concerned Henry Beere, who joined the 30th in Spain shortly after Salamanca, to discover that his brother, Hercules, serving with the 61st Foot, had been killed in that battle. When Henry himself was killed at Waterloo, he left five sisters without male support. An appeal to the Prince of Wales earned the young women a small pension in acknowledgement that their brothers had died for king and country.

As already noted, the sons of vicars constitute a notable group of officers. In the 30th Purefoy Lockwood, Parke Percy Neville and Richard Mayne were all the sons of Irish vicars. More clerically distinguished was the father of Charles Warren, who was Dean of Bangor. Since most Anglican clergymen of the period were the younger sons of gentlemen, and, even if not by birth, attained that status with their degree, it follows that their offspring would be regarded as gentlemen even before they became officers.

These are all predictable backgrounds, but there are others, less predictable and more interesting because they suggest the wider social origins of the officers of the period. David Latouche, for example, was connected to a wealthy Irish banking family of Huguenot descent, responsible for establishing the Bank of Ireland. They also had extensive estates in County Wicklow. David Latouche's distinguished connections did little to raise him in Macready's jaundiced estimation, however. In a damning summary of his character he described him as 'truly despicable'. As for Macready himself, although the son of an Irish actor-manager (and younger brother of the famed actor, William Macready), he was the grandson of a Derbyshire vicar on his mother's side, had been to Rugby, and undoubtedly regarded himself as a gentleman.

Tradesmen occupied a wide and ambiguous position in the social spectrum. There were tradesmen in the ranks and tradesmen among the officers. According to a tale he told William Stewart, John Hitchen had been a wine merchant before he was commissioned into the 17th. Thomas Walker Chambers, who also joined the 30th from half-pay with the 17th, had a trade background. His father owned a herring boat in Lowestoft, while his paternal grandfather was the wealthiest herring-boat owner in Lowestoft, and founder of Lowestoft pottery. Such wealth brought social distinction.

In theory, all the officers, whatever their social background, were Protestants, since only Protestants could swear to the requirements of the Test Act. The Catholic Relief Act of 1791 eased some of the discriminatory laws against Catholics but did not extend to the holding of public office. Many were enlightened enough, however, to recognise that Catholic officers would pose no threat to a Protestant king.

> I have not scrupled to assert that Roman Catholic gentlemen may enlist themselves under the banners of the country. A dispensing rule has very properly been resorted to with regard to non-commissioned officers and private soldiers…[and] the enlightened state of the public mind is such, that Protestant and Roman Catholic gentlemen stand upon the same parade without reference to religious tenets. It must not, however, be inferred from this that the Roman Catholics are no longer liable to informations for thus serving in direct opposition to one of the most stubborn provisions which have been made for the security of the Protestant succession…Every nobleman, or man of independent property, be his rank what it may, who professes himself a Papist, or is known to adhere to the Church of Rome, and consequently is forbidden to take the oath of supremacy, as

enjoined in the mutiny act, is at the mercy of every informer, and may be fined five hundred pounds. As the bugbear of Jacobitism is justly lost, or shortly must be so, in the extinction of the Stewart line, this disheartening stigma upon a very large proportion of His Majesty's most loyal subjects, ought to be removed. It is a galling circumstance to every Roman Catholic gentleman, that whilst he is eagerly stepping forward, with a considerable stake of his own, to co-operate in the general defence of his property, he should only be permitted to shed his blood and risk his fortune by sufferance or connivance.[74]

Many would have echoed these sentiments of Charles James, including Wellington, but the obduracy of George III meant that no commissions could be given to Catholics according to the letter of the law. Not until Catholic Emancipation was achieved in 1829 did the army overtly accept Catholic officers. Yet there were Catholics serving as officers before that date, as James acknowledges.

The reality of the situation was officially acknowledged in 1827, when regiments were required to complete a statement of religious affiliation for both officers and men. By this date, most of the Irish officers of the two-battalion period had left the regiment. Among those remaining was William Sullivan, who had joined as an ensign in 1803, and whose early career was blighted by the wreck of the *Jenny* in 1806, followed by eight years as a prisoner of war in Verdun. In 1827 he was the only officer to be returned as a Catholic but it is probable that others who had since departed were of the same religious persuasion. Presumably, Sullivan and others of the same denomination (including his two brothers, who were commissioned into other regiments) took advantage of the Indemnifying Act, passed annually, which postponed the need to swear the Protestant oath of allegiance.

Although motives for seeking a commission were many and varied, once the commission had been obtained pay, purchase and promotion was the trinity which subsequently occupied an officer's thoughts.

That purchase was a contentious subject is brought out by a short letter to *The Royal Military Chronicle* in 1811; this made the point that 'It is to be regretted that interest and money are often of more consequence than real merit, in the promotion of officers.'[75] Although the key word here is *promotion*, the implicit concern is *purchase*, the system by which a man of wealth could buy his way into the army and then up through the officer ranks. Purchase did indeed lie at the heart of the officer system, both for those who could afford to buy their way up the ladder, and for those who could only hope to step into dead men's shoes. However, money alone was not sufficient to get a man into the army as an officer; he also needed a recommendation. As James pointed out in his *Regimental Companion*:

The usual mode of entering into the British Army is by a regular form of letter, which is issued from the adjutant general's office. Printed copies of these letters lie in the hands of the several agents, and may be had, upon application, by any gentleman desirous of commencing a military career. The purport of this official document is to certify the intentions of the individual to the Commander-in-Chief, of his being willing to abide, in the fullest sense of the word, by the prescribed rules and regulations.[76]

The application had to be supported by a letter written by a field officer holding a commission in the army and took a form similar to James' example:

'SIR,
I beg leave to recommend Mr A.B. as a gentleman fully qualified to hold an ensigncy in His Majesty's regiment of ....
(SIGNED) ...'

There are only two direct references to this system in the various documents that concern the 30th, and both relate to Benjamin Walter Nicholson, who obtained an ensigncy in the 13th Foot in 1805. In December 1809 he stood a court martial in India on a variety of charges. As part of his defence he offered the court the information that his candidacy for a commission had been supported by two influential patrons, a general and a member of parliament. This had relevance because one of the charges accused him of ungentlemanly conduct and he was obviously making the point that a man with such powerful influences behind him could not be considered ungentlemanly. Of course, there may also have been an implicit hint that he had powerful connections. Some years later, in a half-pay statement, he made direct reference to one of these patrons, the Dublin banker and member of the Irish parliament, David Latouche, son of the founder of the Bank of Ireland.

Assuming that the candidate intended to purchase his commission, for there were other routes he might follow, then he had to pay £400 for an ensigncy in a line regiment, as against £900 in the Guards, and £1102.10.0d for a cornetcy. Further amounts then became necessary as he advanced up the promotion ladder. Even £400 was a vast sum of money for the time but this was one of the virtues of the system according to many. An officer caste supported by the ownership of property (which meant wealth) was unlikely to be seduced by radical political ideas or influenced by sedition. The gentleman officer could be relied upon to support the constitution, but he could also be expected to possess the qualities which fitted a man for command. This point was specifically discussed in another letter to *The Royal Military Chronicle* in 1812:

Gentlemen of fortune have alike their claim to honourable merit, when they partake of the calamities of war. Much, therefore, may be urged on the advantages resulting from inducements which promote the entry of the above into the army; and, I am far from imagining, that any argument could prove that considerable evil arises from the (possibly) rapid promotion of these gentlemen. Besides, they are in general well educated: and inclination, when seconded by genius, must acquire for them soon a perfect knowledge of the profession, than officers otherwise circumstanced can possibly be supposed to possess.[77]

To consider purchase a little further, however, once a candidate for a commission was in the army it remained the surest path to promotion when allied to seniority. Indeed, a frequent punishment for more minor misdemeanours was to place the offending officer at the bottom of his rank within his regiment. Money could and frequently did play a deciding role in promotion. To take a hypothetical situation, should Captain Smith decide to retire from the service, the senior lieutenant, Brown, would be offered the option to purchase the vacant captaincy, thus becoming the junior at that rank. Assuming that Brown did not have the means to pay the difference between his lieutenancy and Smith's captaincy, which in 1810 would have been £950, the offer would then be made to the lieutenant next in seniority, Jones. Should he also be an impoverished veteran, the vacant captaincy might eventually go to the wealthy Compton-Barnett, who had already bought himself promotion on a previous occasion above several impecunious ensigns. Thus Compton-Barnett leapfrogged to a captaincy over the claims of his two seniors, whose only realistic hopes of promotion were active service and dead men's shoes.

This injustice to long-serving but penurious officers caused much consternation. 'Mentor', in the letter quoted earlier, continued:

Should there not be some regulation so far in favour of veterans, as to prevent them from falling under the command of men young enough to be their children? Might not something of this kind be effected, even without altogether doing away with the present situation of purchase?[78]

As another correspondent wrote, everyone knew the officer who had 'marched and countermarched from Acton to Ealing, from Ealing to Acton' and who, despite never having been in action, still finished up a major-general, while others had 'borne the summer's parching heat, the winter's chilling cold; expended their youth amidst toil and hardships, and been lavish of their best blood in the service of their country,' but never progressed beyond subaltern rank.[79] This was not just the fault of the purchase system in general, however, but also because the step between lieutenant and captain was so expensive. Since a lieutenant's pay was 6/6d a day, with another shilling added after seven years' service, an impecunious officer had little hope of finding the money to buy his way to the next step of the ladder.

The other evil in the system, as it was generally perceived, was the rapid or undeserved promotion of young men with money and influence but limited experience or ability. Ironically, Wellington provides one of the best examples of the system in practice, and would seem to justify it, but for one Wellington there were many incompetents who progressed at a similarly fast rate. In 1809 the Duke of York, as Commander-in-Chief, introduced regulations which stipulated the minimum period an officer had to serve at each rank before he could progress to the next rank. The time spent as a subaltern was extended to three years, and another four years were to elapse, at least two spent as captain, before the officer could acquire a majority. Finally, nine years' service in total had to be completed before promotion to lieutenant-colonel.

Having dealt with this problem, the duke then sought to abolish the most pressing abuse of the system, over-payment, by which vacancies were put up for auction as retiring officers, who undoubtedly regarded their commissions as investments for the future, sought to realise their assets at the highest possible price. His first attempt, in 1804, banned overpayment on threat of dismissal. Five years later the Commons Act was passed to give the regulation parliamentary support. Cashiering was the penalty. Yet there were no convictions, despite the known and frequent incidence of the abuse. In 1824 it was reckoned that only a tenth of purchased commissions were obtained at the official price.

The abuse certainly caused widespread concern among those with a purer approach to promotion, or lacking the means to pay over the odds, perhaps. James wrote:

> Although the sale and purchase of commissions are countenanced by government, and the prices of those commissions are regulated by the King's authority, yet there are various ways through which young men of fortune and connexions may get over the head of veteran officers...Purchase and sale are terms unknown in the navy. We should be happy to have it in our power to say, that in this course of time, the word *purchase* will be erased from the vocabulary of military men...[80]

Elsewhere, James pointed out that officers were required to attest upon their honour that they had not paid above the regulation price, to which he added the sardonic comment: 'We have, however, known several instances in which this pledge has been forfeited. So much for signatures upon honour!'[81]

There was a more positive aspect to this overpayment, however. Commissions beyond the rank of ensign had two values, the official price sanctioned by the government, and what may be termed the regimental price, which was determined by how much men were prepared to pay for promotion. This could actually help poorer officers; their contribution to making up the difference might well be smaller if their wealthier fellow officers were prepared to pay more than their fair share of the total sum demanded by the retiring officer. Of course, there was a simple solution, which no-one at the time had the power to implement, even if it was considered. As some correspondents of *The Royal Military Chronicle* pointed out, if officers were paid a pension, then the need to realise the cost of their commissions would no longer be so crucial to their future prosperity.

Furthermore, there was a shady underworld in the business of obtaining commissions, particularly first commissions, and this caused as much concern as the abuse of the system by serving officers. Commission brokers (also known as army brokers), who were often former officers with good connections, functioned usefully for those prepared to pay, even though their activities were illegal. With their carefully nurtured connections they could obtain endorsements for their clients or give relevant information to officers wanting to purchase or exchange into another regiment. They also liaised between official army agents and would-be purchasers. They seem to have been particularly active in 1793–4 and 1804, both periods of rapid expansion of the army through augmentation.

In 1806 the employment of army brokers was specifically banned by a clause inserted into the Army Act of that year. The penalty for an army agent who used the services of a broker was to lose his function as an agent for that particular regiment, while the offending officer would have his promotion cancelled. Initially, this attempt to ban the trade in brokered commissions had no effect. Lack of evidence meant that not a single broker, agent or officer was prosecuted. Three years later, however, after the scandal which obliged the Duke of York to resign as commander-in-chief, when it was discovered that his mistress, Mary Ann Clarke, was acting in effect as a commission broker (a means she used to fund her prodigious extravagance), a Brokerage Act was passed and rigorously enforced.

There was widespread sympathy for York, who was cleared of involvement by an investigating committee of both Houses of Parliament. When he resumed his former position in 1811, compliments were paid to his integrity. A Soldier's Friend, writing in *The Royal Military Chronicle*, commented: 'The Commander in Chief has hitherto acted very judiciously in his promotions, having almost uniformly promoted the eldest and most deserving officers whenever he had the opportunity.'[82]

Similarly, 'J. P.' claimed:

> There cannot exist a doubt, that the regulations as directed by his royal highness the Duke of York, are just and reasonable; but the infringements and innovations by different means and for different purposes, appear to me so truly disgusting, that much cause is given for grievance.

This last letter was an extended complaint not against brokers but against misuse of the brevet system. In theory, this was a means by which impoverished officers could be rewarded for meritorious service by being given a higher rank within the army than their regimental rank, which effected precedence but not pay. Precedence, though, was crucial to promotion. J. P. felt the system was open to abuse when (as happened in 1812) young men were recommended for brevet rank by senior officers who wished to ingratiate themselves with the influential connections of these young men. J. P. commented further:

> The officers of the army should be bound together by every possible means of promoting friendship and a good understanding. Merit rewarded is at all times

admired in the army; but surely unjust innovations cannot be otherwise than disgusting, and productive of contrary effects to those we would desire.[83]

This long letter elicited several replies, all agreeing with the writer. J. P. himself calculated that in the brevet of May 1812, after Ciudad Rodrigo and Badajoz, the twelve captains promoted to majorities had averaged six and a half years in the army. Again the essential point was the resentment of long-serving officers as they watched men of less experience, possibly of lesser merit, but possessed of influence through their family connections being fast-tracked, to use the modern term, to high rank.

Another reason why promotion, and the attendant question of purchase, so exercised the minds of officers was the link between promotion and pay. Once again, the letters written to *The Royal Military Chronicle* make clear that many officers considered themselves underpaid. In November 1811 one correspondent suggested that junior officers deserved anything between an extra shilling a day (for captains) and two shillings a day (for subalterns) to raise their pay to a reasonable level. The writer calculated that such an improvement could be achieved for £374,125 per annum, a sum large enough to give pause. He argued, however, that low pay prevented men of property from considering the army as a career since the rewards were too trifling to attract them, thus depriving the country of potential officers of merit and ability.

This was an unusual argument because the most common cause of complaint was the difficulty of surviving on such low pay. For example 'Miles Britannicus' wrote a month later:

> A large portion of British officers have no other income than their stipulated pay; and when it is considered by their countrymen that both time and constitutions are given up exclusively to their professional duties, ought not the recompense to be that of liberal subsistence?...The rank of serjeant [sic] is infinitely better paid than that of subaltern; his bread and meat are delivered at a settled and low rate; arms, uniforms, and accoutrements are granted him by government; no ostensible appearance of dignity is required from him. If the officer be careless in his dress, society, and manners, he loses a portion of the respect due to his situation; the requisite subordination is diminished, and one link is broken in the perfect chain of discipline.[84]

There is merit in this argument when the cost of uniform alone is considered. James gives the following figures, which he presents as averages for the trade in London:

Best regimental hat, complete	£3.13.06d
Regulation sword	£2.12.06d (up to £3.11.0d)
Regulation sword knot	9/-

Long patent silk sash	£1.11.06d (up to £3.03.0d)
Regulation gorget with rosettes	10/6
Bleached sword-belt	12/-
Making an officer's coat	8/- (up to 10/6d)
Waistcoat	2/6d (up to 3/6d)
Breeches	3/- (up to 3/6d)

This list includes only the bare essentials, and would not take an officer very far in his military career. As J. A. (John Anderson) of the Royals wrote in 1811:

> We are necessarily obliged to dress more exclusively than other people, to keep up the appearance and respectability of gentlemen, and to associate with such; it may indeed be said that we enjoy 'splendid misery'...We seldom get a dinner, exclusive of wine, for less than the day's pay of an ensign. Supposing a young officer to join his regiment fully equipped with everything necessary, he cannot then possibly subsist on his pay.[85]

James quotes some figures for messing, taken from various regiments. For example, in one marching regiment, a regiment without a permanent headquarters, every officer was required to pay 10/6d a week, irrespective of rank, and to contribute to extras, which included fruit, beer and wine. This sum was exactly two days' pay for an ensign. There was a further annual contribution of 10/6d for furniture and utensils, and five guineas upon a new appointment or promotion. A different system, employed by a fencible regiment, required each officer to pay 1/3d for a meal, with extra to cover the cost of fruit and drinks. The amount required upon appointment or promotion was regulated so that field officers paid three guineas, while staff officers paid only half a guinea. Whatever the method adopted by a regiment, however, mess bills could become an embarrassment for the cash-strapped officer. While serving in India, where expenses tended to be higher because of the more lavish social lifestyle, Macready found himself in serious financial difficulties and had to resign from the mess for a while.

To make the problem absolutely clear, one has only to set regulation prices of commissions against officers' annual pay. In 1806, the annual pay for officers and steps in promotion in a line regiment were:

Rank	Pay	Commission
Ensign	£95.16.3d	£400
Lieutenant	£118.12.6d	£150
Captain	£191.12.6d	£950
Major	£292.0.0d	£1,100
Lieutenant-colonel	£310.05.0d	£900

These figures demonstrate that pay was hardly likely to be the inducement which took men into the army as officers. Nor was an impecunious officer likely to be impressed with the arguments which John Anderson cited in a letter deriding a Commons committee set up to investigate officers' pay. One member even asserted that

> officers go into the army from the honour of the service, and not for a subsistence; another cannot conceive the necessity for an increase in pay, because we have never collectively memorialed; but how little do the sons of affluence know of the collective misery of that useful body, to whom they are so prodigal of thanks, while they almost deny them the necessities of life...The British army, at this present moment, borne down and debased by unmerited poverty, possesses the rudiments of the finest army in the world. Do away with purchase entirely; cease to consider property a criterion; let there be no reward but to military merit; and you will have an army, which the French will not only not venture to menace again on our own shores, but which, virtuously conducted, will give liberty to the world.[86]

Few officers would have disagreed with Anderson's sentiments.

Chapter 8

An Officer's Life – Work and Play

Although purchase provoked such strongly antagonistic feelings, the experience of the officers of the 30th make clear that it was not the only, or even the most common, route to a commission. From a sample of seventy-seven officers whose records have survived, over a quarter of the total who served during the two-battalion period (or a third if the *paper* officers and the twenty medical staff are excluded), a clear impression emerges that the majority of officers neither obtained their first commission nor achieved promotion through purchase. Only eight officers bought all their ranks, while forty-six never used the purchase system. Of these forty-six, however, many never rose above the rank of lieutenant, which makes sense when the cost of a captaincy is noted. The twenty-three who used both systems tended to buy their captaincy or majority, the two slowest points of promotion.

Since it was possible to gain a commission and subsequent promotion without purchase, although initially the candidate still needed the recommendation of two backers, it is useful to consider the other routes a would-be officer might follow. At times when the army was desperate for officers in the augmented corps or new regiments the purchase system simply would not provide the necessary manpower. This explains why so many officers who served with the 30th during the Revolutionary and Napoleonic Wars, particularly after the collapse of the Peace of Amiens in 1803, were commissioned without purchase.

A single entry in *The Royal Military Chronicle* for 1811, covering a period of five months, demonstrates how the system of entry and promotion worked in practice:

April 2nd: Captain Robert Douglas, 36th Foot, captain of a company *vice* Beaumont, placed on half-pay of the 36th Foot.

April 16th: Ensign Hughes, from the Portuguese service, to be ensign without purchase *vice* Garvey, promoted.

April 23rd: Ensign Purefoy Lockwood, from the Tipperary Militia, to be ensign.

April 30th: John Edmond Brooke, gent. to be ensign, by purchase, *vice* Baker, promoted in the 80th Foot.

May 7th: Lieutenant John Garland to be adjutant, *vice* Stewart, promoted.

July 2nd: To be lieutenants without purchase, ensigns William Pennefather, James Eagar, John Napper, Richard C. Elliot, A. W. Freear, John Rumley, W. A. Brisac, and Andrew Baillie.

To be ensigns without purchase: Edward Parry, gent. *vice* Elliot; ... Stephens, gent. *vice* Brisac; and Samuel Robert Poyntz *vice* Baillie.

July 23rd: to be lieutenant without purchase, ensigns George Teulon, Robert Daniell; and ensign and adjutant George Stephenson: to have the rank of lieutenant; ensigns P. P. Neville, and John Roe, from the 61st Foot.

To be ensigns, gentlemen cadets Edward Boyd, from the Royal Military College, *vice* Teulon; Jonathan Flude, from ditto, *vice* Daniell; and George Darling, from ditto, *vice* Neville.

30th July: lieutenant-colonel Charles Turner, from the Royal West India Rangers, to be lieutenant-colonel without purchase; major Norris William Bailey, from de Meuron's regiment, to be major without purchase, *vice* Hamilton, promoted in the Royal West India Rangers.

13th August: ensign Theophilus O'Halloran, from the 54th Foot, to be lieutenant, without purchase.[87]

This list reveals several possibilities for the impecunious young man. He might volunteer from the militia, as did Purefoy Lockwood, whose service earned him an automatic ensigncy in the regular army. At least thirteen other militia volunteers were commissioned into the 30th by this route. In addition, he might serve as a volunteer, messing with the officers and marching with the men, in the hope that he would be rewarded with the next vacant ensigncy. As we have seen, the three sons of Arthur Poyntz all served as very young volunteers and one of them, Samuel Robert, appears in the list above. Francis Tincombe joined the second battalion in the autumn of 1810 and finally obtained his commission without purchase early in 1812. Two years later Edward Macready hoped to follow the same route when he joined the second battalion in Flanders. Not only did he quickly obtain a commission, helped by the untimely death of Lieutenant Flude, but his conduct at Waterloo so impressed the senior officers of the battalion that he was promoted to lieutenant before others who were senior to him on the list of ensigns.

Three young men at the Royal Military College were commissioned into the 30th without purchase, although only Flude actually joined the regiment, to die two years later of typhus fever. They were all the sons of army officers, this being another criterion that avoided the purchase system and which was also applied at times to the sons of long-serving and distinguished NCOs. Even if Arthur Poyntz had not risen to quartermaster, it is probable that his three sons would still have gained commissions.

It is significant that only one of the new ensigns, John Brooke, actually paid for his commission. Similarly, in relation to promotion, fourteen ensigns, two from outside the regiment, were promoted to lieutenant without purchase. Indeed, it is rare in this period to find an ensign who paid for his first promotion.

The departure of Captain Beaumont to the half-pay list of the 36th Foot because of ill-health suggests another possibility. He exchanged with Captain Douglas of the same regiment. Douglas, however, was on full pay so when Beaumont went on half-pay he created a vacancy in the captains' list of the 36th. The man who replaced him paid the difference between the value of the half-pay and full-pay commissions, thus giving Beaumont some money with which to fund his retirement.

Exchange, as in Beaumont's case, was a route into a particular regiment, although not into the army. Promotion could often be more easily achieved by moving to a regiment that was on active service and likely, therefore, to suffer casualties. Although the transferred officer became the junior in his rank, if he had come from a regiment where there was little officer movement his chances of promotion improved in a more active unit. For example, when James Spawforth transferred from the 8th Garrison Battalion into the 30th in 1809 he was aware that he was joining a regiment with one battalion in India (and its high death rate) and the other in the Peninsula. Although he remained in command of the depot throughout his four years with the 30th, he still moved up the promotion ladder within his rank.

It was possible, however, that an officer might transfer, or exchange, out of a regiment for more personal reasons. Although there is no evidence of this as a motive for officers coming into the 30th, one officer claimed to have left the regiment because he was dissatisfied with the way he had been treated. When Lieutenant Alexander Fettes exchanged with J. W. Brydges into the 14th Light Dragoons he was motivated by a sense of grievance that a vacant captaincy had been given to Donald Sinclair. Fettes was senior to Sinclair in the regiment, having joined in July 1803, whereas Sinclair joined nine months later. His resentment was clearly conveyed in letters he wrote in 1830 when trying to sell his half-pay commission:

> I joined the 30th Regiment of Foot in 1803 and was on active service with the Regiment in the East Indies, until the year 1812 when I came home on leave on urgent family affairs and during my absence Lieutenant Sinclair (also in England on Sick Leave) was promoted to a Company vacant by the death of Captain Jackson [who had been lost at sea] and which ought to have been given to me as Senior Lieutenant of the Regiment.

He was undoubtedly justified in complaining; he was, after all, a long-serving officer who seems to have done his duty by the regiment, most of the time in India. There is a problem with dates, however, which makes the situation less straightforward. According to the records, Fettes' exchange with Brydges is dated the 7th July 1814, which is the same date that Sinclair was promoted to captain *vice* Roberts, a prisoner of war who was rewarded for his long incarceration in Verdun with a majority. He too had been moving up the list of captains even while *hors de combat*. Unless Fettes had some prior warning that Sinclair would get the captaincy, it is difficult to see how it provoked him to seek a transfer. Furthermore, he transferred with an officer on half-pay, which suggests that he was looking for a form of retirement. Nevertheless, his pride may well have been hurt by the preference shown to Sinclair, and the resentment, festering over the years, became in his own mind the motive for his departure.

The half-pay list was expensive, so any means of shortening it appealed to the government. Thus at periods of augmentation officers on the list were encouraged to return to full pay without purchase in order of seniority. Since many of them went on the half-pay list unwillingly, usually because of reduction, as in 1802, it is no surprise that several officers who joined the 30th in 1803 came from half-pay. As already noted, Lieutenants Thomas Walker Chambers and John Hitchen had both been placed on half-pay with the 17th Foot when that regiment was reduced in 1802. A year later they joined the 30th. They were both good officers. After their promotion to captain, Hitchen was given command of the grenadiers and Chambers, the light company, the two elite companies of any battalion. Indeed, Chambers seems to have been an officer of exceptional talent, and his death at Waterloo was a sad loss to the regiment.

A transfer had to be abandoned if the officer could not raise the purchase money involved, and this may explain why some of the officers who are listed in the monthly returns as having been promoted into the 30th *vice* a departing officer never actually arrived. A rank-for-rank exchange, on the other hand, should not have involved any financial dealings unless an officer from a line regiment, where commissions were cheaper, was exchanging into a cavalry regiment or the Guards. Nevertheless, exchanges could fail. In 1812, Robert Daniell exchanged with Lieutenant Stewart of the 37th and was struck off accordingly. The May monthly return, however, recorded that the exchange had failed and Daniell was taken back on the strength of the regiment. No reason is given.

As with Fettes' departure, there must be some question about Daniell's desire to leave the 30th, which he had joined in 1791 as a private. It was generally agreed that life for an officer commissioned from the ranks could be difficult, even for one who had served for seven years as quartermaster sergeant. In Daniell's case, however, he had been strongly recommended for an ensigncy without purchase in 1810 by his commanding officer, Minet, supported by other officers of the battalion. Certainly, he never made another attempt to leave the regiment, finally going on the half-pay list in 1818, by which time he was 46 and had survived Toulon, Egypt, Badajoz, Salamanca, Villamuriel, Quatre Bras and Waterloo, as well as suffering the loss of his family in a shipwreck.[88]

Daniell's career illustrates another route by which men might obtain a commission. It has been estimated that at least 5 per cent of all officers rose from the ranks. If this number is taken to include the predictable number who became quartermasters and adjutants, then it is not particularly noteworthy. The paper strength of a battalion was forty-seven officers, excluding the medical staff; thus 5 per cent is less than three officers per battalion. If only field and company officers are considered, the number of officers promoted from the ranks is even lower, just 2 per cent. Working on the supposition that the quartermaster would always be a promoted sergeant, the company officer promoted from the ranks was a rarity. The promoted sergeant would find himself numerically and socially at a disadvantage among officers who had come into the regiment by any of the other possible routes. He might become a gentleman upon gaining his commission, but he would not have been born one.

Daniell appears in the list from *The Royal Military Chronicle*, promoted from ensign to lieutenant without purchase. He would have understood the situation of Robert Hughes, also in the list. This former sergeant of the Buffs had been commissioned into the Portuguese service as a reward for good service. An ensigncy in the 30th took him one step further, giving him the kudos of a regular British army commission.

Not everyone agreed with the commissioning of sergeants, however. The young Macready believed that 'They labour under an evident inferiority of manners and ideas, and affect to elevate themselves by a domineering severity.' He made the point more strongly when recording the death of Ensign Ledge in India, describing him as

> a poor fellow whose good conduct was his ruin by causing his promotion from an excellent and respectable Sergeant Major to a useless and besotted officer. His fate afforded another instance in support of the opinion I have broached in the 2nd chapter of the error and, in fact, injustice, of not providing particular corps for the reception of these men. In such regiments they would meet people of manners and ideas consonant to their own, and form a society happy in itself and respectable in the eyes of the world, for who would not admire and rejoice in the gladness of such sacred bands of the valiant and deserving.[89]

The question of manners certainly coloured his opinion of Robert Hughes:

> While at Carlisle I met Hughes of ours – we were never very intimate nor yet on kind terms – our societies were different – however tho' I always thought him vain to folly & less vain than illiterate – I respected him as a fellow of undaunted gallantry – he had been a private soldier & was still a mere mercenary.

This opinion softened after Hughes had praised Macready to his brother, telling William Macready that 'he's a credit to you'.[90] Nevertheless, whatever his prejudices, Macready had frequent dealings with promoted sergeants because he was serving in a regiment with more than the average number, seven at the time he joined in 1814 not including the two quartermasters. Whatever his own reservations, they were not shared by either Minet or Hamilton.

Robert Hughes later wrote in a letter which accompanied his half-pay statement of 1828:

> I have the honour to submit for your kind consideration the length of my services and allow me to observe it was in consequence of not having interest or money to purchase I was allowed to remain for so long in half-pay.

This was a problem for all promoted sergeants. Hughes, in fact, returned to full-pay service and in 1843 was eventually promoted lieutenant-colonel in the 1st West India Regiment, a rare distinction for a man from the ranks but one that was shared by two other promoted sergeants who served with the 30th, Samuel Bircham and Henry Craig.

Bircham makes an interesting case study. He was a son of the regiment, his father having risen from the ranks to sergeant. He enlisted as a boy drummer and rose rapidly to the rank of sergeant. In his half-pay statement of 1823 he wrote:

> in 1793 [aged 23] I was engaged four times with the army of Toulon in the south of France. In 1794 I was at the capture of St Fiorinza Bastion and Calin in the island of Corsica. In 1795 I was at two naval engagements when serving as a marine under Admiral Hothand [Hotham]. In 1798 I commanded the brigade of artillery attached to the late Sir John Moore in the rebellion of Ireland and was engaged in the county of Waterford on which occasion my conduct met the entire approbation of that officer. In 1799 and 1800 I was at the siege and final capture of Malta. In 1807 I accompanied an expedition under Sir E Pellew and Colonel Lockhart to the island of Java and destroyed the Dutch shipping and forts etc in the port of Gressie and on my return from Java in 1808 and 9 I accompanied my regiment against the Rajah of Travancore. I was presented with my first commission as a reward of meritorious conduct in the field of battle of France under the command of Brigadier General Lord Mulgrave on the 1st and 15th September 1793.

He might have added that he and another sergeant on the latter occasion safely brought off a detachment of the 30th from Mount Faron (Toulon) after all the officers had died or been disabled by wounds.

He added as a footnote,

> I first commenced my military career in 1780. In 1781 I accompanied my regiment (30th) to Charleston South Carolina when I was present at several skirmishes etc with the enemy. I was at the battle of Quinly Eutar Spring under the command of Colonel Stewart, the Buffs. In 1782 I went to the West Indies where I continued with my regiment until 1791, nine years previous to obtaining

30th Foot, private, 1806. (*Queen's Lancashire Regimental Museum, Preston*)

30th Foot, sergeant, 1807. (*Queen's Lancashire Regimental Museum, Preston*)

30th Foot, officer, 1806. (*Queen's Lancashire Regimental Museum, Preston*)

30th Foot, company officer and private, 1815. (*Queen's Lancashire Regimental Museum, Preston*)

30th Foot, colonel and officer, 1818. (*Queen's Lancashire Regimental Museum, Preston*)

30th Foot, fifer, 1816. (*Queen's Lancashire Regimental Museum, Preston*)

Recruiting party of the 33rd Foot.
(*Michael Crumplin*)

Major Charles James, late of the Royal Artillery Drivers, author of *A Universal Military Dictionary* and *A Regimental Companion*.

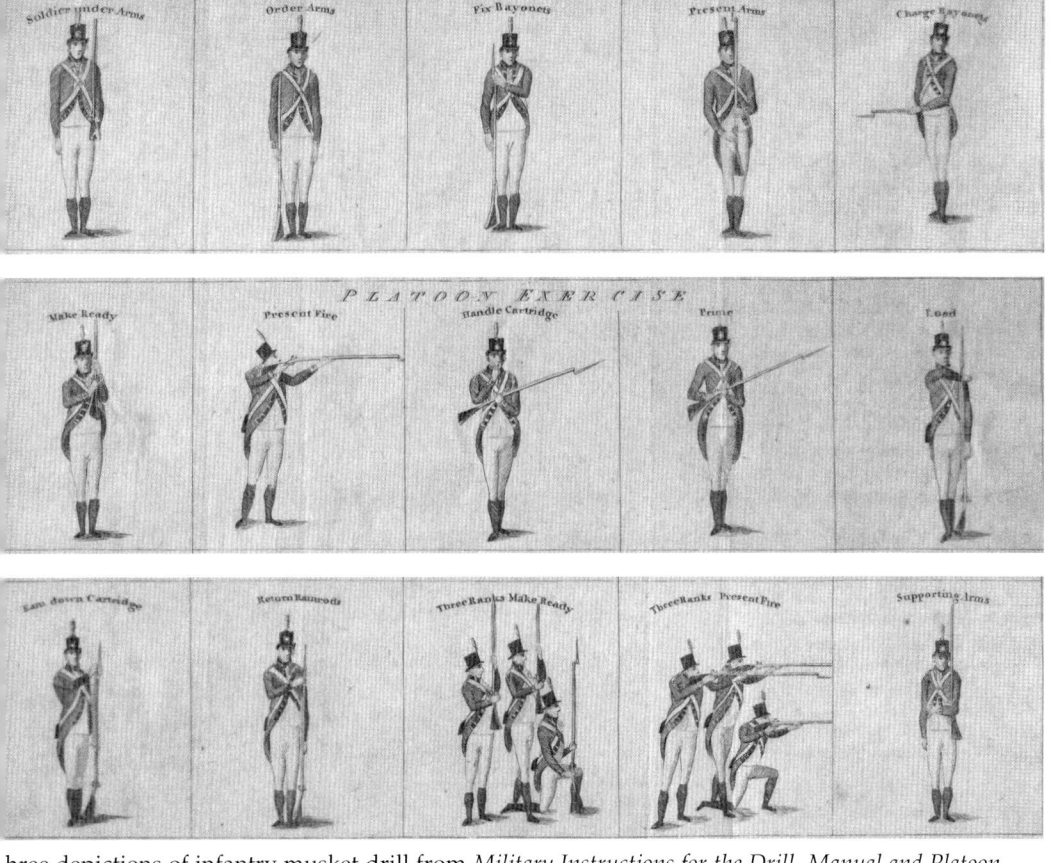

Three depictions of infantry musket drill from *Military Instructions for the Drill, Manual and Platoon Exercise*. (*Denham & Dick, Edinburgh, 1803*)

Infantry Drilling by J.A. Atkinson, 1807. (*Philip Haythornthwaite*)

Royal Barracks, Dublin.
(*Sue Knox*)

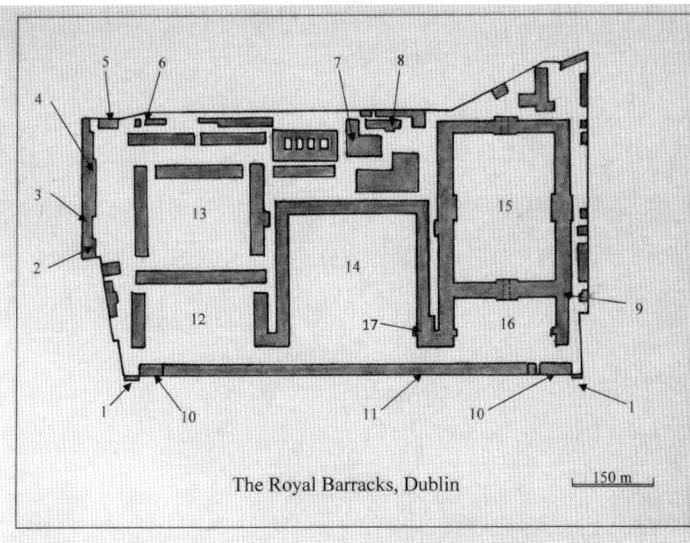

Royal Barracks, Dublin, plan.

The Royal Barracks, Dublin

1 Entrance	9 Barrack master's quarters, stores and office
2 Barrack sergeants' Quarters	10 Guardhouse
3 Armourers workshop	11 Barrack master's quarters
4 Officers' stables	12 Cavalry square
5 Washhouse	13 Stable square
6 Soldiers' privies	14 Royal square
7 Canteen and cookhouse	15 Palatine square
8 Barrack sergeants' quarters	16 Brunswick square

Troops in Bivouac near the Village of Villa Velha, on the Evening of the 19th of May 1811. Engraved by C. Turner after Major T. St Clair. (*National Army Museum, London*)

Camp Scenes. Etching by W.H. Pyne, published 1803. (*National Army Museum, London*)

Baggage Wagon. Aquatint by J.A. Atkinson, 1807. *(National Army Museum, London)*

Soldiers Marching. After Thomas Rowlandson. *(National Army Museum, London)*

my commission in battle. I lost my father and two brothers in the service and never had leave of absence for one month.

When Bircham wrote this statement he was anxious for further service, having been placed on half-pay upon reduction. Before that he had risen to the rank of major, and every step had been without purchase. His letter seems to have had some effect because after spending some time with the 1st Royal Veteran Battalion, and then another period on half-pay, he joined the Ceylon Rifles without purchase, and eventually became lieutenant-colonel of that regiment.

Reference has already been made to the Royal Military College, whose graduates automatically received commissions without purchase. This establishment, welcomed as 'a most excellent opportunity for instructing young men for the army...the good effects of which will soon be known',[91] was established at High Wycombe in 1801, the inspiration of a French *émigré*, General François Jarry, who was its first inspector-general. The original purpose was to improve the education of young officers, but a year later a junior department was set up 'for the instruction of those who from early life are intended for the military profession'. The correspondents of *The Royal Military Chronicle* wrote approvingly of the new military schools. Typically, T.J. suggested that

> The early age at which young gentlemen enter the army is probably the cause of the frequent instances which occur of officers, whose conversation betrays a slight and insufficient education, both as to those acquirements which every gentleman would wish to possess , and of branches of knowledge which are more immediately connected with a military life.
>
> Marlow and Wycombe are rapidly effecting a very desirable change in this respect, not only by the numerous accomplished officers which they produce, but the desire of knowledge which has thereby been disseminated through the army. Officers, even of the rank of lieutenant-colonel, feeling the deficiency of their first education, return to school to make themselves masters of subjects which greatly increase their value and importance, and open for them a shorter and more splendid road to preferment and distinction.[92]

The remainder of the letter, however, decries the inadequate military education that most young officers received, a problem that was widely recognised.

The foremost requirement demanded of an officer was an awareness of his duty. For example, according to the standing orders of the Gibraltar garrison, 1803, the commanding officer of each corps was required to declare that every captain and subaltern under his command was capable of performing the duties required of him. Any officer considered incapable was to be kept from guard and garrison duties until he had been thoroughly instructed, under the direction of the adjutant. Similarly, any newly-arrived officer was not to be put down for any public duty until his competence had been ascertained.

In practice, most officers learnt their business 'on the job' unless they had been to the Royal Military College. Nevertheless, there was some required reading:

> As soon as a young gentleman joins a regiment, he must provide himself with such books, as may be recommended to him by the commanding officer. He must read with great attention, the *Articles of War*, and the *Act* of Parliament *for punishing Mutiny and Desertion*, which empowers his Majesty to make those articles for the better government of his army. He must have copies of the *Rules and Regulations for the formations of field exercises, and movements of His Majesty's forces, General Orders and Observations on the movement and field exercises of the Infantry, The manual and Platoon Exercises* and *General Regulations and Orders*. All these works are, by command, to be in the possession of every officer in his Majesty's service, and commanding officers of regiments are responsible that it is obeyed.[93]

Thomas Reide, writing specifically for the instruction of young officers, suggested that some basic competencies were required. He instanced a knowledge of several foreign languages (listing French, German, Spanish and Italian), mathematics, to support the study of fortification and tactics, riding and fencing, and drawing, to execute plans and charts. Once the novice was with his regiment, he should keep a journal of daily military occurrences into which he would also insert all general and regimental orders. This requirement was certainly practised in some regiments, although there is no evidence for the 30th. William Stewart's journal, however, makes clear that there was considerable attention given to the subalterns, to make them fit for duty, while General Graham's decision to send the young volunteer, Edward Macready, to the 2/30th in 1814 was based on his knowledge of Hamilton's skill in bringing young officers up to scratch.

Furthermore, a young officer was instructed to attend all parades and field days, learn to mount guard, and regularly attend divine service. When he attended morning and evening roll-call he should make sure that the men of his company were present, sober, clean and have their arms and accoutrements in good order, an ideal which was not always realised in practice. It was one of the most frequent reasons for men from the ranks appearing before regimental courts martial, which links to another of the young officer's duties, to learn both regimental and general court martial procedure through observation. The regularity with which Ensign Carter recorded in his journal his experiences of regimental courts martial suggests that he took this duty very seriously.

Offences might not lead to a court martial; a reprimand was often a suitable substitute. The officer, however, should deliver them gently. Reide pointed out to the novice that it was unmanly to lose one's temper or strike a soldier. (In fact, this seems to have been a more common failing among NCOs than officers.) As well as reprimanding, however, the officer was also required to investigate complaints from the men. If the problem proved intractable, he should consult his captain or the adjutant, who was, among his other duties, a mentor for young officers.

The junior subalterns were also required to observe the proper forms of subordination within the officer hierarchy. This should be enforced by the commanding officer in order to preserve discipline and the young officer was expected to recognise its necessity.

James instructed officers commanding companies to hold a private parade before a general parade to satisfy themselves that arms, dress and accoutrements were all in good order. He also advised them, for their own benefit and the benefit of their men, to put the company through the manual and platoon exercises on occasion after the private inspection. This would be an opportunity for ensigns to learn the appropriate words of command:

> At private inspections, the officers, particularly the subalterns, should frequently exercise themselves in calling the roll of the company. They will, by these means, become acquainted with the names of the men, and insensibly acquire a military tone of voice.[94]

During field manoeuvres officers were expected to know their respective positions and how to hold their swords during the different manoeuvres. 'Officers leading platoons or divisions, especially in echelon, should be very exact in preserving their distances; regulating themselves in such a manner, as never to overlap, or to be too wide from the preceding platoon or company.' Furthermore, when marching, 'Great attention must be paid to the uniformity of step, and squareness of their platoon, and that the men march firm and steady…' When the battalion charges,

> The officers upon the flanks of companies, particularly the captains must be cool and collected, directing all their attention to the preservation of a good line. They are to remember that their business in all movements of the battalion, most especially when ordered to charge or fire in advancing, should be confined to their men…

Word of command 'must be given loud and distinct, not hurried, though no time should be lost in delivering them'.[95]

Guard duty was one of the most important of the officer's responsibilities because

> No circumstance so strongly marks the character and discipline of a regiment as the conduct and management of its several guards, and the maintenance of the strict order among its sentries. Young officers should, above all others, be scrupulously exact in the unequivocal discharge of this important duty; from the exercise or neglect of which much good or evil must hereafter ensue, under the conditions of actual service.[96]

As the Gibraltar standing orders make clear, when on guard duty an officer was fully responsible for the conduct of the men, whether of his own or some other corps. Any breaches had to be reported, and the offender confined. If an officer failed to do this, it was as if he himself had committed the fault.

When on duty, officers had to be

> particularly attentive to visit every thing charged to the guard, together with the officer, or non-commissioned officer, who he is to relieve; and satisfy himself, in the first instance, whether all is complete or not, before he suffers the old guard to march off.[97]

Of particular concern to the relieving officer should be the order and cleanliness of the guard-room. He was also to make sure that he received the book of orders. Any failings in both these respects were to be reported to the commanding officer of the old guard, and they were also to be noted on the schedule which he would sign for the officer or NCO he relieved.

Having completed these formalities, the officer then visited the sentries to ensure that they understood their orders:

> that they are on no account permitted to eat, drink, sit down, smoke, whistle, sing, read, quit their arms, lean upon the muzzle of their firelocks, go into their sentry-boxes, except in raining weather, or address themselves to any person, either military or inhabitant, except in the execution of their duty.[98]

As for the officer, he could only absent himself from the guard-room when visiting the sentries. Nor was he permitted to amuse himself or allow any amusement (such as gambling or drinking) in the guard-room. Finally, having completed his period of duty, the officer reported the details of his guard to the field officer of the day.

Reide, in his *Treatise*, identified a range of duties specific to camp, garrison, quarters, and even on board ship. For example, when in camp, the general of the day was responsible for proper regularity and discipline overall, while the brigade field officer supervised the camp of the brigade. The captain of the day supervised the cleanliness and regularity of his regiment, as well as parading guards and piquets, ordering roll-calls, and reporting to the commanding officer. A subaltern assisted the captain, while also having responsibility for inspecting the men's messes and producing a written report on the quality and preparation of the food. The captain and the subaltern were also required to visit the regimental hospital at different and uncertain hours.

Piquet guards paraded at beating the retreat. They might be under the command of a single subaltern, or up to three officers, in which case one of them would be a captain, and consisted of fifty men. They were responsible for security, thus they needed to stay awake throughout their period of duty, ready to fall out at any time. This, as Macready discovered in Flanders, could prove problematic and officers might take extreme measures to keep themselves awake, such as stopping anyone and everyone who came within their orbit.

Garrison duty was similar to camp duty, while the size of the guards and the number of officers required when the battalion was in quarters would depend upon circumstances. If the men were quartered within one small area, there would obviously be a more limited requirement than if they were dispersed over a wider area. Shipboard duties posed particular problems, of course. Consequently, 'The greatest care is necessary from every officer embarked on board ships destined for foreign service, not only to preserve their own health, but likewise that of the men under their command.'[99] Nevertheless, the assumption was that significant aspects of military life such as parades, drill and ball-firing should still be maintained.

An officer was also expected to be familiar with the march of a regiment, military funerals and, as we have seen, military courts. Drill and field exercise were a further regular part of his life. As *The Rules and Regulations* (1804) dictated:

> The complete instruction of an officer enlarges with his situation, and at least takes in the whole circle of military science. From the variety of military knowledge required of him, his exertion must be unremitting, to qualify himself for the progressive situations at which he arrives.[100]

General David Dundas, in his drill book, pointed out that

> an officer who cannot thoroughly discipline and exercise the body entrusted to his command, is not fit, in time of service, to lead it to the enemy: he cannot be cool and collected in the time of danger; he cannot profit of circumstances, from an inability to lead others; the fate of many depends upon his ill or well acquainting himself with his duty. It is not sufficient to advance with bravery; it is requisite to have that degree of intelligence, which should distinguish every officer according to his station: nor will soldiers ever act with spirit and animation, when they have no reliance on the capacity of those that do conduct them.[101]

Young officers were to make it their business to attend and observe field exercises. These exercises followed a prescribed pattern, starting with exercises of the line, including passage of line and retreat in line, because 'on a just and quick formation into line almost every movement depends'.[102] Other exercises involved changes of front, formation into square or oblong in order to encounter cavalry on open ground, echelon movement, column, counter-marching, firing and charging a line. All these depended upon words of command from the battalion officers, so familiarity was crucial. Indeed, it was an ability to form quickly into square that saved the 2/30th from the fate of the other battalions in Halkett's brigade at Quatre Bras. For the benefit of inexperienced officers Reide provided eighty pages of instruction in his *Treatise*, including a clear digest of the commanding officer's word of command, and the words of command that were required from the company officers at every stage of the exercises.

A Handbook for Officers, based on the 1807 regulations, summed up how these commands should be given. On the assumption that expectations of exactness created effective soldiers, the officer should aim to give all commands 'in the full extent of his voice', even when addressing a small number of men. This not only avoided confusion, but also maintained a proper relationship between officers and men. The same source also expected officers to know what was required of a recruit or a soldier. He should expect to be examined by his commanding officer on his knowledge of the 'movements' and must be prepared for extra drill if his knowledge were imperfect. He should also understand the principles that underlay the manoeuvres and recognise the faults that might emerge.

To sum up, the good officer put the comfort of his men before his own. He used the expertise of NCOs consultatively but still recognised that decisions must be his own. Finally, he acknowledged that there was no such thing as bad soldiers, only bad officers.

There was another side to an officer's life, however, and all four of the surviving journals written by officers of the 30th demonstrate the importance of enjoying one's leisure hours. Not surprisingly, more space is given to this aspect of their lives than the more predictable and humdrum aspects of duty. Being on campaign or going into action was recorded, but the day-to-day business of an officer's life tended to be taken for granted.

Between them, the four diarists, William Stewart, John Carter, James Goodall Elkington and Edward Macready cover the period from 1810 to 1827, taking in the Peninsular War and the Waterloo campaign, Ireland and India. What is interesting, therefore, is the similarity of leisure activities that passed the time for these four very different individuals.

Not surprisingly, socialising was a significant element in their lives, particularly for Stewart and Carter in the Peninsula. Stewart's journal, from September 1810 to May 1811 is regularly punctuated with references to dinners with other officers, particularly during the period when the second battalion was behind the Lines of Torres Vedras. Often the participants were members of the battalion, but there were also occasions when officers from other regiments were entertained by Stewart and his messmates. For example, on the 24th October, only a week after the battalion joined up with the rest of the fifth division, he recorded that Captain Wilson and Lieutenant Rae of the Royals dined with himself, Major Hamilton and Captain Bamford, who were messing together. Four months later his and Bamford's guests were Lieutenants Killet and Balfour, also of the Royals. Perhaps the most memorable of these dinners given for officers of other corps, though, occurred on the 4th January 1811, when Lieutenant-Colonel Belsdin and Ensign H of the 3rd Portuguese Regiment

> dined with us – Had great argument, & my chum the M——r [Hamilton] had a bad fall down his own stairs in consequence of inebriation…Our visitor the Lt-Col also got swamped in a Drain on his way home & only for Ens H would have been lost.

It is interesting to note the number of officers within the battalion with whom Stewart dined: there are specific references to Colonel Minet, Major Hamilton, Captain Hitchen, Captain T. Williamson (who was on the staff), Captain Lynch, Captain Fox, Captain McNabb, Captain Machell, Lieutenant Andrews, Lieutenant Eades, Lieutenant Mayne, Surgeon Hennen, Quartermaster Kingsley, and Mr Tincombe, a volunteer. This last name is particularly interesting because volunteers occupied an uncertain position in the battalion hierarchy. Tincombe, however, was very much part of the social scene, as Ensign Carter's journal also makes clear. Furthermore, the frequency of dinners (rather than just messing with one's chums, as Stewart would have phrased it) is notable. For example, having entertained Lieutenant Andrews, Captain L. Hughes and Mr Tincombe to dinner on the 20th January 1811, he dined at Captain Fox's, along with Captain Lynch and Mr Tincombe on the 21st, and then entertained Captain Hughes again on the 22nd.

Something of the flavour of these evenings is brought out by Stewart's account of a dinner with Captain Hitchen:

Capt H dined with us & having by the assistance of a little Wine & a Glass of Grogg [sic] nearly got the better of his fatiques [after a long walk] he amused us with many pleasant & laughable stories relative to his Scenes with Excise Offrs when he was a Wine Merchant, as also of a new mode of Duck shooting struck out by himself thro' the means of a Cannon!!!

His story for the trap he laid for a Ganger [revenue officer] was as follows – This Man had once broken over a *private* Cellar which contained private Liquors & the entire proved a legal seizure. The Capt thought it proper to introduce fifty Barrels of Water sealed & done up in the manner of Spirits, Wines etc & employed a person to give information to the Ganger that a fresh supply of Liquors had lately been smuggled into Mr H's stores. The Excise Gentlemen are always greedy of plunder & the bait took, for ere Noon the Door of the Cellar was *broken open* (the key purposely being put out of the way) & fifty Barrels being carried off in triumph Mr H instantly entered a Lawsuit against the Ganger for breaking open his House & for robbing, & recovered treble the value of the first seizure made from him & dispossessed the Gentleman of his situation.

Some mournful Songs & much good humoured conversation finished the Evening.

Ensign Carter, in a similar situation to Stewart a year later, also enjoyed dining with his fellow officers, even though his means fell short of Stewart's resources. He must have welcomed an invitation to dine with Lieutenant-Colonel and Mrs Grey shortly before Christmas 1811. He celebrated Christmas itself with the adjutant, Lieutenant Garland, and Ensign Campbell. The battalion had spent the morning parading for General Walker, who found fault with the movement, the men not sloping their arms properly, called the officers 10 paces in front & told them to examine the men & put them to rights, he found fault with the supernumerary officers, in particular after advancing & retiring in line, we marched home. In consequence of all this palaver he ordered the whole regiment to drill at 8 o'clock every morning.

With this dispiriting activity ahead of them, it is no wonder that the three young men felt the need to cheer themselves up. In good spirits, they 'had a famous jolly time of it, sung several songs, at 9 o'clock we adjourned to Colonel Grey's where we had an eloquent supper, [and] a great deal of jolly rum with which I play my part pretty well'.

The paucity of Carter's resources, as well as those of his messmate, Assistant Surgeon Evans, became apparent the next day.

> The doctor & I were so merry the night before that we asked a whole lot of fellows to dine with us, neither had much money, but the doctor raised 2 dollars, which enabled us to buy a ceg [sic] of wine, this together with the ration rum we got the day before wined us pretty well, the adjutant was also so good as to send up three pints of whisky. We were very much puzzled as to how to get a table and table cloth however I proposed to the doctor that we should bring up some planks which were in the yard & rest them on a chest & made a table, now we did not know how it was possible to procure a cloth. Coming up from the kitching [sic] to my great astonishment I saw the doctor very busy spreading a cloth & bestowing great pains to brush some dirty yellow spots off it. When I asked him where he had raised that he told me that it was one of the sheets which he had taken from the bed & that it would do very well once he had brushed the lice & fleas off. Dinner was served up everyone seemed to enjoy himself very much, after sitting some time & making rather merry the company retired. I forgot to mention that I had employed myself all the morning in making apple dumplings which would have been very good had they not been boiled too much.

Financially, their situation could only get worse. On the 30th December

> Paddy Wire the butcher desired the doctor & me for the payment of a little mutton which we had bought of him in order to make the times appear a little more like Christmas. Neither of us had a farthing to pay him.

The next day, having invited Lieutenant Brisac to dinner, they forgot

> at the moment our great poverty. I left two vints & a half with my servant to buy potatoes. All the money we had between us he managed to get two pound of potatoes which bearly [sic] served us. We had no allowance of rum or wine. Brisac who was pretty flush, volunteered to buy some wine & we very modestly accepted of it.[103]

On the 5th January Carter

> dined with the adjutant, we had part of the band & the company which consisted of Lieutenant Mayne, Ensign Smith, Campbell, the doctor, myself & four Portuguese girls, one gentleman & the old mother danced & made most merry until a late hour.[104]

On the 9th February there was a similar occasion.

> In the evening there was a dance, we subscribed half a dollar each, I tossed up with the doctor who should pay the whole & I won. The rooms were very small & full, half the ladies had the itch. I was very much entertained at seeing the Spanish girls play the castanets.[105]

Carter makes clear that merriment could easily turn into drunkenness. On one occasion,

> Several of the officers who had been drinking at Ensign Lockwood's sallied forth about 2 o'clock in the morning into the street & began to throw stones at Lieutenant Mayne's & Ensign Smith's quarters, it enraged Smith so much that he fired a fowling piece out of the window & hit Lieutenant Garland. Ensign Smith reported this to the colonel, Ensign L[ockwood] was put under arrest.[106]

Another sociable activity was visiting old friends. Stewart's journal contains several references to meeting up with former comrades while behind the Lines. Similarly, Surgeon Elkington recorded some years later how he encountered Captain Roche, formerly with the 30th, in Limerick. They had been fellow prisoners in Verdun and undoubtedly enjoyed their reminiscences of French imprisonment now the war was safely over.

Another activity indulged in by all four diarists was sightseeing. Stewart, for example, took advantage of a period of leave in Lisbon to explore the city. He visited the Tagus and the new fortifications (the third line of Wellington's defences) with Captain McNabb and Quartermaster Kingsley, and the famous library in the Plaça Comércio. He was impressed by the size and stock of the library, and also the dimensions of the square itself, while he considered the equestrian statue of King Joao I the finest he had ever seen. On the last day of his leave, he visited the church of St Roche with Colonel Minet, and was deeply impressed by the intricate mosaic work, the gold-studded altar and other features of the place, an unexpected response from an Ulster Protestant. He also visited the lace workshops and silk manufacturers, which he thought every visitor to Lisbon should witness. On his way back to Torres Vedras he stopped off at Mafra, but was sadly disappointed by the palace.

Stewart, in fact, roamed as widely as he could during this period of waiting for Marshal Masséna to withdraw from the Lines. On one occasion he visited the castle of the Count of Vimeiro and lamented the distressing sight of the count's books strewn around by French plunderers. The palace of Runa was the focus of another of his sightseeing expeditions. Even when he was part of the pursuit which drove Masséna out of Portugal, he still took a tourist's interest in the places he passed through, such as Linhares and Guarda.

Macready was particularly interested in visiting battlefields. In Belgium he noted that a march passed Oudenarde, 'the scene of Marlborough's defeat of Vendôme', while a family with whom he was billeted, les Verdures, took him to

> the field of Fontenoy. From the mill of Antoine I could trace the positions of the two armies. To my left was the ground on which the English Infantry successively defeated every corps in the French Army, where the Household were repulsed, and whence Marshal Saxe sent to Louis to repass the bridge of Calonne.[107]

On the departure from France at the end of 1815

> we marched over the immortal field of Crécy. I could plainly trace the position of the English army; and I stood for some minutes at the rude stone cross that marks the death spot of the King of Bohemia. On the crest of the hill, a mill now stands on the precise spot where Edward III viewed the battle. It was worth a year of mere existence to stand upon this sacred spot.[108]

Macready was undoubtedly a romantic at heart.

The battlefield that seems to have affected him most deeply, however, was Assaye, in India. As he records,

> I was fortunate in traversing the field with an intelligent officer, who had previously been over it with one who had distinguished himself in this glorious battle (for this was one of the very few eastern affairs to which that epithet is due).

He then included in his journal a full account of the battle itself, before adding his own experience.

> I crossed the field from the ford of the Kaitna to Assaye, whence I rode on the track of the dragoons across the Juah, a short distance beyond which, the retreat became a rout. About an hundred yards from the right bank of this nullah is a fine Banyan tree, near which the action was most obstinate, and which now serves to mark the spot where fourteen British officers were buried…A whitewashed mud tomb is under that tree, but whether erected to their memory or that of an enemy I could not learn. My feelings were variously excited, and while I admired the accidental fitness of the emblem that overshadowed the gallant fellows, I

could not help breathing out a curse on the neglect which has left them without a more legible testimony of their deeds.

Exploring his feelings, Macready added:

> I consider it a happy coincidence in my career, that in all the countries I have visited it has been my good fortune to tread those fields most hallowed by the valour of my countrymen. In Flanders, France, and India, I have traversed the fields of Oudenarde, Fontenoy, Malplaquet, Crécy and Assaye, with an accelerated pulse, and a heart proudly throbbing for the honor [sic] of old England. In every age and every clime has the courage of her sons shone brave and brilliant, and tho' she may one day decline in strength and greatness, the congregated mass of her fame shall flourish, and rival in history the days of Roman and of Grecian glory.[109]

Such sentiments would probably have been shared by most of Macready's fellow officers.

Elkington, like Stewart, had the instincts of a tourist. In the spring of 1814, after Napoleon's first abdication, he took advantage of seven days' leave to visit Rotterdam, the Hague and Delft in company with Colonel Bailey, Paymaster Wray and Captain White. On April 27th he recorded how they

> Visited Delft, saw the beautiful monument erected to the Prince of Orange, perhaps the most magnificent in Europe, afterwards to the Hague, where we remained, visited the Palace, (called the house in the wood), left cards on our Ambassador, Lord Clancarty, who invited us to dinner the following day.

Three weeks later he visited Louvain, 'a singular old City with its quaint Gothic Hall, and fine Church, large breweries were established there. It is situated in a deep valley its canal communicates with Malines.' More prosaic than Macready, Elkington was, nonetheless, careful to record his impressions as he travelled around. For example, on the 3rd August

> in the even to Ghent, a large fine City, with wide streets, magnificent churches, some fine houses, supposed to have been built by the Moors, still remain. It has a famous piece of Artillery, fine canals, large prison, walks and rides; few towns have suffered more than this in its trade and population by the transfer to France.

Carter, in the winter of 1811 and spring of 1812, was not well situated to visit local sights, nor does he seem to have possessed the tourist's eye. Neither Linhares nor Guarda, which he passed through on the march, evoked any comment from him. He did, however, enjoy walking, a favourite exercise of many officers. Evans was his usual companion, and their walks seem to have been sociable affairs. On one occasion they 'met with two priests who played us several tunes on their guitars, gave us some lemons, walked home with us & gave us a general invitation to their houses'.[110] A week later

> the doctor & I took a long walk met with two ladies who greeted us with preserved fruits, they detained us for some time, we went into a garden hard by filled our pockets & hands with oranges & came home.[111]

The most indefatigable walker was Stewart, whose journal is regularly punctuated with accounts of the walks he took in the Torres Vedras area. Indeed, he believed walking to be a healthy exercise; those who pursued a sedentary life in the filth of the town 'were the first victims to fever & disease of all kind'. On one occasion he took a long walk with Ensign H of the 9th which involved using trees to cross two rivers. He also records a day when he went fowling with Captains Bamford and Hitchen before visiting the Queen's Palace and Garden, north of Torres Vedras:

> My companions noted me *Conductor* for the remainder of the Days excursion, & on this occasion I assumed to myself a thorough knowledge of the Country! Having conducted them thro Roads, over Mountains, & across Villages until I began to tire, I was at length obliged to confess that my topographical abilities were not *quite* so perfect as I had supposed them to have been!! In some degree, however, Capt B & I were excused by the reflection that Capt H was on this occasion amply repaid for having taken us a much more unpleasant walk on a former occasion by way of showing us Game. It was evident he made a *game* of us.

The reference to game links to another favoured activity, hunting. There are no references in the journals to hunting with hounds, although Wellington's predilection for this activity is well known. Stewart makes many references to other forms of hunting, however. In December 1811 he went fowling with Bamford on the 1st, and nine days later he went coursing with Bamford and Colonel Egerton of the 44th. He also went fowling with Bamford on the 11th January, when he 'killed a firm large hare'. Obviously, such a kill was a welcome supplement to army rations, so it is no wonder that Stewart and Bamford went fowling on a day's halt during the march to Spain.

For Macready in India hunting was a recreation. On Christmas Day 1822, 'a roving party, christened per se "The Rangers" and consisting of Backhouse, James, Mansel, Stuart, and myself took the field or rather the jungle for a campaign of six weeks against all game from quails to royal tigers.' Macready was appointed caterer and accountant general, George Backhouse, master of the revels. By the end of the expedition they looked like brigands. On one occasion a Muslim even mistook them for robbers, and began to strip off to show he had no valuables.[112]

Time passed slowly in India, and diversion was needed to avoid sinking into that lethargy which could drive a man to drink. Macready himself devised one unusual way of passing the time, an intellectual contest with Lieutenant Ralph. They called themselves Sarpedon and Emulus, and exchanged thoughts for a considerable period. He was also persuaded to tread the Jaulnah boards, which he did with some reluctance, provoked by a report that Major Dalrymple

> had prevented our officers joining the theatricals. To contradict this silly rumour, Neville, Gregg and I came forward, and the blood of the McCready's [sic] so bravely bore me up that, to borrow the complimentary phraseology of our Adjutant-General, I succeeded 'à la merveille'. I was flattered by the receipt of several play books, and notes requesting me to fix on any part I chose, but my determination was taken. I had strutted my little hour, and was resolved no more to expose myself to the attacks of men 'sworn foe to witticism, by men called criticism'.[113]

He kept to this resolution, even though his journal makes clear that plays were regular occurrences.

As were the races. These were a regular event. In 1822, he noted that the races were poor and the Cambridge Cup, with a prize of 1,000 rupees, was walked over. It is no surprise, however, that racing was a favourite activity in the often static life of the officers in India. It is more surprising, perhaps, that Stewart refers to racing on the drill ground at Torres Vedras.

What else could one do to pass the time? Obviously, there were the risks of gambling, although there are no references to it in any of the journals. Both Stewart and Macready tried to learn the language of the country where they found themselves. Stewart obviously persevered with Portuguese. Kept at home by 'uncommonly Rainy and Stormy' weather, he spent the last day of January 1811 'studying Portuguese all Day'. A month later, a misty, gloomy day caused him to amuse himself 'reading, writing & studying Portuguese as usual'. It would be interesting to know whether he subsequently devoted the same effort to learning Spanish. Macready, however, seems to have been more interested in the young woman whom he hired to teach him Hindustani than in acquiring a knowledge of the language.

At times one senses a desperation in the means employed to create amusement. Captain Machell, in Portugal, for example, won money in a 'leaping match' with Lieutenant Boyd of the 4th, while Captains Bamford and Hitchin set up a wager about the state of their respective companies' necessaries, which Bamford won. Just as the men were best motivated when there was the chance of action, so the officers welcomed the call to arms. Yet action came rarely, duty was predictable and repetitious, so it was necessary to make one's own amusements to counter the potential tedium of an officer's life.

Chapter 9

Crime and Punishment

The law military, of which I propose to speak, comprises a body of rules and ordinances, expressly laid down and presented by competent authority, for the government of the military state, considered as a distinct community; attaching to the members of such state, in their individual as well as collective capacity; regulating the conduct of each in all that concerns him in his primary and relative duties; in what he owes to himself, to others, and to the society of which he is a part.[114]

This statement, written in 1816, reminds us that when a man joined the army he became subject, in his military capacity, to a set of 'rules and ordinances' different from those pertaining to the civil law. Although his civil rights remained sacrosanct under common law as a common citizen of a common state, he found himself in addition subject to a particular law which imposed new obligations on him in his role as a soldier.

The source of this accumulative law was the Articles of War and the Mutiny Act. Sir William Blackstone wrote in 1765 that

> Martial Law [being] built upon no settled principles…is…in truth and reality no law…and therefore it ought not to be permitted in time of peace, when the King's courts are open for all persons to receive justice according to the law of the land.[115]

This claim inevitably set up a tension between civil and military law which had a detrimental effect on army discipline until 1792, when an appeal against the Mutiny Act by a sergeant accused of sanctioning a fraudulent enlistment was ruled inadmissible. Thereafter, it was generally acknowledged that the Mutiny Act governed the discipline of the British soldier.

The Articles of War, contained in the Mutiny Act, covered all aspects of military life 'for the better government of the army in the Kingdoms of Great Britain and Ireland, dominions beyond the seas, and foreign parts dependent upon Great Britain'. In other words, wherever his service took him and whatever his rank, the soldier was controlled by the Articles. Indeed, it must have been some consolation to soldiers in the ranks that even generals could be, and regularly were, tried by court martial for their shortcomings. The Articles could be amended at the pleasure of the king, but they had to be confirmed annually by parliament under the Mutiny Act. They were read to the men at least once a month so that they could not plead ignorance. Should a soldier be able to prove that they had not been read to him, he could not then be tried by a court martial.

In 1816 there were 124 Articles which may be summarised into twenty-two sections, although only those relevant to crime and punishment will be considered here.

The first four articles sought to enforce regular and properly conducted *Divine Worship*, and to restrict the soldier's tendency to blasphemy, profanity and sacrilege, while two further articles controlled the behaviour of chaplains. Although these were not articles which often brought soldiers to trial, Joseph Lole, of the first battalion in India was accused of 'unsoldierlike conduct when marching to a funeral', for which he was sentenced to two weeks in solitary confinement; William Kertland, of the same unit, received fifty lashes for being 'drunk for divine service'.

The section on *Mutiny* comprised a variety of offences: speaking disrespectfully of the king and the royal family; showing contempt towards a general or other commander-in-chief of His Majesty's forces; conventional mutiny, or sedition, or murmuring against authority (known as mutinous conduct); standing by while mutiny or sedition was committed; disobeying the lawful commands of a superior; striking or threatening with a weapon. These were amongst the most serious offences a soldier could commit, although it was the last two that seem to have brought men most often to a court martial. For example, Daniel Frost of the first battalion was tried by general court martial for 'mutinous expressions to Sergeant Abbott' and was sentenced to 400 lashes, of which 300 were inflicted. Joseph Kennedy, also of the first battalion, received 200 lashes for 'riotous conduct when a prisoner and striking Sergeant Preston'. Many of the instances of disobedience and threatening or violent behaviour in India seem to have been committed in a state of drunkenness, while in the second battalion, where this kind of mutinous behaviour was less common, there was no association with alcohol. Nevertheless, William Derry was sentenced to seventy-five lashes in Portugal for 'disobedience to orders' and received fifty, while Thomas Bradley received 150 lashes in Flanders for 'unsoldierlike conduct, striking Corporal Connell'.

A further five articles dealt with record-keeping, for which regular *Musters* were required. These articles stipulated the frequency of musters, and included the precise regulation of furlough and temporary leave of absence. The overall responsibility for accurate compilation rested with the commanding officer and the adjutant, but the penalty for any officer who knowingly signed a false certificate of any kind was cashiering. Linked to the previous section was the section on *Returns* which comprised another four articles. Failure to complete a return honestly was punished by cashiering because 'It is the duty of every officer to return things as they are', and it was presumed that an officer would know 'what from the duty of his office he is bound to know.'[116]

Desertion was defined as 'a wilful abandonment or departure by any officer or soldier of or from his station, regiment, or corps, without leave; and without the intention to return'. This last phrase was crucial, as court martial papers and regimental records make clear. There were five articles which together covered desertion by men who had enlisted, punishment for officers who countenanced the presence of deserters, and for soldiers who persuaded others to desert. Less obvious cases of desertion, although technically described as such, covered apprentices who enlisted but did not deliver themselves to the army at the end of their apprenticeship, men who enlisted into a second corps without legitimate discharge from their first, or absconders from recruitment parties who had received their enlistment money. A distinction was also made between desertion in time of war, and in time of peace.

The endemic nature of the problem is made clear by the official returns for the army as a whole. For example, in 1803, a period of army expansion after the collapse of the Peace of Amiens, there were 4,404 desertions, and this number rose to 7,081 two years later. The 30th returned their highest number of deserters in that period, while both battalions were in Ireland, but the number fell dramatically once the first battalion had sailed to India and the second battalion was on active service in the Peninsula. Also, a man returned as a deserter one month frequently made a re-appearance the following month. Sometimes the reason was legitimate, as in the case of Francis Fahey. Men who had fallen ill while returning from furlough were initially returned as deserters but subsequently a note would explain the reason for their absence. More commonly the cause of absence was drunkenness, and a depressing number of courts martial in the first battalion note this fact. Taking the army overall, though, desertion was more common on home service than service abroad.

The five articles which covered *Quarrels and Sending Challenges* had the precise aim of preventing private quarrels, particularly between officers, which were seriously detrimental to the good conduct of the regiment. Consequently, 'no officer, non-commissioned officer, or soldier shall use any reproachful or provoking speeches or gestures to another, upon pain, if an officer, of being put in arrest; or, if a non-commissioned officer or soldier, of being imprisoned'.[117] Sending a challenge to fight a duel led in theory to the cashiering of an officer (corporal punishment in the rarer instance of a non-commissioned officer or soldier committing such an offence), whether or not the challenge was actually accepted. Similarly, it was an offence to countenance a duel taking place, while anyone involved in carrying a challenge or in the conduct of a duel was considered as guilty as the actual participants.

A proviso, obviously framed to prevent duels, stated that if an officer was killed in a duel no officer of his own regiment could succeed to the vacant commission. Furthermore, anyone involved in a duel would be charged with homicide. Some distinction was made, however, between a spontaneous duel, for which the charge would be manslaughter ('the sudden heat of the passions') and one fought after a cooling-off period. This would be regarded as murder ('the malice and wickedness of the heart').[118]

There was only one fatal duel involving an officer of the 30th, in Gibraltar in 1809 when Richard Heaviside killed Lewis Mountford of the 47th. In India the situation was different. There were no fatalities, but several duels took place, always between officers of the regiment. Lieutenant Jones was twice tried for offences under these articles, and was suspended on both occasions. Lieutenant French, also twice court-martialled for duelling, was not so lucky. Suspended for the first offence, he was cashiered for the second.

Five articles dealt with the contentious issue of *Quarters* and quartering troops. Before the widespread building of permanent barracks, billeting was confined in all but the most exceptional circumstances to innkeepers, ale-house keepers and the keepers of livery stables in order to placate the civilian population. The purpose of the five articles was to prevent abuse of the system by military commanders, to prevent fraud, and to provide redress for victims of violence or extortion committed by soldiers. This was a sop to the civilian population. Thus the punishment for accepting bribes, for quartering soldiers in private houses, or for interfering with the duties of magistrates (who were responsible for the billeting of soldiers) was cashiering for an officer and demotion to the ranks and corporal punishment for a non-commissioned officer. Officers were also responsible for keeping good order in quarters and bringing any wrongdoers to justice. One example which demonstrates this is the case of Michael Moran who was tried for 'unsoldierlike conduct, mistreating the woman where he was quartered' while the second battalion was in Flanders. He was sentenced to 200 lashes, but commuted his sentence to service abroad for life, as allowed by the Mutiny Act.

On the other hand, the articles also prescribed fines for anyone liable under the Mutiny Act to receive or victual a soldier. Similarly, any civil officer who refused to superintend the billeting of soldiers or who accepted a bribe not to quarter soldiers was fined. The very existence of these articles, and their even-handed awareness that transgressions might exist on both sides, reminds us of how little the army was respected by the civilian population, except when it was far away winning battles.

Of Crimes Punishable by the Law were two catch-all articles that reminded the soldier he was still subject to

> the known laws of the land – by making officers of all descriptions subservient to and aiding in the service of the process of the civil courts, to bring alleged offenders, or debtors of the military class, within reach of the arms of the civil justice.[119]

The first article specifically required an officer to arrest and deliver a soldier under his command to the civil powers. An officer would be cashiered, under the terms of the second article, if he protected anyone from his creditors on the pretence of being a soldier, or by claiming that he was performing all his duties as a soldier, when this was not the case. On the other hand, soldiers had some protection against fraudulent claims, in the form of costs, since it was against the public interest to be deprived of the service of soldiers who had been wrongfully arrested for debt. Furthermore, the debt had to exceed £20 for the arrest to proceed.

Captain Peter Hawker, who was a prisoner in Verdun after the loss of the *Jenny*, managed to run up debts in the town while he enjoyed the liberty given to prisoners on parole. When he returned to England in 1814 he was immediately sued for debt.

More seriously, a handful of soldiers in the 30th were surrendered to the civil powers on charges of murder. Although the details were not recorded in regimental records, the *Leinster Journal* reported that Sergeant Edward Laughron was hanged at Mullingar for the murder of his wife while Macready mentioned in his journal the case of a soldier who suddenly turned against an Indian, calling him a blackbird and shooting him.

Officers and soldiers alike might find themselves suffering from the oppressive acts of their superiors and *Of Redressing Wrongs* was designed to protect them from any abuse of authority by specifying a procedure for complaints. The first article enabled an officer to take action against an unjust or despotic commanding officer. His first step was to send a written complaint to the officer who was perceived to have abused his power. If he received no redress, he could carry his complaint via his commanding officer (who was obliged to report it) to the commander of the forces. The commander of the forces was equally obliged to examine the complaint and report it to the king. Should the commanding officer refuse to process the complaint, the officer could then pursue the matter on his own behalf. If the commander of the forces decided not to follow up the complaint, the complainant could then petition the king directly.

Soldiers with complaints against an officer also had to carry them to the commanding officer, who was obliged to assemble a regimental court martial. There were some restrictions on the complainant, however. He had to be under the direct command of the officer against whom he lodged the complaint and only a single complainant was allowed to bring a grievance. The court martial was then required to satisfy the grievance, but not to punish the officer. Should either party be dissatisfied with the findings of the regimental court martial, the next step was a general court martial. To prevent frivolous complaints, also termed vexatious or groundless, a failed appeal to a general court martial involved punishment for the appellant. Thus there was protection for those in authority, who were obviously peculiarly vulnerable to false accusations.

A soldier of the first battalion who made use of the process 'for redressing wrongs' discovered that it could prove a painful experience. Thomas Allen was tried by general court martial for a 'frivolous complaint against Captain Cramer and insubordinate conduct'. His punishment was 500 lashes.

The set of six articles *Of Stores, Ammunition etc* was mainly applicable to quartermasters, paymasters and commissaries, and was designed to prevent fraud, embezzlement and misappropriation. The frequency of these offences is borne out by court martial records, although no staff officer of the 30th was ever charged with such a misdemeanour. The punishment for peculation and other offences against the articles ranged from dismissal and making good the loss to the pillory, imprisonment and transportation for life. It was also an offence for an officer who had public money in his possession not to disburse it appropriately, although paymasters, agents and clerks were given a month's grace since they dealt with larger sums of money and complicated payment processes. Peter Condron, who was a company paymaster sergeant in the first battalion was tried for 'making away with subsistence, dishonesty, and not paying wages'. He was reduced to the ranks, with stoppages, presumably until he had reimbursed the missing money.

A lesser offence against these articles, for non-commissioned officers and soldiers, was to misuse ammunition, horses, arms, clothes, accoutrements or regimental necessaries, the punishment being a flogging or imprisonment. This was, in fact, one of the most frequent reasons for a man appearing before a regimental court martial. In the first battalion, as recorded in eight inspection returns, 111 men were charged with offences such as losing or selling their necessaries, or damaging their musket or their accoutrements. In the second battalion there were twenty-five such offences, recorded in five inspection returns. On one occasion, while in Castello Branco, six men of the battalion lost or destroyed their blankets.

Of Duties in Quarters, in Garrison, or in the Field was another catch-all section, a group of twenty-one articles which sought to control behaviour 'recognized for the most part under the usages and customs of war, and the regulations or ordinances of the Crown; though some of them are distinguishable under the enactment and direct sanction of the legislature'.[120] In other words, custom, royal prerogative and parliamentary authority all played a part in the framing of these articles which ordained the proper behaviour of the soldier, whatever his rank. They covered matters as diverse as damage to property (such as chopping down olive trees in Portugal for firewood) to being more than a mile from camp without written permission, or requiring another to perform a nominated duty. Absence from guard, parade, exercise or other assembly without permission, drunkenness, quitting a post or falling asleep when on duty were all serious offences. The last two carried the death penalty when committed within proximity of the enemy. Violence, which included homicide, maiming and wounding, forcible detention, assault and battery, and robbery of the person would certainly be liable to the death penalty if committed on campaign. Indeed, soldiers caught by Wellington's provosts *in flagrante delicto* could be strung up without trial. Two soldiers of the second battalion were lucky to escape lightly when accused of striking an inhabitant at Tynaart in Holland. Francis Riley and William Irwin were each sentenced to 100 lashes and received fifty.

Another group of offences within this section included violating a safe conduct, betraying the watchword or countersign, creating a false alarm, giving intelligence to the enemy or treating with them, and giving relief to or protecting the enemy. All were punishable by death. Other capital offences specific to campaigning were abandoning a post to go in search of plunder, throwing away arms or ammunition, misbehaving before the enemy, which included abandoning or surrendering a command, deserting the colours or fleeing before the enemy. For all these offences, accessories were regarded as guilty as the principals.

Administration and Justice related directly to the exercise of justice, so it is not surprising that there were twenty-eight articles dedicated to the processes by which military justice was implemented, and to defining actual crimes. These articles specified the composition of courts martial, general, regimental and detachment, the role of the Judge Advocate General and his deputies, how the voting for a decision was to be carried out, requirements for the swearing of oaths, the punishments that could be imposed, with the regulations concerning their execution, and the process of arrest. Since the whole procedure of military justice was derived from these twenty-eight articles, they deserve separate consideration.

Two articles on *Troops in the East Indies* had some relevance for the first battalion because they defined the relationship between regular and East India Company officers. They gave precedence to the former, irrespective of date of commission, when both were employed on detachment, courts martial, or other joint duties. Regular and Company officers could sit together as members of a court martial, often a necessity when there was insufficient of either to form a court. The procedure, however, was in accordance with the army to which the defendant belonged.

A single article stipulated that *Troops on Board Ships of War* were to be regarded as subject to naval discipline under the command of the senior officer of the ship. What this implied in terms of naval courts martial was highly contentious, however, and never satisfactorily resolved in this period. Most troops travelled in transport ships, and it is clear from the second battalion records that the normal application of the Mutiny Act pertained in such situations. Thomas Jones was tried by regimental court martial for 'threatening Serjeant Brien in the execution of his duty' while aboard ship on the return from Portugal. He was sentenced to 200 lashes, of which 175 were inflicted. Similarly, William Pratt was sentenced to 100 lashes 'for striking Serjeant Cline in the execution of his duty', again aboard ship.

A final five articles *Relating to the Foregoing Articles* acted as a commentary on the preceding 114 articles and served as protection for the soldier. The first of them limited punishment to offences specified in the Articles themselves, as enabled by the Mutiny Act, although the second referred to offences of a secondary nature not included in the Articles for which a charge against good order and military discipline might be brought. The charge of unsoldierlike conduct covered many of these unspecified offences, although it was often linked to a more specific offence, or there was an explanation which made clear what was to be understood by the term. William Scotton of the first battalion was accused of 'unsoldierlike conduct in quitting guard', even though quitting guard was an offence in its own right. For this he was sentenced to solitary confinement for a fortnight. Daniel Rice was tried for 'unsoldierlike conduct, out of barracks, improperly dressed, beating a native woman'. The last of these was an offence under another of the articles, but 'out of barracks improperly dressed' might well be described as offending against good order and military discipline. This behaviour resulted in Rice being confined in the black hole, the name for solitary confinement suggestive of its condition, for seven days. Perhaps two of the most bizarre instances are those of Jeremiah Cox and John Sharpe. The former was tried for 'unsoldierlike conduct in attempting to strangle himself' and the latter, 'for unsoldierlike conduct in trying to hang himself'. Their respective sentences were 500 and 300 lashes, which demonstrates the change of attitude over 200 years to attempted suicide.

This last set of articles gave military courts considerable discretion, particularly by the article, introduced in 1811, which permitted imprisonment as an alternative rather than just an addition to corporal punishment. Comments on inspection reports make clear that many inspecting officers regarded it as a preferable punishment. In January 1813 General Wetherall wrote in his report on the first battalion: 'As solitary confinement would lessen corporal punishment I beg leave to suggest that a certain number of cells for this purpose be erected which in Cannanore might be done with little expense.' A year later Vaumorel was able to report that 'The necessity of frequent punishment has been much superseded by the adoption of solitary confinement.' Later that same year, however, General Wetherall commented:

> It appears...that eighty-two men have been tried by Regimental and General Courts Martial on a large proportion of whom I am concerned to observe corporal punishment has been inflicted but which I hope and trust will hereafter be superseded by a more lenient and less disgraceful measure, that of solitary confinement.

The second battalion, with far fewer offenders, generally received approving comments, although none made any reference to solitary confinement, probably because a corps on the move would have found it difficult to implement. Instead, General Hatton wrote in November 1813:

> No irregularity has occurred in the Proceedings of Courts Martial or in the execution of the sentences awarded by them, the sentences appear to have been proportionate to their crimes...The officers are reported zealous and assiduous in maintaining the discipline of the Regiment.

Two years later Colonel Bilson observed that 'the proceedings & execution on the sentences of Courts Martial appear to be regular, and the Commanding Officer reports that measures are adapted to prevent frequent punishment.' Whatever these measures were (no alternative to the lash is detailed), they appear to have been successful.

The further summative article reiterated that

> the Rules and Articles of War shall be read, and published once in every two months at the head of every troop or company, mustered or to be mustered in His Majesty's Service; as an injunction that they shall be duly and exactly obeyed by all officers and soldiers.[121]

Such was the military law that one commentator believed held

> over the military institutions of all surrounding nations a proud and commanding superiority; eminent as those great and inseparable results from the law (admitted and admired in other lands), the discipline of our armies, and the steady and reasoned valour, arising out of the sense of its protection, of every soldier composing them.[122]

The Mutiny Act, because it was the means by which the Articles of War were annually promulgated, took precedence over the articles themselves. It was the Mutiny Act which identified the specifically military offences that carried the death penalty, for both officers and men. These may be summed up as fomenting mutiny, or being an accessory to mutiny, misbehaving before the enemy, serious dereliction of duty, disobeying or using violence against a superior in the execution of his duty, and deserting His Majesty's service. Obviously, offences that were capital under criminal law also carried the death penalty when heard in a military court.

Two circumstances made the application of military law crucially important. The first was the diligence of officers, or rather the lack of it, since it was widely acknowledged that a common cause of indiscipline was the failure of officers to control the men. A serious contributory cause was the prevalence of absentee officers. Despite the Articles of War, the Adjutant-General did not have the power to enforce the presence of officers with their regiment; he could only harry them with letters. Although steps were taken by the Duke of York, as Commander-in-Chief, to amend this situation, it still remained a problem, particularly when many senior officers had distracting political and social interests. The monthly returns of the 30th contain many references to officers absent without leave for protracted periods, although sometimes there might be good reason for this. Major Chambers and Captain McNabb were returned as absent without leave for many months after they were killed at Waterloo, evidence of how long news took to travel from Europe to India.

In extreme cases, the absentee officer might eventually be 'dismissed the service'. Ensign Andrew Perry was commissioned into the regiment in November 1808. He first appears in the monthly returns of the second battalion in August 1809, as recruiting in Cambridge. Three months later the second battalion (in Gibraltar) thought he was at the depot in Hull, although depot returns do not mention him. By March 1810, he was supposed to be 'on command' in England, along with

Ensigns Herring and Light. The three young men were then ordered to the depot to embark for India in June, at which point they all became effective in the first battalion. Herring and Light reached India in October but Perry was not with them. Instead he was 'supposed on way to join'. For the next six months this became 'on way to join'. The following month, May 1811, he was returned as absent without leave for the first time. In March 1812 he was 'supposed to be with the second battalion', although two months later he was once more returned as absent without leave. Finally, in June it was record that 'Ensign Perry [had been] struck off the strength of the 1st Battn 25th May 1812, his commission being cancelled.' Presumably enquiries were made, and it was finally discovered by the authorities that Perry had abandoned his military career (without surrendering his commission). The news reached the second battalion rather earlier. In September 1811 they recorded that his commission was vacant, Perry himself having been 'superseded, absent without leave'.

The men might be a problem for the effective running of the army, no less than the officers. A letter to *The Royal Military Chronicle* of April 1811 made the following observations in comparison with the French:

> With us, the military profession has gradually lost its evidence for these last forty years; and our soldiery, although still composed of true British stuff, is not recruited from the same class of the community that fought under a Marlborough and a Peterborough. At that epoch the sons of respectable farmers and tradesmen were proud to be numbered in the ranks of our army; but now the idle and very necessitous form the bulk of the common soldiers; and, sad to say, the scum of jails are too frequently sent as a punishment to be the champions of their country! Under such degrading circumstances, it is not at all surprising that the respectability of the profession should suffer, and that a common soldier should be looked upon with contempt, which even his officers do not escape altogether.[123]

The writer then suggested that growing prosperity and the increasing demand for workers, accompanied by rising wages, had been instrumental in devaluing the soldier. His suggestion for making military life more attractive was to abolish corporal punishment, an attitude widely supported by the civilian population, if not by the army. It was believed by many senior officers, including Wellington, that the scum of the earth, those incorrigibles in every battalion that constituted the king's hard bargains, could be controlled by no other means. Yet, as we have seen, many inspecting officers advocated the desirability of alternative punishments. James, in his *Regimental Companion*, argued:

> it is warmly to be wished, that the disorderly and refractory part of the army could be brought to a proper sense of duty, by punishment less humiliating that the laceration of human shoulders. There are few instances where severe, or even

moderate corporal punishment has had the desired effect. It is a common observation, that when once a soldier has shewn his bare blades, he becomes gradually callous and insensible to shame.

In a footnote he added: 'Solitary confinement, extra fatigue duties, etc might be substituted, and for great offences, shooting should be resorted to'[124] – which was the French solution. John Shipp, twice commissioned from the ranks, commented succinctly, 'If we flog one devil out, we flog fifty in.'[125]

Radicals, in particular, often advocated the French approach to the problem of indiscipline as a more enlightened solution. Sir Francis Burdett, to make the point, suggested that the threat of imprisonment or even execution (as used by the French) was more humane. He described the lash as 'a dreadful instrument of torture...Every lash inflicted by it is, more properly speaking, nine lashes. These pieces of whipcord, not such as Gentlemen use to their horses, but each of them thick as a quill and knotted.' Palmerston, Secretary of State for War and the Colonies, retorted that he was sure men brought to the halberds (about to be flogged) would be obliged to the Honourable Baronet when they were told that as a result of his intercession they were not to be flogged. Instead, they would be shot.

Surprisingly, there were some voices in the ranks who accepted the view that corporal punishment was the only means of controlling the otherwise uncontrollable among their fellow soldiers. Benjamin Harris of the elite and well-regarded 95th Rifles concluded sadly: 'I detest the sight of the lash; but I am convinced the British army can never go on without it.'[126] This view pertained until 1868.

Those who opposed corporal punishment, or at least its widespread use, generally recognised one all-important consideration; good officers (and NCOs) meant good discipline and fewer punishments. Officers who knew their men, who did their duty and did not absent themselves from their units at every opportunity were more likely to be in command of well-disciplined troops. When Macready joined the first battalion in India he found discipline lax and the attitude of the officers dilatory compared with the recently disbanded second battalion. He later softened his view as he came to understand the conditions of the place, but the regimental court martial records do, in fact, support his initial response.

Whatever the arguments about the form punishment should take, it was acknowledged that the enforcement of military discipline had to be pursued with vigour and vigilance. Neither officers nor men were immune to temptation, although the nature of their offences was different. Whereas the man in the ranks might find himself on charges of theft, violence, unsoldierlike conduct, being absent without leave, to say nothing of the perennial problem of losing, damaging or selling military property, the officer was more likely to be accused of failing to do his duty, or of overstepping his authority. He might be involved in a dispute with a fellow officer or charged with financial misconduct. There was one offence that linked officers and men, however. Hard drinking was endemic in early nineteenth-century society, and drunkenness was often the result for both men and officers. Not only did it prevent a man from doing his duty, whatever his rank, but it also tended to lead to other offences, quarrelling between officers and assaults by soldiers.

Two government officers had responsibility for ensuring that the system of justice promulgated by the Mutiny Act was applied as defined by parliament. The Adjutant-General, Sir William Fawcett and later, Sir Harry Calvert, dealt with all matters of discipline, as well as all military regulations and applications for leave of absence. He was in fact, if not in title, the inspector general of the British army. The civilian Judge Advocate General, also known as the Judge Martial, had supreme control of martial law, including the jurisdiction of military courts. He and his deputies were responsible for ensuring that military courts did not contravene civil law, which had precedence, and for providing advice on military legal matters. He received minutes of general courts martial, and his deputies were responsible for taking down the proceedings *seriatim et verbatim*.

These two officers supervised a system which functioned with reasonable efficiency, although the problems associated with active campaigning and the soldier's tendency to commit more crimes when serving abroad often caused a serious backlog of unheard cases. Francis Seymour Larpent, who arrived in Portugal in 1812 as Judge Advocate to the forces in the Peninsula, was a civilian judge from the Western Circuit with little experience of military life. His journal, which is actually a series of long letters to his stepmother, chronicles the problems he faced and his near total incomprehension of military conduct. He wrote from Freneda, Wellington's headquarters during the winter of 1812:

> I really for the last month have been too busy to write. During the last week, before Lord Wellington went away, he kept me hard at work, and left directions to try and clear off and get rid of all the cases pending for Courts-Martial. About thirty-two cases were made over to me, some of near two years' standing. We have now a Court sitting at Lisbon, one in the second division in Coria, one in the seventh in Govea, and one here which I attend myself, four miles from Fuentes d'Onore....I have been writing near seven hours a day for these three weeks, circulating copies of the charges to prisoners, to the Courts, and to the prosecutors, and much of my labour is thrown away by the sickness of the prisoners and witnesses.[127]

These delays and inconveniences could be to the advantage of the accused. At least one miscreant was pardoned because of the good behaviour of his unit in a recent action.

Another difference between the army at home and the army abroad on active service was the way it was policed. At home, in garrison abroad or in the colonies the military authorities, supported by the civil powers, seem to have coped effectively with the rounding-up of offenders. When the army was on the move, however, and battalions were amalgamated into brigades a more rigorous form of policing was required. This was the function of the Provost Marshal, who was

> an officer appointed to secure deserters and all other criminals; he is often to go round the army; hinder the soldiers from pillaging, indict offenders, execute the sentence pronounced, and regulate the weights and measure used in the army when in the field.[128]

His staff comprised a lieutenant's guard (a subaltern and thirty cavalry who were available to the Provost Marshal in the discharge of his duties), a clerk and an executioner. The guard was relieved on a forty-eight-hour basis, possibly to save it from too close and prolonged association with the 'Bloody Provost'. The guard went on rounds twice a day. In addition, assistant provosts were employed in the Peninsula and in Flanders. They were staff sergeants, or sergeants who were granted the pay and allowances of ensigns, and at least one was attached to each division. The total number varied but it rose to as high as twelve, which indicates the importance Wellington attached to maintaining discipline.

Wellington's concern is evident in letters he wrote to Lord Castlereagh in May and June of 1809. On the 31st May he wrote:

> The army behave terribly ill. They are a rabble who cannot bear success any more than Sir John Moore's army could bear failure. I am endeavouring to tame them; but if I should not succeed, I must make an official complaint of them, and send one or two corps home in disgrace. They plunder in all directions.[129]

By the 17th June his complaints had become more urgent, as some extracts from his letter demonstrate:

> It is impossible to describe to you the irregularities and outrages committed by the troops. They are never out of sight of their Officers, I may almost say never out of sight of the Commanding Officers of their regiments, and the General officers of the army, that outrages are not committed; and notwithstanding the pains which I take, of which there will be ample evidence in my orderly books, not a post or a courier comes in, not an Officer arrives from the rear of the army, that does not bring me accounts of outrages committed by the soldiers who have been left behind on the march, having been sick, or having straggled from their regiments, or who have been left in hospitals....In the first place I am convinced that the law is not strong enough to maintain discipline in an army upon service. It is most difficult to convict any prisoner before a regimental court martial, for I am sorry to say that soldiers have little regard to the oath administered to them; and the Officers who are sworn 'well and truly to try and determine *according to the evidence*, the matter before them,' have too much regard to the strict letter of that administered to them...

> The authority and duties of the provost ought, in some manner, to be recognized by the law. By the custom of British armies, the provost has been in the habit of punishing on the spot (even with death, under the orders of the Commander in Chief) soldiers found in the act of disobedience of orders, of plunder, or of outrage.
>
> There is no authority for this practice excepting custom, which I conceive would hardly warrant it; and yet I declare that I do not know in what manner the army is to be commanded at all, unless the practice is not only continued, but an additional number of provosts appointed.

He claimed that even the presence of a Provost Marshal and four assistants was not sufficient to control the troops, since 'there is not an outrage of any description that has not been committed on people who have universally received us as friends, by soldiers who never yet, for one moment, suffered the slightest want, or the smallest privation.' There was an urgent need for

> a regular Provost establishment, of which a proportion should be attached to every Army sent abroad. All the foreign armies have such an establishment ...while we, who require such an aid more, I am sorry to say, than any of the other nations of Europe, have nothing of the kind exception a few sergeants.[130]

Wellington got his way. By 1810 he was referring to seven or eight provosts, and the numbers continued to rise. He could not resist commenting upon occasion, though, that other armies managed with only two. If he was thinking of the French armies, however, he might have remembered that the offences which most concerned him in his own army, plundering and abusing the local population, were actually tolerated in an army which 'lived off the land'.

Whether their numbers were ever adequate, the assistant provosts certainly made their mark on the army. The summary justice they administered to those caught in the act, most outrageously in the opinion of many the threat to flog soldiers' wives and shoot their donkeys when they refused to remain in the rear, earned them the nickname 'Bloody Provost'. Any man caught red-handed in the act of plundering could be hanged without trial. In time, being flogged came to be known as being 'provosted'.

This system took time to establish itself, however. In February 1810 a general order was required to establish the powers of the provosts. They were to take charge of prisoners confined for offences of a general description, preserve good order among soldiers and followers of the army, and punish those caught committing breaches of discipline, where they had witnessed the offence. Where indiscipline was strongly suspected, they were to report to the commander-in-chief, who then decided the appropriate action. This explains why some men of the second battalion, taken by the provost for suspected plundering after Waterloo, were pardoned by Wellington on account of the good conduct of the battalion during the battle.

One further duty of the Provost Marshal was to supervise executions. For a hanging he would use his own executioner, a man who was kept reasonably busy since there were about forty hangings in the Peninsula. When the offence was desertion to the enemy, the ritual was death by firing squad, witnessed by the whole division. The actual firing squad comprised men from the deserter's regiment. Whether it was the inaccuracy of Brown Bess or the reluctance of men to aim straight at a former comrade, the Provost Marshal's pistol often administered the *coup de grâce*.

Whatever the circumstances of a soldier's arrest, there was a strictly specified procedure which then had to be followed. He was first sent to the barrack-guard, or its equivalent, where he was relieved of his musket and sidearms and his crime was set down in writing. Only a commanding officer could confine a man in the black hole, where the prisoner was limited to bread and water and had to keep himself and the prison clean and fumigated. Once the man was under guard, in the black hole or elsewhere, a copy of his crime was delivered to the adjutant, who passed it on to the commanding officer and the man's company commander. During the period between arrest and trial sergeants on duty were required to keep the prisoner sober. Failure to do so was a serious offence. The names of all prisoners were posted at the guard-house entrance.

A different procedure was followed for officers that implicitly recognised their status as gentlemen. They could be 'put in arrest' only by their commanding officer, and were unlikely to find themselves in close confinement unless the charge was serious and there was reason to suspect that they might abscond. Generally, an arrested officer enjoyed the right to freedom within certain limits, provided that he had surrendered his sword and given his word of honour. Were an officer to break the terms of his parole before being set at liberty he would be cashiered.

Confinement was meant to last no more than eight days, or until a court could conveniently be assembled. This was a theoretical proviso because it might take considerably longer than eight days to convene a court to hear a serious case. Even assembling the witnesses might cause protracted delay, as Larpent's letter makes clear. Nevertheless, when Lieutenant Nicholson pointed out that he had been unfairly treated by being held under an arrest for thirteen weeks, there was some justice in his complaint.

A man could be tried by one of four different courts martial, depending upon the charge and his status. The first of these was a court of enquiry which, as its title suggests, did not try cases but investigated circumstances to establish whether an offence had been committed. The other military courts were all concerned with testing innocence and guilt. Regimental courts martial (or garrison court martial where officers of the same garrison sat together) heard only minor cases like drunkenness, disobedience (rather than mutiny), and petty breaches of discipline committed by NCOs and men in the ranks. They were summoned by a commanding officer, without royal warrant. The adjutant kept a roster of officers required to attend, made all the arrangements, and was required to be present. The

RSM was responsible for providing a corporal and a file of soldiers to escort prisoners from the guardroom. Regimental courts martial usually consisted of a captain as president and four subalterns. The maximum penalty was 500 lashes. Oaths were not introduced until 1805 and, if Wellington is to be believed, caused more problems than they solved.

When NCOs and soldiers committed more serious offences, or when an officer was charged, cases were heard by general courts martial. These courts were convened by royal warrant and could inflict a wider range of sentences, including the death penalty. Since these are the papers that have survived, their procedure will be considered in more detail in a later chapter. Warrant officers could be tried by detachment courts martial, with at least five sitting officers, only two of whom could come from the accused man's regiment. A field officer sat as president, and the sentence had to be confirmed. A warrant officer could only be reduced or subjected to corporal punishment if he had enlisted as a private.

Field or drum-head courts martial took place when a battalion was moving rapidly or about to go into action. They dealt with cases that required an urgent response and took their name from the drum that served the members as a table. Only serious offences were likely to be heard in this manner. Similarly *ad hoc* was the company court martial, which a captain could summon to try the most trivial offences. This was the system of military justice. It now remains to be seen how it worked in practice.

Chapter 10

You Stand Charged...

Private Richard Key was a Lincolnshire man who had enlisted in April 1806, probably as a result of the recruiting activities of the party based in Sleaford. He was undoubtedly one of the king's hard bargains, and when he faced a court martial in December 1816 it was neither for the first time, nor the last. He had already been tried on eight previous occasions and had been sentenced to a total of 1,000 lashes, as well as four weeks' solitary confinement and two months of extra drill. On this occasion, he was charged with

> quitting the fort without leave, being drunk and rioting in Blacktown, and grossly abusing and striking Serjeant Bibby a violent blow on the head which occasions the loss of one of his teeth, when in the execution of his duty the 8th instant.

The fort was Fort St George, where the first battalion was stationed, and Blacktown was an area of Madras inhabited by Indians but popular with British soldiers because of the availability of arrack and women. Three days after the offences were committed Key was obliged to face the consequences of his drunkenness.[131]

He was confined on the orders of the commanding officer, Lieutenant-Colonel Vaumorel, who issued the warrant for the trial on the 9th December. While Key was held in confinement, the Adjutant, Lieutenant George Stephenson, organised what is, somewhat unusually, described as a general regimental court martial. This involved nominating the officers who would constitute the court, summoning the witnesses (or evidences) and giving the prisoner a copy of the charges. The actual trial followed the protocol of a general court martial because of the seriousness of the offences, particularly striking an NCO in the execution of his duty. The court, however, comprised only officers of the 30th, although officers from other corps would undoubtedly have been available. The number of members, nine, was the minimum for a general court martial, and the president was a field officer rather than a captain, as would have been usual for a regimental court martial. Furthermore, there was a deputy judge advocate. In regimental courts martial the adjutant performed this function. There were several other trials that followed the same pattern, indicating that regiments were given the power to deal with their most serious miscreants in this way. The implications were for sentence rather than procedure.

The presiding field officer was Major Samuel Bircham. The eight other members were four captains (Tongue, Harper, Skirrow and Cramer), two lieutenants (Jones and Carden), and two ensigns (Leardet and Ledge). It was a formidable court, and Key must have been aware that he was facing men who were well acquainted with his past misdemeanours.

The officers were familiar with the appropriate seating for the *court*, which was the term used for the sitting officers. The president was in the middle, with the other officers to the right and left of him, seated accorded to their seniority, while the deputy judge advocate sat at the bottom of the table, facing the president. The court functioned as a body, and any of the officers were able to ask questions.

The deputy judge advocate in this case was Brevet Major Murray, who was responsible for the proper conduct of the trial. Once the prisoner had been brought into the court, the deputy judge advocate read the warrants that authorised the assembling of the court and his own appointment. He then informed the prisoner of the identity of the members before asking: 'Have you any objection to being tried by the members of this court?' Since only a brave or foolhardy private soldier would have made any objection, it is no surprise that Key simply replied: 'No.'

The deputy judge advocate now administered the oath to the president and the members. They were reminded that they should 'well and truly try and determine, according to the evidence in the matter now before you, so help you God'. In response, they each swore:

> I, A.B., do swear that I will duly administer justice according to the Rules and Articles for the better Government of His Majesty's Forces, and according to an Act of Parliament now in force, for the Punishment of Mutiny and Desertion, and other crimes therein mentioned, without partiality, favour, or affection, and if any doubt shall arise which is not explained by the said Articles, or Act of Parliament, according to my conscience, the best of my understanding, and the custom of war in the like cases, so help me God.

This was the oath that Wellington believed officers took too seriously.

It was unlikely that there was any partiality or affection for Private Key, but there were occasions when an officer might show some partiality (in accordance with his oath) by testifying to the good conduct of a soldier. In August 1816 Denis Toner was charged with desertion from the 36th Foot, fraudulently obtaining sixteen guineas as bounty, and then enlisting in the 30th Foot. When he was arrested in Dublin as a deserter, he denied being attached to any regiment. Toner now claimed he had admitted himself a deserter from the 36th and wanted to rejoin, but instead he was sent to the 30th in India. He supported his case with a series of character references, including one from Major Bircham, who was actually the president of the court. Bircham described him as a 'clean and well-behaved Soldier', while two other officers added 'willing', 'good', and 'well-behaved'. The court had no choice but to sentence him to 500 lashes, but the confirming officer pardoned him, only requiring him to be put under stoppages until he had repaid the sixteen guineas. There is no doubt the recommendation of three officers worked in Toner's favour.[132]

To return to Key's trial, after the president had administered the oath to the deputy judge advocate, the latter read the charge to the prisoner and invited him to plead. 'How say you Private Richard Key are you guilty or not guilty of the above charge?' Key replied: 'Not guilty.' We may wonder why a man who had little chance of proving his innocence should plead not guilty. The Judge Advocate General, however, had clearly expressed the opinion that prisoners should be encouraged to plead not guilty so that all the facts of the case could be heard by the court.

This might prove impossible upon occasion, as the trial of Samuel Lickler also in 1816 demonstrates. Lickler was charged with quitting the fort [Fort St George] without leave when on guard and making away with the chief part of his necessaries. Tried by a general regimental court, where he pleaded guilty, Lickler was sentenced to 500 lashes. Colonel Ogg refused to confirm the sentence, however, because he was

> of opinion that Court Martial, notwithstanding a prisoner pleading Guilty, should always examine Evidence when to be had; to enable him to weigh and appreciate the degree of Guilt. A Man through ignorance may plead Guilty to a Charge which when examined into may be found accompanied by Circumstances that in some degree extenuate the Guilt. I will thank you to let evidence be taken in this trial.[133]

The Court used Tytler's *Essay on Military Law* to justify their decision not to take down evidence:

> If the prisoner plainly and explicitly confesses the crime with which he is charged, nothing remains for the court but to pronounce judgement, but as, in such circumstances, the awarding of a capital or most rigorous sentence is peculiarly painful, the court, not only for the ease of their own minds, but in humanity to the prisoner, who may perhaps be influenced by an illusive hope of mercy, will not willingly record such confession, or preclude the unhappy criminal from ample time and opportunity of retracting it. If, indeed, the special facts and circumstances of criminality be set forth in the charge or indictment, and the prisoner shall voluntarily and freely make a confession of his guilt of the whole of those circumstances, though fully certified by the court of the consequences of such confession, it would seem that all further investigation is of course superseded.[134]

Since this was the situation in Lickler's case Ogg then confirmed the sentence, but halved the punishment.

The witnesses were in court to hear the first part of the proceedings against Key, but now all except the first prosecution witness withdrew. It was a characteristic of courts martial that no witness heard the testimony of other witnesses. This did not prevent collusion, of course, as we shall see in another case.

The oath was now administered to the first witness ('evidence'), who was required to depose the whole truth. In some cases, the first witness would be the prosecutor but in this straightforward case Major Maxwell acted as both deputy judge advocate and prosecutor. In the former function he was also required to take down the depositions *seriatim et verbatim,* either the actual words or as reported speech.

The first prosecution witness was Sergeant Bibby, the victim of Key's attack. His evidence was reported, that

> on the 8th inst. he was in Blacktown, and was asked by Serjeant Robertson to accompany him and he would show him something that would astonish him. On his doing so, Evidence saw the prisoner stripped in the street and drunk. On recommending Serjeant Robertson (the Market Serjeant) to call for assistance of the police to take him to the Main Guard the prisoner ran to him and struck him a blow on the face which knocked out one of his teeth and made use of very abusive language to him.

Once the deposition was completed, it was read back to the witness to check its accuracy.

The second prosecution witness was Sergeant Robertson, who supported Bibby's evidence without adding any further details. Finally, a third witness, Adjutant and Lieutenant Stephenson, was called into court to confirm that the prisoner had no official permission to quit the fort on the 8th December.

Key was now invited to offer his defence. This gave him the right to justify his actions, call upon his own witnesses, and re-examine the prosecution witnesses. He had no witnesses of his own, but he resorted to self-justification and re-examination. He used a weak excuse, common among soldiers charged with drunkenness, 'that he does not recollect any of the circumstances that happened in Blacktown'. He admitted that he had left the fort without permission, possibly hoping that a confession would appease the court.

He then recalled Sergeant Bibby, who was reminded of his former oath, asking him, 'At what hour was it that you say I struck you?'

'As near as I can judge it wanted about a quarter to four in the afternoon.'

Since Key did not follow up this point, it is impossible to know why he thought it necessary to recall the sergeant.

After the completion of the prisoner's defence, the court was cleared so that the deputy judge advocate could read the proceedings to the members. In a complex case there might be protracted discussion of the relevant issues, but it is unlikely that much discussion followed this case. Judgement was then delivered, starting with the most junior officer, in this case Ensign Ledge, thus preventing him from being overawed by the decision of his seniors. Officers were also required, on oath, never to reveal the opinion or vote of any fellow officer.

After this, probably brief, interlude the court reassembled and Major Bircham pronounced the verdict and sentence:

> The court finds the prisoner Richard Key guilty of the crimes preferred against him, and by virtue of the Articles of War do therefore sentence him to receive six hundred lashes at such time as the approving officer may please to direct. [This was a hundred more lashes than a regimental court could have awarded.]

The sentence was signed by the president and the deputy judge advocate before being countersigned by the approving officer, Colonel Ogg. The papers were then despatched to London, and signed by Major Barrow, the Deputy Judge Advocate General to His Majesty's Forces.

It is significant that Key, unlike more fortunate offenders, received no remission of his sentence, a power vested only in the approving officer. Key's record and the seriousness of the offence left little scope for mercy.

Ensign John Herring underwent a very different experience from Key when he stood a court martial at Trichinopoly in December 1810, even though he was also charged with drunkenness.[135] As an officer he was tried by a court of fifteen members, in addition to the president, two more than the minimum requirement. The warrant was authorised by General Sir Samuel Auchmaly, Commander-in-Chief of both His Majesty's and the Honourable Company forces serving under the Presidency of Fort St George. The court itself comprised eight regular officers, five of them from the 30th, and six East India officers. The president was Lieutenant-Colonel Bruce of the 19th Foot, and the deputy judge advocate was Captain Coombs of the 25th Native Infantry.

Following the usual procedure, the warrants were read in the presence of the prisoner and the witnesses. Given the opportunity to object to the members, Herring chose not to. He was then reminded of the charge against him: 'placed in arrest...for scandalous and infamous conduct unbecoming the character of an Officer and a gentleman, in appearing on the public parade of the Regiment, and when for guard, on the 18th instant in a state of intoxication.' The charge was signed by Major Christopher Maxwell of the 30th, acting as prosecutor, and dated the 25th November. It was countersigned by the Adjutant-General of the Army in India and dated the 12th December. Thus Herring had been under an arrest longer than the stipulated eight days.

Invited to plead, Herring pleaded not guilty.

Maxwell now presented the case against the defendant.

> I was Commanding Officer of the parade of H.M. 30th Regiment on the evening of the 18th November; the prisoner was for guard, the Captain of the Day came and reported to me that he was in a state of intoxication and perfectly incapable of doing his duty. I ordered the Adjutant to place the prisoner under arrest, and to put the next officer on duty in his place, which was accordingly done. I then reported the circumstance to the Commanding Officer the first opportunity I had. I did not see the prisoner myself.

At this point the deputy judge advocate exercised his right to question witnesses in order to elucidate what he obviously considered important facts. Maxwell was asked to identify the officer of the day (Captain Jackson). He was also asked whether he had another authority, apart from Jackson's report, for considering the prisoner to be unfit for duty. Maxwell replied that he had instructed the adjutant and the quartermaster to see Herring and report on his state, and the adjutant corroborated Jackson's opinion. There was further questioning. Did the adjutant's inspection precede the prisoner's arrest? No, it had happened at the same time. Did the adjutant have any discretion about arresting the prisoner? No, Maxwell had no reason to doubt Jackson's report, but wanted witnesses to support it. What was the exact report? 'That he, the prisoner, was perfectly unfit for duty from intoxication and that Mr Poyntz the Quarter Master had gave him the same opinion.'

Several points are worthy of note. Firstly, each of Captain Coombs' questions was written down and read back to Maxwell before he was required to give an answer. Secondly, Coombs was fulfilling another of the judge advocate's duties by clarifying evidence for the members of the court. And thirdly, he clearly wanted to establish whether the prisoner, in contravention of legal norms, had been presumed guilty. This, in turn, demonstrated an additional duty, that he should protect the interests of the prisoner.

The first prosecution witness was Captain Jackson, who, once he had been sworn in and reminded of the charge, testified that

> On the 18th November I was Captain of the Week and on the evening parade I went up to the guard for the purpose of marching it off: the Adjutant informed me that the guard was ready, but observed 'look at your officer'. I consequently took particular notice, and observed him to be intoxicated; in consequence of which, I made a report of the circumstances to Major Maxwell commanding the parade, who ordered the prisoner to be relieved immediately.

The deputy judge advocate's questions to Jackson established that the time was about half past five and that the signs of intoxication were 'very unsteady in marching, and staggering very much'. Jackson also added that he had observed clear signs of drunkenness at the commencement of the parade, 'in marching the officers to their guards, and throughout the whole of the guard marching, but I did not report it, until the conclusion of the guard parade'. Coombs suggested that the unsteadiness and staggering might be the effect of some sudden attack. Jackson, however, was adamant that it was caused by excess of liquor, although he could not remember noticing any words or actions on the prisoner's part indicative of drunkenness.

Still Coombs persisted, no doubt aware that the prisoner's military future depended upon the outcome of the trial. 'You had most probably some orders to give to the guards under arms, such as wheeling or marching etc. What manner were those operations performed by the prisoner?'

'In a very unsteady manner and when the guard was ordered to halt he nearly fell.' Jackson then added, in response to another question, this time from a member of the court, that the distance from the guard room to the guard was about 120 yards, and the prisoner had marched about half this distance when Jackson halted the guard and relieved him. There then followed yet more questions from the court as they sought to establish the exact sequence of events.

The final question to Jackson came from the prisoner, as was his right, even before he began his own defence. 'You have stated that I nearly fell, might this not have been caused by some impediment, such as a stone or something of that kind?'

'I cannot positively say, but from former circumstances I thought not, I observed nothing.'

The prosecution continued to establish an increasingly damning and unequivocal case against Herring through a sequence of witnesses. The Adjutant, George Stephenson, supported Jackson's testimony and then, in response to a question from Coombs, very much a terrier at worrying the witnesses, he described the prisoner as looking wild and being unsteady in his walk.

> While marching and in the act of giving the word of command, either to carry or support arms, I do not exactly remember which, he almost fell, that is, staggered; and likewise, when I was conducting him up to his room I was fully convinced both by his walk and everything else that he was intoxicated.

'Everything else' was too vague for the advocate general; he wanted some precise detail.

'He said, he would appeal to all the Officers of the Regiment or some of them, I am not exactly certain which. He said, he was confident he was fit for duty.'

'In submitting to the arrest, or when going with you to his quarters, was the prisoner's language incoherent and unconnected, or that sort peculiar to a state of intoxication?'

'His language was not particularly incoherent; he seemed sufficiently collected to know what he was about. He appeared to me, sensible to his situation, and to feel very much the effect of being placed under arrest.'

Again there were questions from the court designed to clarify exactly what had happened, and where everyone was at the relevant time. The most significant point they elicited from the adjutant was that Herring had been warned for duty in battalion orders the previous day.

The quartermaster, Arthur Poyntz, added a further point to Herring's detriment, that he had 'inspected the Guard without waiting for the Captain of the Week to shoulder [arms] which convinced me, of his being in a state of intoxication'. Poyntz also added, although not in answer to an actual question, that the unsteadiness of Herring's walk was so noticeable that 'the men of the band remarked it, and smiled, they tittered and laughed'.

The prosecution case now moved in a different direction, to establish that Herring had been drinking on the afternoon in question. Ensign James Light, junior to Herring by one day and whose career had exactly matched Herring's, was called upon to give his evidence. Having established that he was the officer sent to relieve Herring, and that he noticed him stagger when given this information, he was then asked by Coombs why he considered the prisoner to be intoxicated.

'From his appearance, his unsteadiness, and my knowledge that he had been drinking.'

One can imagine the court's response to the final part of this statement. The judge advocate, however, merely asked, 'What was your knowledge of his having been drinking?'

> On the morning of the 18th I had invited Mr Herring to take his tiffing [sic] with me, but as he excused himself, I went to call on Mr Hutchinson where I found him, and he claimed of it being a [illeg] to be on duty after just having come off guard. I then cautioned him to be moderate, in drinking, or he would achieve a scrape. The Orderly Corporal then came, with the orderly book, to warn Mr Herring for Guard. Thinking him incapable of reading the orders, I read them to him. He said, that he knew before, he was for guard.

This was already seriously prejudicial to Herring's case. Prompted by the judge advocate, Light added further: 'I perceived when I first went in, that he had been drinking, and he was drinking when I was with him. I cautioned him to beware and he said there was no fear, he had not been drinking much.' Prompted again, Light continued,

> There were three of us and I think two bottles of wine were opened while I was there, and they were drinking one when I went in. When I came away a portion of the second bottle remained. It was past three when I left the house.

Time enough for Herring to have drunk considerably more before he appeared on the parade ground.

Light's testimony brought the prosecution case to a close. Called upon to present his defence, Herring immediately exercised his right to seek an adjournment, so that he could prepare his case. He requested a week, which was granted after some deliberation by the court; but he was warned that the following Thursday he should come to court prepared to defend himself.

This was one of two rights enjoyed by defendants, who could write their opening statement of innocence and then read it to the court. Alternatively they could request that it be read by the judge advocate. His other right was known as an *amicus curiae*. At this period defendants were represented neither by counsel nor by a defending officer. They were obliged to speak for themselves. An *amicus curiae* could sit or stand near the prisoner, however, and instruct him what questions should be asked, or write them down and deliver them to the judge advocate to read, with the court's permission. If this procedure were adopted, such questions would be inserted into the minutes, with the relevant answers.

As a system it probably worked well for officers, who could pay for advice if it were not forthcoming in any other form, but it is unlikely that many private soldiers benefited from an *amicus curiae*. As they were not officially part of the court-martial procedure, their presence and contribution to the defence was never separately minuted. If Herring had such assistance, however, some of the judge advocate's questions might have come from this source.

Although Herring requested a week's adjournment, he actually received a fortnight because of the indisposition of Captain Coombs. Whereas an indisposed member of the court could be replaced, there could be no substitution for the judge advocate, even when he was not prosecuting. In the present case, it would have been difficult to find anyone as diligent in his duties as Captain Coombs.

On the 4th January 1811, at ten o'clock (nine o'clock being the earliest hour at which a court martial could be heard) the court reconvened and called upon Ensign Herring for his defence.

Whatever his other failings, Herring was definitely not short of words. His defence statement must have tried the patience of the court, since each point was made and then elaborated. He was fighting for his military life, however, which justified his prolixity. He made four initial points: his literary skills were limited because he was not accustomed to public writing; if he deviated from the correct procedures it was caused by lack of experience of courts martial; although he had drunk a few glasses of wine, he was not drunk; and any aspect of his behaviour which gave the impression of drunkenness was caused by shock when he was relieved. He then set about summarising and answering the prosecution case, as was usual.

He pointed out that Major Maxwell's testimony was based on hearsay, apart from his claim that the adjutant had reported him drunk, a detail about which Lieutenant Stephenson seemed uncertain. He made something of Captain Jackson's delay in relieving him, and suggested that if he inspected the guard at 'ordered' instead of 'shoulder arms', it was a mistake anyone could make. 'Stagger' was a difficult word to overcome, but he claimed it was a natural shrinking back in horror when Light relieved him. He did, however, make much of the adjutant's testimony that his speech was not incoherent. In his version, this became that he was perfectly calm and collected while distressed by what was happening to him.

Herring then demonstrated particular animosity towards the quartermaster. Having established that it would have been impossible for the band to play, and titter, and laugh all at the same time, he suggested that if they were laughing, Poyntz was the object of their amusement 'for he is constantly trusting [sic] himself close to the Guard, pulling their pouches, and making extraordinary observations'.

The most virulent attack, though, was directed at Ensign Light, whose evidence was probably the most damning. This was a *soi-disant* friend whose behaviour in court he asked the members to recall:

> it was evidently his anxiety to say much more than was required of him, or even related to the charge; he states every minutiae that could in any instance have injured me, in the eyes of the court…this is the Gentleman, who before and since my arrest, has pretended to be my particular friend.

His intention now was to prove Ensign Light a liar, and his first step was to establish the state in which he left Lieutenant Hutchinson's house, having drunk at most a third of a bottle.

Before calling his own witnesses, however, he pointed out that Light's evidence alone suggested he was seriously intoxicated. The others concentrated on the unsteadiness of his walk, which he explained away as habitual. 'At all times I have an unsteady nervous method of walking, occasioned by a severe nervous fever, followed by a scarlet fever, from which I had only just recovered, prior to my embarkation to this country.'

He finished his statement by reminding the court that his future depended upon their judgement. He also explained why he would not be calling anyone for a character reference. He had been with the battalion but three months (having arrived in October with Ensign Light); but two months when he was placed under an arrest. He also pointed out that he had served the king eight years, four as a volunteer in Ireland, and had never been arrested, or even censured during that period. (Herring was only 22 at this stage, which certainly raises some questions about his claim.)

Herring's first witness was Lieutenant Emmanuel Hutchinson. There was an immediate objection from the prosecution, the nature of which was not inserted into the minutes of the trial. (Hutchinson himself was under an arrest, although since he resigned from the regiment before being brought to trial, the charge remains a mystery.) The usual procedure was now followed. The court was closed to consider the objection, so that the prosecution's reasons could be discussed. Then Major Maxwell was informed that his protest had been overruled.

Hutchinson supported Herring's story in all its particulars in response to the questions put to him by the defendant. Mr Herring was sober when he came to Hutchinson's house, and he was still sober when he left, some time before Light departed, which contradicted Light's testimony. He was also aware that Herring had a nervous, unsteady manner of walking. He further contradicted Light's claim that he had been obliged to read the orders from the orderly book because Herring was in no condition to read them himself.

At this point the court had to weigh the evidence of Hutchinson, well-disposed towards the prisoner, against that of Light, apparently ready to introduce any claim that would demonstrate Herring's guilt. They may have resolved part of the problem when they heard the evidence of Corporal William Prigmore, who not only deposed that Ensign Light had not read the orders aloud but also agreed that Mr Herring had not seemed intoxicated when he brought the orderly book to him.

Herring then called four sergeants, John Brown, Richard Bourke, Francis Garland and John Doman, who between them demolished much of the prosecution case. None of them had been aware of the band laughing, as claimed by the quartermaster. One of them deposed that Mr Herring had marched steadily, in time with the music, although they all noticed how he had inclined to the left. As Sergeant Burke phrased it, 'I think that you did not march very steady to your guard, but leaned on one side of your foot, and seemed a little inclined on one side.' None of them, however, had associated this with intoxication. 'I thought it might be adduced through carelessness as anything else,' Bourke added. Perhaps without recognising the significance of his reply to a question from the judge advocate, Bourke also said,

> At the time the Captain of the Day ordered him to inspect the guard, the guard was ordered at arms. He seemed to hesitate a little as if he did not know what to do. He then walked through the ranks, and took post on the right, in front of the Guard.

A member of the court took up this point. 'Is it not customary for the Captain of the Day to give orders for shouldering arms previously to ordering the Subaltern to inspect the men?'

'Yes, I think it is.'

This crucial point was confirmed when Sergeant Brown was recalled and supported Bourke's account. Sergeant Garland, who deposed next, also endorsed the confusion of orders. In other words, Herring's hesitation, interpreted as drunkenness, now had a different and plausible explanation.

Herring next called on his fellow officers for support. Lieutenant John Perry recollected talking with him for about ten minutes some time before guard mounting without noticing anything untoward about his behaviour. Lieutenant Donald Sinclair, sitting as a member of the court, agreed that 'He has a kind of uncertain walk which I cannot describe. I have often observed it.' (Sinclair, having given evidence, could not then return to his function as member of the court.) Lieutenant John Tongue made a similar point. 'I have always observed that he has a kind of nervous manner, a peculiar method of putting down his foot when walking. I have remarked it to others, and others to me.'

The defendant now closed his case, and the court was adjourned until Monday, 7th January, when the verdict was delivered:

> The court having maturely deliberated upon the evidence produced in support of the charge, and what has been urged and adduced in support of the defence, are of opinion, that the charge against the prisoner, Ensign John Herring, has not been proved, and do therefore acquit him of the same.

Was there some debate about the verdict? The evidence was certainly problematic. Either Hutchinson or Light was lying. Were the non-commissioned officers, whom the prosecution had failed to call, more reliable witnesses than Jackson, Poyntz, Stephenson and Light? Whatever the discussion that lay behind the verdict, it was obviously influenced by what had been seen and heard in the court room. Whether it was unanimous is impossible to ascertain. Such information was not entered into the minutes of a court martial. Members who voted for a majority guilty verdict, however, would be the only ones to suggest an appropriate sentence. At the same time, the number that found the defendant not guilty would be added to the number advocating the lightest sentence. When a man was found guilty but received a light sentence the court may have been fairly evenly divided.

Six months later John Herring faced similar charges, was found guilty and cashiered. Which raises the question, was he lucky first time round or did the deep drinking which was commonplace in India become a habit he learnt all too quickly?

There is one clear link between the court martial of Herring in India in 1810 and that of Captain Thomas Leach five years earlier in Dublin.[136] Both were accused of being drunk on duty. Herring's case was internal to the regiment, however, while Leach's accusers were men who did not belong to the 30th, men with whom he came into contact as Captain of the Castle Guard on the 18th July, 1805.

The president was (Brigadier) General James Leith and the court comprised officers of the 16th and 17th Dragoons and the 26th Foot, two lieutenant-colonels, two majors and ten captains. This composition reflected Leach's rank. There was no prosecutor because the men who had instigated the case and gave evidence against Leach were all non-commissioned officers and other ranks. Consequently, the prosecution was conducted by the deputy advocate general, Robert Leslie, Judge Martial. His contribution was perfunctory. He merely asked each witness whether he had seen Leach on the night of the 18th, and whether he considered him to be drunk or sober. All the witnesses replied in the affirmative to the first question and claimed that Leach was drunk. It was then left to Leach and the court to establish the details through further questioning.

The first witness was Sergeant John Westen of the 82nd Regiment, who was Sergeant of the Staff of the Castle Guard on the 18th July. In reply to Leach's questions, he claimed that the evidence of drunkenness lay in 'your saying that the Guard were worse than Blacks, and though they were big men, that little men were as good, or better'. Westen also stated that he had witnessed 'your unsteadiness in the Guard house. By your coming into the Guard house, and turning the men out, and when you fell against the door.' Westen also explained why the men had been turned out:

> You desired the men to turn out at a little after nine o'clock, and to take off their great coats. The men were helping each other to roll them and in consequence of that confusion you kept the men out with carried arms until the Field Officer came, about 11 o'clock. You again turned the men out after twelve, I cannot say why. You reported the men to the Field Officer, and particularly the men of the 36th Regt.

In response to further questioning, Westen denied there had been anything exceptional about the men's behaviour. He also denied bringing a message from the men of the 36th 'imploring Leach to accuse them of improper conduct rather than placing them on extra duty'. Questioned by the court, he conceded that it might be possible to make a mistake about a man being drunk, although 'I thought he was to the best of my knowledge'.

Earlier in the proceedings Leach had asked a question which seemed irrelevant. 'On your oath, did you desire some of the Grenadiers of the 82nd Regt who were present, when called upon before the court, to be all of the same story with Barnet McGrady?'

'I deny it punctually [sic],' was Westen's response.

The second prosecution witness was Robert Pollock, sergeant in the Tyrone Militia. In reply to Leach's initial question, whether he was supposed drunk by his words or his actions, Pollock answered:

> By both. You ordered the Guard to be turned out at 9 o'clock, which they did. Coated as is usual in the Garrison after retreat beating. You ordered them to turn in again and uncoat immediately, the men did turn in and uncoat, and you ordered them to turn out again in five minutes with their coats rolled in marching order. The men were grumbling, there was noise in the Guard house to a certainty. When the noise was in the Guard house you ordered the men to turn out again. The Guard did turn out again. You ordered me and the other Serjeant to fall in on the flanks, and a little to the front, and other officers in the centre, with directions to seize, and bring to you any man who should speak. Before we had time to pitch on any person, you fixed upon two men of the 36th Regt and placed them Centinels [sic] at the Gate. You kept us under arms then until the Field Officer came about eleven. You then reported the conduct of the Guard to the Field Officer.

At this point, there may be some question how Leach's behaviour suggested drunkenness rather than exasperation, particularly when Pollock conceded in response to a question from the court that noise 'must have been heard by every person in or near the Guard house, and every person in the Guard house must have been sensible that there was discontent'. Including Sergeant Westen, since he and Pollock 'were together at the Guard house, and walking backwards and forwards. I heard the noise and the grumbling. I suppose he might have heard it also.' When questioned further, he then explained, 'I thought him [Leach] drunk for acting contrary to the rules of the Garrison,' although he admitted the men had behaved in an unsoldierlike manner, as an act of defiance against the orders Leach had given them.

It was now apparent that there had been trouble with the Castle Guard on the night of the 18th July, and Leach had punished them by keeping them under arms until the Field Officer arrived. According to Westen, he had turned them out again at twelve. Crucially, though, the court would have to decide whether this recalcitrant behaviour was a response to the drunkenness of the officer on duty or had been provoked by an order to remove their greatcoats, 'contrary to the rules of the Garrison'.

Pollock's assertion, that Leach's drunkenness was proved when he contravened the rules of the garrison, was supported by the third prosecution witness, acting corporal William Wainhouse of the 82nd. He had come to the same conclusion because Leach was 'staggering in the open yard, and by the unnecessary trouble you gave the Guard, and the expressions you made use of, by saying to the Guard, they were worse than a troop of Blacks, and not like soldiers'. In answer to a question from the court, Wainwright added, 'I heard some of the men say that the Capn ought to be confined as being disguised in liquor, and giving the Guard so much trouble. This happened immediately before the Field Officer came.' Furthermore, Leach 'was more drunk [at about half past one] then when he turned out the Guard at half past nine, he staggered in the yard to and fro'.

The final prosecution witness, Private Daniel Finlay of the 36th, provided some detail of what had initially provoked the disturbance, in answer to Leach's question, 'Was it from my words or actions you supposed me drunk?'

> From both. At 9 o'clock the Guard was coated. You desired the men to uncoat, and said the night was too warm for great coats. There was some noise in the Guard house, by the men calling out Roll for Roll. You went into the Guard house and ordered silence. The men went on. I suppose they did not hear you, on which you turned out the Guard. You asked what was the cause of the noise. Serjeant Westen said that he did not know of any noise, than the men calling Roll for Roll, about the great coats. You turned in the Guard in about ten minutes, saying that you would make an example of anyone who made a noise. There was some noise after that. You turned out the Guard again, and the Guard remained under arms, with shouldered arms and carried arms for nearly half an hour.

'Roll for Roll' was the cry used when one soldier desired another to help him roll up his greatcoat.

Finlay also provided the court with what he believed to be another instance of Leach's drunkenness, when he came to my post, about half past one o'clock, when I was Centinel [sic] with the other two officers, and Corporal of the Guard. I and the other Centry stood on our posts as ordered, when we saw the rounds coming up to us. You found fault with the manner of the other Centinel stood on his post, and saluted. You said the man was drunk. The man replied it was hard for him to be drunk, as he had been Centinel three hours. You ordered the man to be confined.

The question of whether the men of the 36th had sent a message to Leach also arose. According to Leach, this message was 'apologising for their improper conduct, and requesting to be excused from extra duty'. Finlay quibbled over the exact nature of the message, which he had only heard of. In his version, the man maintained 'that it was hard they should be put on extra duty, not deserving it, and requesting to be relieved of it'.

This ended a somewhat inconclusive prosecution case in which it was significant that no officer had been called to give evidence. The following day Leach began his defence with some rather surprising testimony. His first witness was Private Joseph Tyrrell of the 82nd, who deposed that

When Serjeant Westen fell in the Grenadiers of the 82nd Regt to go to the Regimental Court Martial which was sitting on the trial of Richard James a Grenadier of the 36th, he desired them all to be of one story, and to let Barnet McGrady speak first, because he would deliver himself, and knew better than any other man.

Richard James was the sentry arrested by Leach. It is difficult to imagine there was no connection between his being put on a charge, for which he had to answer at a regimental court martial, and the accusation of drunkenness against Leach. This connection becomes even clearer when Tyrrell named both Sergeant Westen and Corporal Wainhouse as being involved in the conversation he had overheard.

Leach's remaining five witnesses were all officers. Each one testified that Leach was sober on the night in question and they also contributed details of what had actually happened. Ensign Hill of the 82nd described how when he visited the sentries at eleven o'clock

one of the Centinels did not stand to his front, and carry his arms as he ought, he kept walking about with his arms folded over the butt of his musket. I desired him to stand as he ought, and carry his arms. He complied in a sort of way, and said he had been badly treated by being put on extra duty. It occurred to me that the conduct of the Soldier was wilful, and disrespectful, and I reported the matter to you.

Then, when Hill went the rounds with Leach, 'Everything was correct until we came to the same Centinel; his name was Richard James of the 36th; he acted as he had done before.'

Hill also recalled the disturbance in the guardroom, which was described more graphically by Lieutenant Alexander Crawford of the 16th Dragoons. He informed the court that the conduct of the men was

> very improper and insolent. They were huzzaing. When about twenty minutes after nine you ordered the 36th out in front of the Guard, they were knocking the butts of their firelocks on the ground. The men of the 36th would not remain quiet until you ordered them to shoulder arms. I was not present when the whole of the Guard was turned out, I was then in the lower Castle yard. It was in the Guard room I heard the men huzzaing, the noise was so great that it might have been heard in the lower Castle yard. I was sitting in the Officers room when it began, and I started off my chair.

This testimony was supported by Ensign Robert Duncan of the 82nd. Tyrrell was his servant so he was probably the first to hear about the conspiracy. He

> came up to the Guard house at about half past nine, the men were sitting outside the Guard room, and appeared to be very discontented. You ordered them to go into the Guard house. They made a great noise then, shouting and huzzaing; you then ordered them to turn out. The men made a great noise by striking the butts of their firelocks against the stones, on which you ordered them to shoulder, and kept them shouldered about half an hour.

Hill and Duncan both testified that the NCOs did not do their duty. According to Hill, 'they were as dissatisfied as well as the men. I heard one of them say, they were allowed to put their coats on at that hour; it was Sergeant Westen who said it.'

Major James McDonald of the 17th Dragoons, field officer on the 18th July, suggested that a trivial matter, which Leach thought he had contained, was exacerbated by the subsequent sullen behaviour of Private James:

> At a little after eleven o'clock – you were Captain of the Guard – you reported to me that the Guard had been irregular, but then quiet. I asked you if it was so serious that I should report it. You said they were principally men of the 36th Regt and you would mention it to Col. Burne [the commanding officer], out of respect to the 36th Regt and to Col. Burne, and particularly as the men of the 36th were generally so well conducted.

In other words, if James had accepted his punishment of extra duty without complaint, he would not have been put on a charge, and there would have been no conspiracy against Leach.

Before Leach addressed the court, somewhat unusually at the end of his defence, he called one last witness, Captain Richard Tribe of the 82nd. Having established that they had known each other since 1797, Leach asked him, 'Do you know, or have you observed, that I was subject to some hesitation in my speech?'

'I do know you are subject to hesitation in your speech.'
Leach now turned to the president and members:

> Mr President and Gentlemen of this Honourable Court, I flatter myself the Evidences I have produced on my behalf are sufficiently strong to leave no doubt in your minds of my innocence, particularly when compared with that of the men who have in so many instances contradicted themselves. I will not trouble this Honourable Court with any comments, but leave my case intirely [sic] in their hands, not doubting, when every circumstance is considered, but that an honourable acquittal will be the result. I will conclude by returning my sincere thanks to this Court, for their kind and impartial hearing, and indulgence to me during my Trial, which I can assure them, will be ever considered with heart felt gratitude.

The usual process followed. The prisoner withdrew. The court was cleared and closed. The minutes were pondered over, although probably not for long. Then came the verdict: not guilty, an honourable acquittal. One further point was made, however:

> The Court thinks it necessary to mark their opinion of the Evidence for the Prosecution, and particularly the Evidence of Serjeant Westen and William Wainhouse, which appears to have originated in a spirit of insubordination, and to have carried on in pursuance of a malignant combination against Captain Leach in the execution of his duty, and in opposition to truth and consistency.

Leach was the only officer of the 30th to find himself the victim of a 'malignant combination' of non-commissioned officers and men in the ranks. In his case the defence evidences quickly destroyed the story told against him, but his case demonstrates the vulnerability of an officer who provoked resentment, even when the matter was as trivial as not being allowed to wear greatcoats on a warm evening. It also demonstrates that NCOs and men in the ranks could bring a charge against an officer, even though to do so might prove risky.

Taken overall, however, the records of these three courts martial, as well as many others, demonstrate that the exercise of military justice was practised with a strong sense of duty and fairness, qualities often missing in the more perfunctory approach of many civil courts. Few soldiers, of any rank, could claim that they did not receive a fair trial.

Chapter 11

The Law of the Lash

Between 1803 and 1817 the two battalions of the 30th underwent dramatically different experiences. Nowhere are the effects of these differences more apparent than in their respective crime and punishment records. For crime, all courts martial records are relevant, but for punishment the regimental courts martial tell us most about the ethos of each battalion. In the regimental courts, the choice of punishment lay with the regimental officers, while any commutation of a sentence was the privilege of the commanding officer. Unlike a general court martial, there was no confirming officer to question the verdict or change the sentence.

Regimental courts martial records were first included in inspection returns in 1812, and between 1812 and 1816 it is possible to compare directly the figures and details of a battalion serving in India with a battalion that saw active service in the Peninsula and Flanders, as well as a short period of home service.

Between January 1813 and October 1816 there were 604 trials by regimental court martial in the first battalion which produces an average of fourteen a month across the forty-one months. The second battalion, between June 1812 and October 1815 (thirty-four months, because the inspection return for March 1815 is missing) court-martialled 113 men, an average of three per month. Before too much is read into these statistics, however, it must be remembered that the senior battalion was always larger than the junior. Nevertheless, the size discrepancy was never more than two to one, and usually rather less, which suggests the simple conclusion that misdemeanours were more prevalent in the first battalion.

Only at one point do the numbers of men on trial approach parity. In the inspection period from December 1814 to June 1815, the first battalion put fifty-four men on trial, their lowest return. Between March and October 1815 the second battalion tried forty-two men, by far their highest figure. Significantly, thirty of those cases were heard between April and June; thus the tension of waiting for a renewal of war, which was assumed to be inevitable, may explain the misbehaviour. Nine of the offenders in this period were pardoned, compared with only one in the post-Waterloo period, which suggests that Colonel Hamilton understood the effect of this pressure on his men's conduct.

It was obviously more difficult to maintain discipline in India. A survey of other regiments stationed in India makes this clear and also confirms that the 1/30th was not an exceptionally ill-disciplined corps. Macready's first impressions of them, when he arrived in Madras in 1818 are interesting:

> The men of the first battalion appeared well drilled and set up, but were terribly emaciated and had a dissipated (or what the French would call demoralised) appearance. They were considerably superior to the other regiments on the Madras establishment but being accustomed to the strict discipline and orderly behaviour of our troops at home, and totally unacquainted with the license which custom has made the right of the English soldier in India, I must confess I was sadly prejudiced against them on our first acquaintance.[137]

Not only were regimental courts martial more frequent in the first battalion; there is also a marked difference in the nature of the offences committed by the men of each battalion. This can be linked to their different service experiences.

Nearly half the men put on trial in India were accused of drunkenness (often combined with other offences), against only a fifth in the second battalion. This may be explained quite simply by the availability of liquor and the nature of the liquor. Arrack is a spirit which was cheaply purchased, and was even supplied to the men in the canteen. According to Colonel Ogg, who inspected the battalion in May 1816, this had a detrimental effect on discipline:

> I beg leave to draw Your Excellency's attention to the increase in Trials by Courts Martial since the establishment of a regimental canteen, the Number of Trials during the last six months is 144, and during the previous six months when there was no canteen only 105.[138]

There was, however, a note appended: 'The officer commanding the 30th subsequently prohibited the sale of spirits in the canteen' (whereupon the number of trials in the next inspection return decreased to eighty-nine). The discrepancy is undoubtedly explained by the effects of alcohol in a hot climate. In the Peninsula raw wine was available; while not so devastating to sobriety in its effect, it nevertheless explains why five of the eighteen men tried between June and December 1812 were charged with being 'drunk on duty'. Similarly, between April and October 1815 nine men out of fifty-four were found guilty of drunkenness. Again, the cause may have been cheap wine or, more likely, gin. The figures, however, are still nowhere near as high as those of the first battalion, and it may be assumed that whatever the effects of cheap wine and gin, they did not compare with the power of arrack to overset a man's wits. As Richard Key's general court martial demonstrated, spirits could lead to some very bizarre behaviour.

The most frequent offence in the second battalion was being absent without leave, or similar misdemeanours such as failing to appear on parade. This only became a problem after the return from the Peninsula. There were five cases between January and November 1813, all in the six companies which had come home early. Overall, this group of offences accounts for over a fifth of the charges. On the other hand, the men of the first battalion were proportionately less inclined to absent themselves. Only 11 per cent were charged on these grounds, and the charges were often linked to drunkenness. Going out of barracks without permission in order to obtain arrack, or failing to return, having been rendered incapable by drink, was a frequent event. Duties and parades were missed, but this is different from the second battalion, where men would take themselves off for days rather than hours. Of course, drink may have been the motive for the initial absence and the cause of the delayed return, but the subsequent charges do not make this explicit. Obviously, a man who had allowed himself time to sober up could be charged with absence without leave but he could not be charged with drunkenness.

'Making away with regimental necessaries' appears with similar frequency in both battalions, 14 per cent of charges in the first and 12 per cent in the second. 'Making away' generally meant turning necessaries into cash, and it is safe to assume that the cash was for drink. There was also a similar rate of charges for using abusive language, showing disrespect, or direct disobedience. In the first battalion, however, the disrespect was often directed at an officer whereas there is only one instance of this in the second battalion, where NCOs were more likely to be the target. This seems to confirm Macready's opinion that

> This brave corps...was not more distinguished by its professional exertions, than by the cordial and brotherly unanimity which pervaded its internal regulations. The men were devoted to their colours and their officers; neither, while the regiment [battalion] existed, had they been known to shrink from either; the officers, scrupulously attentive to their soldiers, entered with feeling into their wants and wishes, and received a pleasing return when circumstances threw the power of obliging into the hands of the private.[139]

Two areas where there is considerable discrepancy are the catch-all 'unsoldierlike conduct' and theft. The former is an imprecise term, and was often tagged onto another offence, such as 'failing for duty' or 'rioting in barracks'. As a stand-alone charge, there were fifty-two instances in the first battalion and ten in the second. It was more likely to be linked to other offences in the junior battalion where it constitutes a fifth of all charges against little more than a tenth in the first battalion.

The difference in frequency of theft is even higher, 13 per cent of all charges in the second battalion, against 5 per cent in the first. However, there is an equally noticeable difference in what was stolen. In the first battalion money and clothing constitute all but three of the cases where the stolen property is identified, with one case of a man stealing another man's necessaries and two cases of stealing arrack. There were three cases simply described as stealing, of which two were 'on suspicion'. In the second battalion there was only one case of money being stolen, and one of clothing, a shirt, but a further nine cases are simply described as theft, four of them 'on suspicion'. More significantly, recalling Macready's reference to unanimity, men in the first battalion stole from their fellow soldiers and this did not happen in the second battalion, except in the case of the shirt. Being on active service, which implied sharing hardships and danger, may have bred an *esprit de corps* which was lacking in India.

There was one instance, in the second battalion, of a private stealing from an officer. This never came to court, however, because William Sloane absconded.

So much for what may be called the predictable offences. Indicative of how life was lived in India, compared with Europe, are some of the rarer offences the soldiers committed. 'Not reporting to a surgeon when suffering from a venereal disease' does not occur in the records of the second battalion, but venereal disease was a problem which inspecting generals often commented upon in India.[140] Nor do we find any examples of malingering in the second battalion. Other offences peculiar to the first battalion were mistreating another soldier's wife, or a sepoy, or abusing a native, male or female. One soldier was charged with throwing his bayonet at his wife's head (and missing, presumably, since he was not charged with murder). In every inspection return there were incidences of fighting or rioting in barracks; in one case, provoking disorder by bringing a dog into the barracks. There was also much spreading of lies, false report and malicious gossip.

All this implies much about the soldier's life in India. Combined with the attacks on and thieving from fellow soldiers, it suggests boredom, frustration, and a definite lack of fellowship. Before the picture becomes too depressing, however, it must be remembered that soldiers' wills often attest to high levels of comradeship. Nevertheless, cases of suicide and attempted suicide demonstrate that life in India could become unbearable for the few.

Equally striking is the difference in both the scope and the degree of punishment inflicted by the two battalions. A mere reading of the sentences imposed is, in fact, misleading. When the sentence included flogging, the average number of lashes imposed in the first battalion was 224, against 183 in the second, not a great discrepancy. The number of lashes actually inflicted, however, a statistic also included in the inspection returns, shows a greater disparity; 217 in the first against 119 in the second. Before deciding that Vaumorel was more of a martinet than Hamilton, there are several points that need to be considered. For most of the Indian period the battalion was static and in barracks. Men who suffered a severe flogging would definitely need a period in hospital to recover but they could be spared because they were not required for active service, unlike the men in the second battalion. Also, a static unit could impose alternative punishments such as solitary confinement. Where sentences were commuted, this was the preferred substitute punishment although, as we have seen, not as frequently imposed as some inspecting generals would have wished. Thus, Vaumorel either commuted the flogging to some other form of punishment, or let the man suffer the original sentence in full.

Hamilton, however, had fewer options. Three months in solitary confinement, for example, was impossible in a unit that was constantly on the move. He seems to have chosen a reduction in the number of lashes actually inflicted as a means of showing some mercy. For example, two men tried in Steinkerk in April 1815, Pat Wier for being absent from parade and then on morning parade without his pack, and James Hall for making away with his necessaries, both had their sentences greatly reduced, the former from 200 to seventy-three lashes, and the latter from 250 to fifty. The odd number of the first might also suggest the intervention of the surgeon (Elkington in this instance), who could pronounce a man unfit to suffer further punishment. In theory, he would then take the rest of his punishment when he had recovered from the first instalment, but this seems not to have happened in the second battalion. Alternatively, a man might well be pardoned, as happened in eight cases. It was not until the battalion was part of the army of occupation in France that a soldier was ordered to be confined. In October 1815 Private William McDonald was accused of murder. The charge was subsequently reduced to manslaughter, for which he was sentenced to twelve months' confinement. This, however, was imprisonment in the conventional sense, rather than the military punishment of solitary confinement.

Any comparison of punishments must also take note of the number of men who stood trial in each battalion and the sentences they received. Thus the 352 sentences of flogging in the first battalion represent only 52 per cent of the total trials, whereas the eighty-one similar sentences in the second battalion represent 72 per cent. There are some further statistics that are significant. Thirty-eight men were acquitted in the first battalion (of 604 trials) against the eight already mentioned (of 113 trials) in the second. Thus a man had a proportionately higher chance of being acquitted in the second, suggesting that the presumption of guilt may have been marginally higher among the officers of the first battalion. Perhaps because they were often dealing with known recidivists, as we shall see.

Solitary confinement was imposed in 109 cases in India. There had been a tendency to combine flogging and solitary confinement, a practice that the Duke of York banned in 1811. Flogging was commuted to solitary confinement in a further fifteen cases, although there is no pattern as to why this happened, and it may relate to knowledge of the men. There is one instance when the sentence was commuted on grounds of health. Similarly, only one man had 'and stoppages' added to his sentence in the second battalion (against eighty-six in the first), while a further two men were sentenced only to stoppages. Of course, stoppages were imposed to regain the money a man 'owed' to the regiment through losing, damaging or selling regimental property, or through peculation.

Non-commissioned officers, drummers and men in the ranks could all suffer the same punishments, but NCOs and drummers could also be demoted. The comparative figures for demotion in the two battalions are seventy-nine in the first, with four subsequently pardoned, and ten in the second, with three pardons. Reinstatement, however, was more common in the second battalion.

Another option for the men themselves was to commute their punishment to service abroad 'for life' or 'at His Majesty's pleasure', which meant serving in one of the penal colonies. It could be inflicted as a sentence by general court martial, but in the first battalion we have Edward Hart choosing this punishment as preferable to four weeks in solitary confinement after he had been found guilty of unsoldierlike conduct. In the second battalion Jeremiah Hughes chose the same route to avoid a flogging after he was sentenced to 100 lashes for being absent from parade and leaving his arms and accoutrements in quarters.

Solitary confinement was not the only alternative to flogging in the first battalion. Three men had their sentence commuted to extra guard, three NCOs were reprimanded, one was suspended rather than demoted, one man was 'logged', and two drummers had to attend drill with their coats turned inside out. There was definitely a greater repertoire of punishment in the senior battalion but also a greater repertoire of crime.

Finally, there were the fortunate few who were pardoned, nineteen in the first battalion (3 per cent) and sixteen in the second (14 per cent). Sometimes a reason is given, such as 'for weak health' (first) or 'on account of long confinement' (second). One NCO in the second was pardoned and 'restored in consequence of good character'. As we have seen, there was a greater tendency to restore NCOs in this battalion, which may be explained in part by the nature of their offences. Of the seventeen who faced a regimental court martial, five were accused of drunkenness, three in each case with disrespect, disobedience and unsoldierlike conduct, one with extortion, one for being absent without leave, and one for sitting with a drunk soldier. In the first battalion, as with the men in the ranks, there was a far greater creativity in the range of offences, again often leading to multiple charges. Taking just the offences for which there is a single example, they encompassed abuse, of a native, of an officer and of power, malicious complaint and false accusation, and prevarication at a trial. There were four instances of dishonesty or theft, three of being absent without leave, violence and neglect of duty, and two of striking a private and disobedience. By far the largest group, though, more than all the others put together, were the fifty-one cases of drunkenness, which reinforces the perception that drink was the principal discipline problem in India, affecting men and officers alike.

Since the sentences passed by regimental courts martial lay within the battalion's own ethos of discipline, the conclusion may be drawn that the second battalion was easier to discipline, whether on active or home service, than the first battalion in the far more alien conditions of India. More speculatively, it might be suggested that the character and philosophy of the commanding officer had an effect on the punitive ethos of the battalion. This hypothesis may be tested by examining what happened when Hamilton replaced Vaumorel as the commanding officer of the later, single-battalion regiment. Although it is based on just two inspection reports, both totals were markedly lower than any under Vaumorel's command.

Although general courts martial transferred the punishment of crime away from the battalion and the regiment, a useful comparison of the two battalions can be deduced from general courts martial which, of course, include the trials of officers.

The raw statistics seem to tell the same story as the regimental records. In the first battalion, according to the Advocate General's records, there were twenty-six trials with no acquittals and one adjournment, against twelve in the second battalion, with three acquittals. The discrepancy becomes even more marked when dates are added; the recorded courts martial of the second battalion extended over eight years (1809–1816), whereas those in the first battalion covered just five years (1813–1817). Thus these records exclude Lieutenant Nicholson's quarrel with virtually the whole mess, the two trials of John Herring, four officers charged with duelling, Assistant Surgeon Griffin's drunken verbal assault on a magistrate, and several others involving men in the ranks.

A range of offences could bring a private or NCO before a general, rather than a regimental court martial. Whereas officers were more predictable (duelling, drunkenness and dereliction of duty were the most common misdemeanours) the men were more ingenious in their offences against the Articles of War. Once again, though, there was a marked difference between the two battalions. In the second battalion nearly half the offences were committed against civilians. In Gibraltar, Private Fleming was charged with hitting a local inhabitant, but was acquitted. Two men, John Simpson and William Woodhouse, were accused of breaking and entering, and stealing various goods from a merchant's store by drawing them out of a window. A third, Brian Farrell, was charged with conniving at the robbery while standing sentry. All three were found guilty and were transported for seven years. In Portugal in 1812 William Stephenson was found guilty of forcible entry and robbery, and was also transported for seven years. Similarly, Joseph McNabb was found guilty of taking spades and buckets and threatening their owners with violence, for which he was sentenced to transportation for life.

There was one example of violence within the battalion. Private William Macdonald [sic] was tried on the 16th October 1815 at Passy. He was charged with 'murder committed by him...in wilfully and maliciously stabbing Private Michael Laughey, 2nd Battalion 30th Regiment with a bayonet at Paris on the 8th day of October 1815'. The court found him not guilty of murder but guilty of manslaughter, for which he was sentenced to be imprisoned for twelve calendar months. A note was added to the opinion and sentence:

> The court in closing the proceedings think it necessary to advert to the higly improper behaviour of Corporal Baker of the 30th Regiment from which it appears the irregularities which led to the crime committed by the prisoner Macdonald have originated.

Two other courts martial in the battalion were rather more bizarre. John Riley answered an accusation of desertion with a convoluted tale which took him halfway round Europe – and was acquitted.[141] In November 1811 Bailey Smith was charged with unsoldierlike conduct 'for attempting to commit sodomy on William Derry of the 30th Regiment and John Pilgrim of the 4th Regiment'. He was sentenced to 500 lashes for an offence which, like suicide, seriously offended the mores of the times. Smith also faced a regimental court martial in 1812, and was sentenced to 150 lashes for unsoldierlike conduct, although there are no details to explain what this entailed. In April 1813 he finally deserted.

The charges against the men of the first battalion who stood a general court martial might have been more varied, but they were also predictable in the context of India. Most of the men were charged with multiple offences. There were six instances of insolence, threatening language, disobedience or threatening behaviour, and another six of drunkenness. Five men were absent without leave. Four were found guilty of riotous conduct, and another four of striking a sergeant. Since these replicated the charges found in the regimental records, it must be assumed that a greater degree of seriousness led to trial by general court martial.

There were three cases of desertion, all committed by the same man, Private Samuel Lickler, who had joined the regiment as a boy in July 1805. As we have seen, when he first appeared before a general court martial on a charge of desertion in December 1816 there was an additional charge of making away with regimental necessaries. He was sentenced to 500 lashes, of which 250 were remitted, and stoppages. Seven months later he was charged with desertion for a second time, but the trial was adjourned. Just seven days after this he was again charged with desertion and was transported for life. Although there are no further details in the records, and the papers have not survived, it is probable that Lickler deserted before the adjourned court martial could be completed, was caught, and then disposed of in the only way that an unsatisfactory soldier could be, short of execution. The regimental records tell the same story of Lickler. He was obviously one of the king's hard bargains.

Two men in the first battalion were charged with mutiny, an offence so serious that one received 900 lashes and the other three months in solitary confinement. Another two were found guilty of not reporting the death of a fellow soldier who had drowned in a ditch. Since this charge was combined with quitting the fort without leave, we may assume that the dead man drowned because he was drunk. His two companions may have been too drunk themselves to report what had happened or they may have been sober enough to hope that if they kept quiet they would avoid punishment. If so, they were sorely mistaken. Private Morrissey was sentenced to 540 lashes, with fifty remitted, while Private Turville received all 500 of his sentence.

Reference has already been made to Private Allen, who received 500 lashes for making a frivolous complaint against Captain Cramer. In 1816 Private John Wilson, formerly a sergeant, also faced a general court martial for 'Making groundless complaint to Captain Lynch and using threatening language to Lynch.' His sentence of 300 lashes reflects the need felt either to protect officers from such accusations or remind the men of the danger of challenging authority. Wilson had previously been charged with drunkenness at a regimental court martial and reduced, so the resentment against Lynch may have stemmed from this incident.

To complete this survey of general courts martial for the first battalion, there remain those offences for which only one man stood trial: neglect of duty (by a corporal), theft, firing a loaded musket in barracks, attempting to abuse a child, and the soldier who refused to turn his coat when ordered. Private Jeremiah Cox's attempted suicide (tried by regimental court martial) has already been mentioned. A similar case involved Adam Walker, 'for saying he would shoot himself & loading his firelock'. Unlike Cox, he was acquitted.

Finally, Quartermaster Sergeant Richard Bourke was accused of not drawing his allowance of arrack but allowing a certain Sarah Williams to draw it on his behalf and then sell it. He was found not guilty on the second charge and, as it is difficult to identify which Article he would have offended by not claiming the arrack on his own behalf it is no surprise that the court chose to award no sentence.

As has already been mentioned, the king's hard bargains figure in many journals and memoirs of the period, recognised by officers and men alike. Their incidence in the army of the day cannot be precisely identified, although, as already noted, John Colborne (later Lord Seaton) reckoned that a battalion which had less than fifty irredeemably bad characters, men who could not be reformed by any kind of punishment, might consider itself very fortunate. It is impossible to say with any certainty whether the 30th had more or less of these miscreants than the average, although the figures for the second battalion suggest it may have been one of the more fortunate units. The hard bargains are simple enough to identify, however. Their names appear with predictable frequency in the court martial records.

Using this definition, then once again a stark difference emerges between the two battalions and once again it may be ascribed to the different conditions of service. In the second battalion, the highest number of repeat appearances before a court martial between 1811 and 1816 is three, and only three men managed this. Thomas Jones had a problem with authority. In 1812 he was found guilty of disrespect to an officer, for which he was sentenced to 200 lashes but received only fifty. A year later he was charged with threatening Sergeant Brien in the execution of his duty, found guilty, and again sentenced to 200 lashes, of which he received 175. Finally, in 1815 the charge was unsoldierlike conduct and the sentence this time was 150 lashes. He received sixty-eight, which suggests the intervention of the surgeon. Yet Jones has his place among the heroes of Waterloo, dying two months later of wounds he received on the 18th June.

Martin Moran came before a general regimental court in 1812, charged with theft. This court had the power to sentence him to 600 lashes, which suggests the offence was serious. He actually received 325 lashes, harsh punishment by the standards of the second battalion. In 1814 he appeared twice more, this time in regimental courts. The first time, he was accused of quitting his post and lying down in the snow, behaviour that suggests he may have been drunk. The sentence of 100 lashes was carried out in full. The second time, the charge was unsoldierlike conduct for mistreating the woman where he was quartered; as already noted, he commuted his sentence of 200 lashes to service abroad for life.

The third of this trio of miscreants was Jacob Wheele. He was a chronic absentee: being absent from quarters without leave in 1813, committing the same offence in

1814, and in the same year quitting the guard and being arrested on a suspicion of theft. His sentences, respectively, were 200, 100 and 150 lashes. The second and third he received in full, although he was spared twenty-five lashes the first time.

These three offenders assume insignificance when compared with the hard bargains in the first battalion. To enumerate all the men who appeared at least three times before a court martial between 1813 and 1816 would produce fifty-seven names. When the number is raised to five, there are still fourteen serial offenders. It was normal practice for the best men to serve in the senior battalion. If the depot applied such a policy, then the number of repeat offenders suggests how conditions in India could corrupt even the best soldiers. Yet if we move back to the time when both battalions were in Ireland (1803–1805) there were, as has already been noted, generally more men on charges in the first than the second. Whether this means that Colonel Wilkinson was more severe than Colonels Lockhard and Minet, or that the men of the senior battalion had a greater tendency to offend is impossible to say.

Four men made six appearances in court, and two offences dominate: drunkenness and making away with necessaries. There were other, more unusual charges, however: running away from the bazaar with a bag of money, mistreating another man's wife, being found in possession of stolen arrack, and attempting to load a firelock. The picture is similar for Patrick Davy's seven appearances, although he was not only habitually drunk but also obstreperous, resisting arrest, using abusive language, refusing to carry a flintlock, refusing to be placed under arrest, and threatening to shoot a sergeant. Brian Nowlan specialised in unsoldierlike conduct and drunkenness (nine appearances) while Joseph Kennedy frequently resorted to violence. His ninth appearance, however, when he was accused of defrauding a fellow soldier, resulted in an acquittal, which demonstrates that even the most hardened offender still received a fair hearing.

The worst offender was James Lee, who was in court ten times during the three years under consideration. His main offence, covering eight appearances, was making away with necessaries, sometimes combined with absence (although on one occasion this was the sole charge) and drunkenness. He was actually cleared of possessing stolen arrack. He received in total 1,050 lashes, and spent eleven weeks in solitary confinement. He was also regularly placed under stoppages. No punishment, however, seems to have had much effect on this hardened recidivist. Nevertheless, when he was discharged in 1827, despite his conduct being described as 'very bad', he still received a pension.

Having examined some of the hard bargains in the 30th, it is difficult not to agree with John Schipp's judgement that the lash, far from beating the evil out of a man, only hardened his propensity to wickedness. And yet, bearing in mind the conditions and attitudes of the time, it is difficult to see what else could have been done with these disorderly offenders while still maintaining the discipline of the battalion. As a corrective to this depressing picture of incorrigible recidivists, it is important to remember the many men who went once to the triangle (the name given to the three sergeants' halberds lashed together to which a man was tied) and never re-offended, and the even greater number who never faced a court martial. These were the men whose conduct was described on their discharge papers as 'good', 'excellent' or, in Hamilton's idiosyncratic phrase, 'very excellent'. In comparison, references to 'bad' conduct are rare.

So much for the men in the ranks. McCready was rightly proud that during his time with it *his* battalion, the second battalion, had seen no officers court-martialled. He might have added that throughout the period of its existence, no officers were cashiered and only two officers faced a court martial. Duelling, as has been noted, was a capital offence under the Articles of War, as well as under the civil code, so that when Lieutenant Richard Heaviside was charged that he 'did on the morning of the 15th day of December 1809 wilfully and of malice aforethought kill and murder Lieutenant Lewis Mountford of the 47th Regiment of foot with a pistol near Fort Barbara in Spain' he might have expected the ultimate sentence. A conspiracy of silence by the seconds, the two surgeons' deliberately obfuscated testimony and Heaviside's decision to exercise his right to silence once he had pleaded not guilty presented the court with a difficult decision. Even without a fatal outcome duelling was a cashiering offence. Had the court found 'on the balance of probability' they would have had no choice but to convict Heaviside. Yet, although it was established from the surgeon's evidence that Mountford had been killed by a ball from a pistol, it was not proved *beyond all reasonable doubt* that Heaviside fired the shot. To make the sitting officers' situation more difficult, the Gibraltar garrison was a tight-knit community. The members of the court almost certainly knew why the duel had taken place. Whatever the circumstances, their sympathy may have been with the defendant.

The other officer to stand trial was Quartermaster Kingsley, whose court martial has already been discussed. Suffice to say that the battalion rallied round, from Hamilton's testimony, read to the court, to the evidence of the men who had been with him at Moito, where there is a suggestion of some economy with the truth.

In the journals of Stewart, Elkington, Carter and McCready there is clear evidence that the hard drinking which was commonplace in the period was not confined to the men in the ranks. The officers of the second battalion, however, avoided the ignominy of being drunk on duty which led, as we have seen, to the cashiering of Lieutenant Herring. More fortunate was Lieutenant John Winrow, also of the first battalion, who was also charged with drunkenness, more specifically 'being intoxicated and entering an officer's bedroom forcibly'. This first time he was suspended for four months. Five years later he was again found guilty of 'appearing intoxicated on parade', and was sentenced to lose two steps in the lieutenants' list of the regiment.

Assistant Surgeon Samuel Griffin was highly regarded in the regiment, but even he succumbed to the effects of drink, which led him to face a charge of being 'at night armed and using insulting language to a magistrate'. He was initially cashiered, but subsequently received a royal pardon.

If drunkenness was one of the problems in the first battalion, then duelling was the other. Of all the officers court-martialled while serving with the first battalion, only two were connected neither with drinking nor with duelling. The arraignment of Captain Leach has already been considered. The other case involved Captain Thomas Walker Chambers, who overstepped the mark when passing comment on the conduct of Captain Thomas Jackson while both were on detachment and was suspended for three months. The two officers subsequently fought a duel but there was no court martial as a result.

In February 1808 Lieutenant Thomas Jones was charged with 'conduct prejudicial to good order and military discipline in challenging Lieutenant Benjamin Nicholson…to fight a duel, and for upbraiding and posting him for refusing to accept the challenge'. Posting in this context should be taken literally; Jones displayed notices proclaiming Nicholson's cowardice on board the ship that was taking both of them to India. Jones was found guilty as charged and the unavoidable sentence was cashiering. The court, however, made a strong recommendation to the king for mercy on account of his youth and the provocation he had received from Nicholson, who had instigated the original quarrel. As a result, Jones was pardoned.

In 1810 Jones was one of four officers court-martialled for being involved in a duel. Jones acted as a second, along with Lieutenant Harpur, to the combatants, Lieutenants French and Carden. The accused were all found guilty and sentenced to be cashiered, but again a royal pardon was granted. After that, Jones managed to avoid further trouble.

The remaining court martial was undoubtedly the most complex, and the most protracted, lasting five days. Lieutenant Nicholson (who had prosecuted Lieutenant Jones for posting him a coward) stood trial in December 1809, although one of the charges related to events at the end of the previous year. Following the duel between Jackson and Chambers, he took it upon himself to insist that Jackson's apology to Chambers for the earlier quarrel that had brought Chambers to a court martial must become common knowledge in the regiment. At the instigation of General Wilkinson he was charged with 'unofficer and ungentlemanlike conduct in urging at Madras between the 16th day of November and the 1st day of December the repetition of a duel between Captain Jackson and Captain Chambers…and saying that blood must be spilt'. He was further charged with

> conduct highly unbecoming the character of a gentleman in positively refusing to perform an engagement into which he had been allowed to enter at his own request for the purpose of having the proceedings of the Court Martial before which he had been arraigned put a stop to as specified in his letter to me [Colonel Vaumorel] bearing the date the 6th July 1809 and in consequence of which engagement the proceedings of said court were actually put a stop to and he…released from arrest.[142]

This second charge needs some explanation. The engagement referred to was an undertaking to resign from the regiment in return for a recommendation. This would have enabled him to return to Europe and arrange a transfer to another regiment. Nicholson, however, refused to sign the resignation until he had the recommendation. Since this implied that he did not trust Colonel Vaumorel, it is no surprise that Vaumorel took umbrage and placed him on a charge.

The trial was singularly unpleasant for the first battalion because it revealed deep animosity among the officers. Chambers, one of the principal prosecution witnesses, did little to help the prosecution case, and he and Nicholson cast doubt on the veracity of several of their fellow officers. The court, though, seems to have sided with the defence. Nicholson was found guilty only of the second part of the first charge and was sentenced to a reprimand, the mildest of punishments.

The approving officer was General Wilkinson, in command of Southern Division. Early in the proceedings Nicholson objected that, because Wilkinson had preferred the first charge, he should not have this further influence on his fate but the objection was overruled. Wilkinson then refused to accept the verdict of the court, instructing them to reconsider. The court stood firm, however, maintaining that the prosecution had failed to prove the first part of the first charge, without which the comment that blood must be shed lost its more sinister implication. They also agreed that Nicholson had been justified in refusing to sign a resignation before being given the promised recommendation. Wilkinson could object no further, and Nicholson received the following reprimand from General Gowdie, commanding the army in chief: 'I confirm the sentence of the Court and the Prisoner is hereby reprimanded and ordered to be released from arrest.'

There seems little doubt that the highest powers in the battalion (Wilkinson had never fully surrendered his connection with the 30th even after being placed on the general list) were determined to rid themselves of Chambers and Nicholson, who were undoubtedly the focus of some festering ill-feeling in the mess. They succeeded with Chambers, although their loss was the second battalion's gain. Nicholson stayed in India until 1813 when he sailed to Europe for recovery of health. At this point he joined the second battalion, and remained with them until the reduction of 1817, when he went on half-pay.

Obviously, an officer's status as a gentleman which, if not his by birth, he acquired upon being commissioned, protected him from physical punishment. For the men in the ranks, the triangle was a constant threat. If there is a lasting image of military punishment in the early nineteenth century, it focuses on the grim procedure of going to the halberds, an experience which could either corrupt a man for life or convince him that it was an experience which should never be repeated.

'I absented myself without leave from guard for twenty-four hours and when I returned I found I was in a fine scrape, for I was immediately put in the guard room.' The writer, William Lawrence, was sentenced to 400 lashes.

> As soon as I had been brought up by the guard, the sentence of the court-martial was read over to me by the colonel, and I was told to strip, which I did firmly, and without using the help that was offered me, as I had by that time got

hardened to my lot. I was then lashed to the halberds, and the colonel gave the order for the drummers to commence, each one having to give me twenty-five lashes in turn. I bore it very well until I had received 175, when I got so enraged with the pain that I began pushing the halberds...The colonel, I suppose thinking then that I had had sufficient, 'ordered the sulky rascal down' in those very words. Perhaps a more true word could not have been spoken, for I was indeed very sulky. I did not give vent to a sound the whole time, though the blood ran down my trousers from top to bottom...

Perhaps it was as good a thing for me as could have happened, as it prevented me from committing greater crimes, which might at last have brought me to my ruin.[143]

Chapter 12

Disease and Death

As we have seen, one of the duties of the regimental surgeon was to attend when corporal punishment was inflicted, whether imposed by a regimental or a general court martial. It was his responsibility to ensure that men were not flogged beyond their capacity to endure the punishment awarded. To the men in the ranks the surgeon's humanity might be crucially important, but even more critical was his skill in treating the illnesses and dealing with the wounds that were so frequently the soldier's lot.

What was the reputation of the medical men? Young James Bullen, his shattered legs amputated in a desperate attempt to save his life, died crying that the medical men had done for him. After the battle of Fuentes d'Oñoro Lieutenant Grattan of the 88th came upon his regimental surgeon in the process of amputating a man's leg at the thigh:

> he was one of the best-hearted men I ever met with, but, such is the force of habit, he seemed insensible to the scene that was passing around him, and with much composure was eating almonds out of his waist-coat pocket.

This was against a background of 'arms and legs, flung here and there, and the ground was dyed in blood'.[144] It would be easy to conclude from these, and similar, comments that in the army of the Napoleonic period medical treatment was rudimentary, brutal and callously inflicted, but such a view is a misleading simplification. Whatever other progress was made during the long wars, a relatively more efficient medical system was one of its more desirable results. Indeed, the limiting factor at this period was knowledge, rather than intention or, latterly, organisation.

These limitations were crucial, however, because they effectively handicapped the medical practitioners of the period. There were no effective anaesthetics and no antibiotics. There was awareness but no understanding of infection and contagion. These three factors alone indicate why the outcome of medical intervention was, at best, a matter of chance, and why success might ultimately depend upon the attitude and constitution of the patient. Some men did indeed recover from conditions that were normally considered fatal. Moses Dyer of the 2/30th survived an abdominal wound at Waterloo, as did General Walker at Badajoz.

There was a regulatory system in place throughout the wars; a system that, like so many other areas of military administration, consisted of three conflicting layers of interest and authority.

The administrative level was represented by the Army Medical Board, which was established in 1794 on the orders of the Duke of York. The three members of the Board were the Physician General, the Surgeon General, and the Inspector of Regimental Hospitals. Each had his own area of responsibility, but there was considerable overlap and each guarded his administrative territory from his fellow members. Independent of the Board were the Apothecary General, a hereditary post established in 1747, and the Purveyor General.

This system might have worked if the officials were competent, but there is little evidence of efficiency in any of these administrators. In 1807, however, as the result of a commission of military enquiry, the Medical Board was reformed, to consist of a chairman who was 'well-acquainted with the details of military service, both at home and abroad', and two junior members, 'medical officers who have served in the capacities of regimental and staff surgeons in different climates, and on active service'.[145] This emphasis on practical experience was a welcome development and may explain why in 1811 the new Medical Board appointed as head of the medical department in the Peninsula a man of pragmatic and medical talent, James McGrigor. He arrived in the Peninsula in January 1812, fortuitous timing in the context of the hard campaigning that lay ahead. Most of the practical improvements that followed can be ascribed to McGrigor's assiduous attention to detail and determination to improve a perfunctory system.

In addition to the replacement of the former administrators by the new officials of the Army Medical Board, the commission of 1807 offered other recommendations for the greater effectiveness of the system. The process by which medical officers were appointed was changed. Army doctors were to be clearly graded. There was to be greater use of regimental hospitals, rather than the general hospitals where diseases flourished and malingering was a popular occupation. This was a recommendation that McGrigor energetically fostered in the Peninsula. Finally, the supply of drugs was brought under closer supervision, a necessary encroachment on the hereditary privileges of the Apothecary General.

The medical staff attached to the army, rather than to individual regiments, can be described as the executive level of the system. It was they who were responsible for implementing the recommendations of the 1807 commission. At this level, the executives were the inspectors, physicians, staff surgeons, apothecaries, purveyors and hospital mates. These last, however, were the mere drudges of the system.

Inspectors could be responsible for a division or a whole army. They had to supervise the proper enforcement of general orders, so that the whole system functioned efficiently. This involved scrutinising everything from the day-to-day running of the general hospitals to the correct completion of the many returns that the system demanded. Much depended upon the efficiency of the inspector-general, who had overall control of the inspection process. McGrigor's predecessor,

Dr Franck, seems to have been lax in this role, so that medical provision during the early years of the Peninsular War left much to be desired. In contrast, McGrigor inspected everything from stores and accounts to the number of officers and men – and their womenfolk – in Lisbon, returned as sick or wounded. Many of them proved to be malingerers, styled 'Belem Rangers' after the large convalescent hospital where so many of them feigned disability. His solution to this problem was repatriation for those who were unfit for further service and a return to their regiments for the rest, either as fit for service or convalescents who could recover under the care of their regimental surgeons. This solved two problems. Men fit to fight returned to the army at a time when there was a desperate need for extra manpower; and the medical staff required in Lisbon to care for convalescents could be attached to the army.

The three categories on the staff enjoyed very different reputations. Physicians could practise only after they had achieved a demanding academic qualification and were considered, or considered themselves, the elite of the medical profession. They were also able to enjoy lucrative remuneration in private practice, which may explain why there were so few of them with the army. According to an order of 1798, should a physician wish to offer himself for military service, he needed a medical degree from Oxford or Cambridge, or a licence from the College of Physicians in London.

> These, however, were not to be deemed *indispensable* requisites, if the candidates should otherwise have strong pretensions for military service, local knowledge and experience, or other circumstances of special cogency; or if he should be a medical graduate of a University in Great Britain or Ireland, and be found properly qualified in other respects, on one or more examinations by the Physician-General, assisted by two Army Physicians to be associated with him on such examinations.[146]

Surgeons were the mainstay of military medical practice; in the executive level of medical administration they served as staff surgeons which made them available for general service rather than being attached to a particular regiment. They were appointed upon the recommendation of the Surgeon-General, usually from regimental surgeon, and once appointed might find themselves on a general's staff, in a general hospital, or in a garrison hospital. Within the hospital they were under the orders of the physician-in-charge. Indeed, a contemporary commentator defined a surgeon as 'one who cures by manual operation; one whose duty is to act in external maladies, by the direction of the physician'.[147]

Although the prestige of the staff surgeon was inferior to that of a physician, he was far above the hospital mate. These menials of the medical service ranked similar to the regimental assistant surgeon, although they were unlikely to have the responsibility that an assistant surgeon could acquire in the absence of the regimental surgeon. Hospital mates were junior hospital doctors who held their certificates from the Surgeon-General. During the Napoleonic period some attempt was made to improve their status. In 1809 the first commissioned, rather than warranted, hospital mates were appointed. There was also provision for mates appointed by warrant to acquire extra qualifications so that they could be commissioned. In 1813 mates were designated hospital assistants, a parallel to a change made in 1796 when regimental surgeons' mates became assistant surgeons. This change of title was significant enough for Ebeneezer Brown, surgeon to the 30th from 1800–1803, to record in his later statement of service how while serving with the 79th he had implicitly progressed from surgeon's mate to assistant surgeon.

Completing the general medical staff were the apothecaries and purveyors. The former were responsible for medicines and medical stores. They were usually drawn from the ranks of assistant surgeons and hospital mates, and were appointed on the recommendation of the Inspector-General. The latter supervised the buying and supplying of food, clothing, bedding, utensils and medical comforts. They tended to be former purveyors' clerks since their expertise properly belonged to accountancy.

The relative status of these medical gentlemen can be measured by their remuneration. The following figures are based on rates published in June 1807, but later changes maintained the proportionate differences. At the top of the salary scale was an inspector of hospitals, who received forty shillings a day, while a deputy inspector received twenty-five shillings. Both were granted a guinea a week for subsistence. Inspection required travelling, so the inspector received a forage allowance for four horses, valued at forty pounds a year, and the deputy, an allowance for three horses. A physician's income was twenty shillings a day, a guinea a week for subsistence, and a forage allowance for three horses. In contrast, a staff surgeon received fifteen shillings a day, with a weekly subsistence grant of fifteen shillings, and forage for two horses. The inferior status of hospital mates is emphasised by their remuneration, seven shillings and sixpence a day with no additional allowances. Apothecaries received the same rate as staff surgeons, and purveyors, the same as physicians, with the appropriate allowances. These generous rates not only recognised the importance of those who supplied the system but may also have acknowledged the need to give generous reward to those who handled large sums of money.

At the regimental level the medical staff comprised in theory a surgeon and two assistant surgeons. In practice, this full complement was only intermittently maintained, particularly when the situation made extra demands on the medical services. By examining the period when both battalions were in Ireland, and what happened after they went to the unhealthy stations of India and the Peninsula it is possible to make some observations on the strength of the medical provision within a regiment.

For the two years both battalions were in Ireland, the second battalion had only a month when it lacked the full complement of surgeons. In November 1805 it had a surgeon and one assistant surgeon. This situation, however, was rectified in two months and it continued with a full complement until 1807, when again it lost an assistant surgeon. By March 1808 the medical staff was back to full strength, and this remained the situation until the battalion sailed to Portugal in 1809. The first battalion, though, spent only seven months out of twenty-four with a surgeon and two assistants. This was also the situation in India. Although Surgeon Pearse and Assistant Surgeon Piper proved impervious to the Indian climate and the rigours of their working conditions, Assistant Surgeon Griffin returned to Europe for recovery of health after his court martial in 1810, and was not replaced.

When the second battalion arrived in Lisbon in 1809 it was accompanied by the distinguished surgeon, John Hennen, and one assistant surgeon, Edward Brett. To counterbalance the absence of Samuel Piper in India, Edward Purdon (first battalion) was left with responsibility for over 100 men at the depot in Kinsale. These men would later be transformed into recruiting companies, as both battalions were abroad. Both Brett and Purdon were lost to the battalion the following year when the former returned to England for recovery of health and the latter was promoted into the 8th Royal Veteran Battalion. When the battalion sailed to Cadiz it had only Hennen with it. The pressure on Hennen is brought out by the monthly return for October 1810. By this time the battalion had joined Wellington's army behind the Lines of Torres Vedras and Hennen was receiving assistance in his medical duties from a hospital mate called Newton, who was described as 'attached'. Hennen himself fell sick in December, while Brett's absence continued to be covered by sick certificates. Fortunately, Thomas Irwin arrived as assistant surgeon that same month, but, like many of the men, he succumbed to the climate and died two months later. This made Hennen, recently recovered, again solely responsible for the medical care of the battalion.

The situation did not improve during the rest of the year. Hennen was appointed staff surgeon in October, and Dennis Hughes of the 7th Garrison Battalion was appointed to replace him. At the same time, John Evans was appointed to replace Irwin, while Brett was still on the strength of the battalion despite his protracted absence. On paper, therefore, the battalion was at full strength medically. In reality, Hennen left in November 1811 and Hughes did not arrive until March 1812; Brett died in January 1812; and only Evans was with the battalion from November to March. Evans himself was then detached to tend the wounded of Badajoz. He returned in June, only to be detached again to attend the wounded of Salamanca. Not until November did the battalion have three medical men present, when Evans once more returned and Patrick Clarke arrived as Brett's replacement.

Such fluctuations of medical strength seem to have been the lot of most battalions, and the 2/30th was actually better attended than most. Hughes died in January 1813. The four companies kept their two assistant surgeons in the Peninsula while the new surgeon, James Goodall Elkington, joined the six companies in Jersey. Elkington and Evans then remained with the battalion until reduction, while Clarke went on half-pay with the 82nd in January 1816.

Assistant surgeons were usually drawn from the ranks of hospital mates. They would then hope to be promoted to regimental surgeon or to apothecary, although assistant surgeon to apothecary was a rarer progression. Even promotion to regimental surgeon might be long delayed. Wellington wrote to Lord Bathurst in 1812:

> I beg to draw your Lordship's attention to the practice of the Medical Board in promoting to vacancies in this army, instead of promoting the officers on the spot, who deserve promotion highly for their merits and services, officers are selected in England, the Mediterranean, or elsewhere, to be promoted. The consequence is increased delay in their arrival to perform their duties, and all who do arrive are sick in the first instance.
>
> It would be but justice to promote those on the spot, who are performing their duty; and we should enjoy the advantage, and the senior of the department at least would have experience in the disorders of the climate, and of the troops serving in this country, to which climate they would have become accustomed.[148]

This pragmatic reasoning, however, had little effect on those who controlled the system.

Elkington's experience, while not exactly proving Wellington's point, certainly demonstrates that merit was not necessarily rewarded. Elkington, who was serving as assistant surgeon with the 24th, was left behind at Burgos in October 1812 to care for the wounded, being promised promotion as a reward. He was then captured by the French (for the second time) but made an enterprising escape. He returned to England, confident of promotion, but was told there were many other candidates who had a better claim. Using whatever interest he could muster in support of his claim, including an appeal to McGrigor, he was finally successful, and joined the second battalion as the six companies arrived in England from the Peninsula. As he recorded in his journal: 'I was agreeably awoke this morn with the intelligence of my being promoted to the surgeoncy of the 30th Regt. My letter to Dr McGrigor having succeeded – I was directed to join the depot at Berwick-on-Tweed.'

Having reached the rank of regimental surgeon, the medical man might then hope to be promoted staff surgeon, although this was an even less likely step. Just three made this progression during the two-battalion period. Nevertheless, the status of a regimental surgeon was ranked with that of a captain, while an assistant surgeon had the rank of a subaltern. The medical men gained slightly on pay, however. A surgeon received 11/4d a day, against the captain's 10/6d, while the assistant surgeon was paid 7/6d a day, against the lieutenant's 6/6d. (After seven years' service, the lieutenant finally reached parity.) Apart from an advantage in pay, though, surgeons were unlikely to consider themselves as privileged as company officers. They had no power to command, although within the regimental hospital they were expected to receive obedience and respect. And it would be a foolish soldier who provoked the annoyance of the surgeons.

The regimental surgeon had specific duties, beginning with his responsibility for the regimental hospital. Apart from the hospital inspector, who might occasionally visit, no-one had authority over him within his own domain. A well-intentioned general could nevertheless use his authority to deal with an unsatisfactory situation. General Packenham, for instance, found scandalous inadequacies during a visit to a hospital and used his authority to effect improvements. Indeed, all generals were expected to visit regimental hospitals within their command, a duty conscientiously carried out by General Robinson almost as soon as he took command of the second brigade of the fifth division in the spring of 1813.

Within his hospital the surgeon was responsible not only for the treatment of the sick and wounded but also for 'the interior oeconomy', the management and finances of the establishment. A surgeon was judged on his ability to run his hospital efficiently in all respects. There was also a clerical aspect to his duties. He had to keep a record of all medicines dispensed and maintain a book from which a monthly report could be extracted for the Army Medical Board and the Inspector of Hospitals. The commanding officer of the battalion also needed a daily report of the number of sick.

On campaign the surgeon was responsible for his own sick and wounded and for any stray sick or wounded men from other units. He might be required to care for the wounded after an engagement, as happened twice to John Evans and once to Elkington in 1812. While on campaign he was allocated a tent but this might also have to be used as a hospital tent, particularly before the introduction by McGrigor of portable, prefabricated structures.

Another requirement was that he should recommend to the colonel of the regiment that all recruits be inoculated against smallpox. Although there is no evidence of Colonel Manners' response, the only deaths from smallpox during the two-battalion period occurred in the autumn of 1803. Furthermore, there is evidence in the inspection returns that both battalions practised inoculation. In May 1814 Vaumorel reported of the first battalion: 'the vaccine inoculation has been adopted in the regiment.' Six months earlier vaccine inoculation was recorded in the second battalion. This means not that the regiment had just started inoculation but that inspecting generals were now required to establish that it happened. In October 1815 the inspecting general even thought it relevant to note that 'Vaccine inoculation has lately been practised, the matter being received from the Institute in Paris.'

Because the 30th was a typical regiment of the time, its surgeons may be taken as representative of military surgeons generally. By tabulating their careers (see Appendix 1) it is possible to establish a clear picture of the medical establishment at regimental level. During the two-battalion period twenty-three surgeons and assistant surgeons served for periods varying from less than a year to twenty-five years. The average was between five and six years but this obviously obscures some notable differences. On the one hand we have Robert Pearse (1803–1828) and Samuel Piper (1806–1823 and 1830–1834) and on the other hand Frederick

O'Heighen, Thomas Irwin and John Rose Palmer, who served for sixteen months, four months and nine months respectively. Of these, the first two died in service, while Palmer went on half-pay at reduction. According to William Stewart, Irwin was 'universally regretted. He had been but a few months in the Corps, yet his gentlemanlike conduct and obliging manners had secured him the affection of his brother officers.' This reminds us that surgeons were fully accepted in the mess, as is also very clear in Elkington's journal.

Also worthy of comment are Robert Anderson and Nicholas Gernon. Both were superseded after several months during which they failed to join the regiment. Since there is no information about their subsequent careers it is most likely that they preferred civilian to military surgery.

As Irwin's death from 'a dangerous fever' demonstrates, the surgeons were as vulnerable to fatal illness as the men. Four other surgeons died in service, two of them, like Irwin, while serving with the second battalion in the Peninsula. The Peninsular and Waterloo veteran, John Evans, died in India. Described by Macready as 'a good-hearted choleric Welshman', he 'killed himself by drinking'. This is no surprise. In 1812, Ensign Carter recorded in his journal several occasions when he had to put a drunk Evans to bed. On the 27th December

> the doctor dined with Captain Machell & got very drunk, he disturbed me very much when he returned home, so that I was obliged to get up & go in my shirt to the stable & call his servant up to put him to bed.[149]

A significant point is that none of the assistant surgeons was promoted within the regiment, and this seems to have been normal practice. Of the six surgeons, only one, John Hennen, was already serving as a surgeon, with the 7th Garrison Battalion, and he joined the 30th by exchanging with James Kennedy. His earlier promotion to surgeon, though, had followed the usual pattern when he left the 3rd Dragoons for the 3rd Irish Light Infantry Battalion. All the others were promoted from assistant surgeon in another regiment. Similarly, the majority of assistant surgeons began their careers as hospital mate. The two exceptions for whom there is information are Ebeneezer Brown and Daniel O'Flaherty who were appointed directly to surgeon's mates (the earlier title of assistant surgeons), the former probably with a commission into the 79th, the latter definitely commissioned into the 30th. In both cases this happened as soon as they had passed examination by the Royal College of Surgeons and the Army Medical Board.

Even before a man became a hospital mate, he would probably have learnt something of his trade as a surgeon's apprentice. This is true of eight of the nine surgeons of the 30th whose records survive. The period they served varied greatly. Brown commenced his medical education with Mr Charles Curtis RN surgeon, in Edinburgh and remained his pupil for two years. At the other extreme, Pearse studied for six years with Mr William Pearse, probably his father or near relative, who was surgeon and apothecary in Somerset. The average seems to have been five years. Towards the end of, or after, this period they all attended classes at medical schools or with private practitioners, five in London hospitals, two in Edinburgh, one in Dublin, and one in Dublin and London.

To take just two examples of this training, Hennen's classes covered anatomy and surgery, chemistry, practice of physic, theory of physic, materia medica and midwifery, while Elkington studied practice of medicine, anatomy, practical anatomy, surgery, chemistry and midwifery. The next stage for some of them was to serve as a pupil at a hospital: Elkington at St Bartholomew's and Finsbury Dispensary, Piper at St George's, Pearse at the Borough Hospital, and William Fry at Guy's, where he was initially a surgeon's pupil and then a physician's. The final step was to become a member of the Company of Surgeons (before 1800) or College of Surgeons (after 1800) in London or the College of Surgeons in Edinburgh.

An exception to this general pattern was Daniel O'Flaherty, who commenced his studies at 'the University of Dublin' in 1802, 'not having been an apprentice, being then a scholar of this university'. He attended classes at the College of Physicians, although one course covered anatomy and surgery, before becoming a pupil at the Dublin General Dispensary. He was then examined at the Royal College of Surgeons, Dublin, and by a medical board, whereupon he was appointed to the 30th. His next step, while serving with the 30th, was to attend the classes of a Mr Crompton (later Surgeon General) in anatomy and surgery. Then comes a curious divergence; according to the Army Lists, he was attached to a garrison battalion, while according to his own account he was with the second battalion in Portugal. Late in 1810 he commenced another period of study, with Mr Brooks, Professor of Anatomy and Surgery, and as a pupil at Westminster Hospital. He then resumed his military career, in April 1811, as surgeon to the 72nd. Ten years later he wrote in his statement of service: 'I am not a Licentiate of the College of Surgeons, not having been an apprentice.'

It was obviously not unusual to acquire further skills and qualifications later in one's career. Brown received his diploma for surgery in 1793 but in 1803 he also attended classes in anatomy with Mr Brooks, while in 1815 he was MD from King's College, Aberdeen. Piper obtained a degree in medicine from Glasgow in 1830, having received his diploma in surgery in 1806. Elkington attended the Royal Infirmary, Edinburgh as a pupil for nine months in 1817–1818, attending classes in anatomy, midwifery, surgery and physiology. He then went to the Hôtel de Dieu in Paris for a further three months.

Once he had qualified a man might opt for civilian practice but only a limited range of surgical procedures were carried out in civilian life. For a young man with ambition and a sense of adventure army surgery offered a more exciting alternative. William Dent, with the 9th in the Peninsula, wrote to his mother:

> I hope you don't fret at my entering the army. I am perfectly happy, and I see no reason why you should not be so, for I think the army an excellent school for a

young man, who has a desire to excel either in his Profession, or to become acquainted with the manners of the World.[150]

Dent recognised that it could take him years to establish himself in a civilian practice, whereas in the army his expertise would be acknowledged and utilised from the beginning. Furthermore, if an army surgeon chose to retire on half-pay he could use this income to supplement his private practice.

There were some restrictions on a man's chances of becoming a military surgeon, however. From 1803 all regimental surgeons had to be approved by the Medical Board rather than just by the colonel of the regiment. After 1806 mates had to pass an examination at Surgeon's Hall or a similar process conducted by senior army doctors in order to obtain a diploma or army certificate.

Whatever route the young surgeon followed to enter the army, he then had to equip himself for his new life. Like all other officers he had to supply his own uniform. At regimental level this would comprise a straight coat, without facings, but with the regimental colour for collar and cuffs, an epaulette on the right shoulder and with the swallow-tail of the period. Hospital mates and staff surgeons wore a single-breasted coat with black velvet collar (and cuffs in the case of the surgeons). Both uniforms consisted of

> slashed sleeves and skirts, yellow hospital staff buttons, one epaulette on the right shoulder, one button on the collar, and two on the sleeves; cocked hat with black feather, black button, and black silk loop; blue pantaloons and half-boots; black (waist) sword belt, regulation sword and sword knot, as approved for officers of infantry.[151]

Staff surgeons were distinguished from hospital mates by the gold embroidery on their epaulette and by buttons on the cuffs of their sleeves.

These details of uniform belong to the period before 1812, when there were changes across all ranks, the most important being the adoption of a short-tailed coatee and felt shako. This was similar enough to the dress of other officers for Major Bailey to borrow Elkington's coat when he joined the 30th just before Waterloo still in civilian clothes.

The individual surgeon was also responsible for providing himself with his surgical equipment. James included two lists in his *Regimental Companion*, one a 'set of capital instruments for each regimental surgeon' and the other a 'list of a pocket case of instruments, to be constantly kept complete by every assistant'. A surgeon had to make an annual return of his instruments, despite having supplied them himself. When the surgeon went on campaign further equipment was required. Hennen, giving advice to the young and inexperienced surgeon, listed

> Lint, surgeon's tow, sponges, linen both loose and in rollers, silk and wax for ligatures, pins, tape, thread, needles, adhesive plaster ready spread and also in

rolls, opium both solid and in tincture, submuriate of mercury, antimonials, sulphate of magnesia, volatile alkali, oil of turpentine, etc etc

as 'articles of indispensible necessity'. He continued:

> Every surgeon will naturally have the best instruments he can procure; but it may not be amiss to remind him that his knives will often loosen, and his scalpels, more particularly, break from their handles, if not firmly riveted through at least half of their length: an indispensible addition to his case will be a good strop to touch them on when blunted...
>
> About his own person each medical man, of course, carries a pocket case of instruments; and I would strenuously recommend that he never omits a canteen of good wine, or spirits diluted. Many men sink beyond recovery for want of a timely cordial before, during, and after operations...
>
> It is usual also to issue a certain number of what are called field tourniquets to the officers, and to some of the non-commissioned officers, drummers, and other non-combatants. In many instances life has been preserved by these instruments.[152]

Unfortunately, at Badajoz Major Grey neglected to carry a tourniquet with him and bled to death in the breaches.

Military hospitals, of one kind or another, were the focus of the surgeon's working life. Hospital mates, having learnt the basics of their profession through apprenticeship and lectures, might now find themselves in one of the four home-based general hospitals, at Plymouth, Deal, Gosport (Hasler) or Chelsea (York Hospital). This last was where Elkington began his career. In the Peninsula, general hospitals were located at Lisbon (Belem), Oporto, Coimbra, Abrantes and Elvas, among other places. The main difference was that the home-based hospitals were purpose-built, whereas the army abroad used whatever buildings were available, particularly ecclesiastical buildings like convents. Wherever they were located, however, they had a reputation for overcrowding.

Regulations of 1797 established an administrative hierarchy within the general hospitals. The staff consisted of one or more medical men, a sufficient number of assistants, a deputy purveyor, a clerk or storekeeper, a resident mate, a steward, ward-masters and orderlies. There is reference in the regulations to a matron and other female nurses, although these would be found as staff only in the home-based hospitals. On campaign the soldiers' wives were likely to perform this work. Hospitals could function efficiently when they had a full complement of conscientious staff, but this was rarely the case, particularly in general hospitals abroad, where inspection was usually more lax. This, of course, explains the importance of McGrigor's arrival in the Peninsula.

The chief medical officer was required to carry out two daily inspections, at nine or ten o'clock in the morning, depending upon the season, and at eight o'clock in the evening. The orderly assistant surgeon, who was on duty between the same hours, was also expected to make regular visits to the wards. He had to remain on site throughout his hours of duty, and write a report at the end of them. The resident assistant surgeon then took over, visiting the wards at nine o'clock in the evening and making a report to the medical officer when he arrived for his morning visit. The resident surgeon also kept a record of all medicines that were prescribed and dispensed them, possibly with the aid of a hospital assistant once the 'hours of dressing' were over.

The chief medical officer had to ensure that fever patients were isolated in separate wards. There was emphasis on ventilation and cleanliness and where there was evidence of contagion (even though the process was not understood), wards were thoroughly cleaned, aired and fumigated, using fumes from boiling pitch or tar, or from nitrous acid. Bedding and the clothes of infected patients were baked in an oven, or steeped in running water. It was also recognised that convalescents from fever should not be discharged prematurely.

There was, in fact, considerable emphasis on cleanliness in the regulations. Upon admission, patients were to be washed, their hair cut and combed, and they were to be given a well-aired, clean shirt. Their shirts would then be changed twice a week, and their palliasses and sheets at least every two weeks. Should a patient die, the straw from his bed would be burnt and the place where he had lain, scrubbed with soap and water. At least, this was what the regulations stipulated.

Although the hospital mate was under the command of the medical officer, his more immediate superiors were the orderly and resident assistant surgeons, from whom he received instructions on the care of patients. He also came into close contact with the ward master, who was responsible for the proper conduct of the ward. This included such mundane but vital tasks as emptying night stools and chamber pots, opening windows when judged necessary, and sweeping the floors. He also made sure patients were washed, and their hair was combed, before breakfast (at eight o'clock). He had to examine bedding and utensils for cleanliness. He received and reported all admissions, deaths and discharges to the hospital mate on duty. And it was his responsibility to remove the dead as quickly as possible.

The actual business of keeping the wards clean and aired was entrusted to nurses and orderlies, who also cared for and controlled the patients, often assisted by convalescent patients. Any disorderly patients were reported to the medical officer, who could discipline them with a 'low' diet or confinement. They could also be reported to a military officer for appropriate punishment.

So much for the ideal stipulated in the 1797 regulations. Too many accounts from men who found themselves in a general hospital indicate that the ideal was seldom achieved. Few cases were as extreme, however, as the

> criminal neglect which occurred at Plymouth. On a minute examination into the causes of some very serious symptoms of general contagion which appeared among the troops in that district, it was found, the bedding belonging to some wards had never been changed for a series of years.

As the writer commented: 'If half the care were taken of soldiers that is lavished on horses and dogs, the effective rolls of corps would make a better appearance.'[153]

A hospital mate posted to the Peninsula would certainly have found considerable deviation from the regulations in a situation where local conditions and logistical problems determined how the hospitals functioned. Before the arrival of McGrigor, many abuses were simply ignored. As a result the general hospitals were overcrowded and unhygienic, offering treatment that might vary from unsatisfactory to life-threatening. As at Belem, they might be full of malingerers whose presence detracted from the care of the genuinely sick. On the other hand, the hospital situated in a convent at Coimbra was highly commended, which suggests that ultimately it was the staff who determined the quality of the hospital.

Several of McGrigor's innovations made a great difference to the patients. As a first step, he insisted that the condition of the sick should be classified, and the men separated, to reduce the risk of contagion. Further regulations related to the space each patient enjoyed, medical inspection of new patients, and general hygiene and cleanliness. That he considered such regulations necessary says much about the lax regime of Dr Franck.

The hospital mate's next step would be promotion to regimental assistant surgeon. This might come quickly, particularly in the Peninsula. Indeed, in the 30th, it was safer to be a surgeon in India. When promotion came, it took the surgeon from the larger general hospital to a smaller regimental hospital. Here he was responsible for all the men who found themselves in 'the surgeon's report', which included the drunk as well as the sick. Like the larger institution, the regimental hospital used whatever buildings were available, a somewhat *ad hoc* arrangement. For this reason McGrigor introduced portable regimental hospitals, useful both on campaign and when a regiment was quartered in small villages with no suitable buildings.

The new assistant surgeon quickly discovered that the regimental hospital had to remain close to the battalion (thus the advantage of portable buildings) and provide initial care for the sick and wounded. This may explain why fatalities were higher in the general hospitals, because they received the severe cases that could not be treated at regimental level. Furthermore, regimental hospitals, with their own medical supplies, were under the control of the regiment. A conscientious commanding officer ensured that his hospital was efficiently run so that his men would return to the ranks as quickly as possible.

The regimental hospital was equipped with twenty-four stretchers, twelve sets of bedding, and cooking, feeding and ward utensils. Such a hospital was designed to accommodate up to sixty men, with the bedding reserved for the most severe cases. Regimental hospitals were also required to observe the same hygiene and cleanliness regulations as the general hospitals and, with less pressure on their resources, they may have been more successful in this respect. These regulations were the responsibility of the regimental surgeon, but in his absence the assistant surgeon would be held to account.

The general regulations of 1806 set out further responsibilities that devolved on the regimental surgeon. Beyond his responsibility for the medical care of the battalion, he was also directed to keep accurate accounts and complete returns of all medicines used. He had to maintain an exact record of admissions, discharges and treatment, and to certify to the adjutant when a man was fit for service. He was required to visit the hospital twice a day and report to the commanding officer all the relevant details of men unfit for service (including those too drunk to perform their duties). In the context of hygiene, ventilation and cleanliness, he had to find a building large and airy enough to serve as a hospital, making sure there was a source of good water. He also had to inspect barracks or quarters to prevent contagion and ensure adequate ventilation and cleanliness.

As a check on the surgeon, the captain and subaltern of the day visited at different and uncertain hours, while the commanding officer was instructed to inspect the hospital on a regular basis. General officers were also part of the inspection process, being enjoined to visit the hospitals of all the battalions under their command. All inspections were to be thorough. When General Packenham carried out an inspection he discovered that in one regimental hospital the most serious cases had been consigned to an upper room where there was snow on the floor. General Robinson, brigadier with the fifth division in 1813, found nothing quite so bad, but he did urge the purveyor to serve the men good wine instead of bad rum. For commanding officers the duty was even more urgent because 'They ought to consider, that if the regimental hospital, and consequently the care of the sick be overlooked, the most important points of military discipline may be rendered abortive.'[154]

The day-to-day running of the regimental hospital was the responsibility of the hospital sergeant, who took

> charge of the bedding, utensils and other Hospital Stores, and [was] himself answerable to the Surgeon, who of course is responsible to the Public, for any damage or loss. This non-commissioned Officer should be very active and of good character. He was to be selected by the Surgeon, with the approbation of the Commanding Officer, and be exempted from other military duties; nor should he be removed, except in cases of misconduct or inefficiency.[155]

The regular appearance of the hospital sergeant's name as a witness to wills suggests another, unofficial duty. Convalescents and men considered unfit for any other service (possibly aided by soldiers' wives) tended the sick, administered medicines and performed other menial duties. They were considered as attached to the hospital, unless dismissed for a misdemeanour, and could remain in this role for extended periods. James Butler, for example, was returned as a hospital orderly for 150 days, at an extra fourpence a day. (The hospital sergeant received an extra sixpence a day.)

If the surgeons were attached to active service corps they would sooner or later accompany their units into battle. In these circumstances, they would encounter the most *ad hoc* of hospital arrangements, the field hospital. This might be a Quinta, as Grattan recorded after Fuentes de Oñoro, a quarry as at Badajoz, a farmhouse as at Waterloo, when the farmhouse at Mont St Jean was commandeered by the allied surgeons, or the surgeon's tent. In fact, any suitable location would be used.

The surgeons were not bystanders. They went with their battalion into action, even advancing to the trenches during a siege. They would initially be close to the fighting, as was Elkington at Quatre Bras. As the first casualties were carried out of battle, however, the surgeons accompanied them to the temporary field hospitals or dressing stations. Here they dealt with whoever was brought to them, irrespective of unit. Elkington noted in his journal that during the chaos of Quatre Bras

> …during the even, for it was getting dark I dressed many wounded and was at last called to an officer who had received numerous wounds, above a dozen, after having dressed a great number of them, I told him that none of them would kill him, he replied 'but look at this Doctor,' taking up his shirt a lance had entered his side, it was only a muscular wound, he on my telling him that would not settle him, opened his eyes and recognised me, and said do you really think Elkington I shall not die, I then sponging his bloody face found it was my old friend Mizies [sic] of the 42nd that I had left with a compound fracture at Burgos.

John Hennen had definite ideas on how wounded men should be treated depending upon the nature of their injuries and their own temperament:

> Some men will have a limb carried off or shattered to pieces by a cannon ball, without exhibiting the slightest symptoms of mental or corporeal agitation, nay, even without being conscious of the occurrence, and when they are, they will coolly argue on the probable results of the injury: while a deadly paleness, instant vomiting, profuse perspiration, and universal tremor, will seize another on receipt of a slight flesh wound. This tremor, which has been much talked of, and which, to an inexperienced eye, is really terrifying, is soon relieved by a mouthful of wine or spirits, or by an opiate; but, above all, by the tenderness and sympathizing manner of the surgeon, and his assurances of his patient's safety.[156]

If the patient could be persuaded to a calmer state of mind, he would obviously cope better with the treatment he required. This might be little more than simple first aid, or something as drastic as amputation. Assuming he survived this initial stage, he would then be transferred to the regimental or general hospital.

This system was confined to the men. Wounded officers were brought to the field hospital or dressing station with all the other casualties but they would not be transferred to either the regimental or general hospital. Instead, they would have to find their own accommodation. Whether wounded or sick, they were dependent upon their servants or fellow officers for any succour.

Obviously, battles and sieges were rare events. Far more of the surgeon's time was given to the treatment of sickness and disease, which were ongoing challenges to his skill. Nevertheless, the wounds the surgeon treated can be identified (where a man survived) from the details on discharge papers, which often go beyond the mere 'wounded at…'. The majority of wounds that proved survivable were inflicted on the extremities. Of the eighty-eight wounds instanced in the records of the 2nd 30th, sixty-eight were to arms or legs. More specifically, twenty-three were described as wounds to the leg, eleven to the thigh, five to the foot (including frostbitten toes as a result of the retreat from Burgos), one to the knee and one to the ankle. There were fifteen wounds to the arm and twelve to the hand. Eight of these wounds led to amputation, eight legs, two arms, and two that were described as 'of the thigh'. Arm wounds led to contraction of the fingers in two cases. There was obviously less chance of survival from a wound to the head. Only eight are recorded, all suffered at Waterloo. In addition, one man lost an eye while another was totally blinded at Cadiz. Nor was there much hope of survival from a wound to the trunk. Again, only eight are recorded, two to the shoulder, two to the groin, and one each to the breast, side, back and abdomen. This last, suffered by Moses Dyer at Waterloo, is probably the most unexpected of all the wounds that were survived. Yet Dyer lived to claim the General Service Medal in 1848. Finally, wounds might have delayed after-effects. Two men who fell off the ladders at Badajoz continued to serve until 1817, when one was reported to suffer from 'incontinence of urine' and a second from a rupture.

Another man, Daniel Rohan, was not returned as wounded at Badajoz, either in the muster roll or in his discharge papers, and was discharged, like many others, simply for 'reduction of the battalion'. Despite his good conduct, he did not receive a pension. Two years later, however, he presented the following affidavit at Kilmainham:

> I do solemnly swear that in consequence of a wound I received on the head, by a fall from one of the scaling ladders at the storming of Badajoz, I have since been subject to a severe affection of the head, which disqualifies me from obtaining a livelihood by any kind of laborious employment.

(He had resumed his previous occupation of servant.) His claim was supported by statements from three inhabitants of Clonmell, where Rohan was living. There was also a letter from his employer's son that made clear Rohan was not dismissed for misconduct but 'in consequence of his ill health by a wound in his head which he says was received in the storming of Badajoz, and which I believe renders him incapable for doing any active labour to maintain himself'. Furthermore, according to his captain, Richard Heaviside, he was

> a very sober, honest and well conducted man. I further certify that at the storming and taking of Badajoz in Spain in the year 1812 he received a contusion on the head by a fall from a ladder, and I believe the effect of the said wound has often been very troublesome to him.

His employer, Daniel O'Brien, added his own testimony in support of Rohan's claim:

> Daniel Rohan lived with me in the capacity of table servant for several months during which time he conducted himself honestly and soberly; I now discharge him not being competent to active work from a complaint in the head with which he is attacked occasionally. The wound that appears on his head, he told me on engaging in my service, he received at the taking of Badajoz for which he got a medal (he now wears it) and a regimental discharge from the 30th regiment.

Perhaps Rohan was being a little disingenuous in this last respect, and the medal was probably his Waterloo medal, but there seems little doubt that he was incapacitated by a head wound, as he claimed. Certainly, he convinced the Kilmainham commissioners, who belatedly awarded him a pension.

A man might be wounded on several occasions. Although there is no way of assessing their seriousness, Daniel Brennan's four wounds, to the breast and thigh in the Peninsula and to the hand and leg at Waterloo, were recorded as the reason for his discharge, as well as his long service (twelve years). His conduct was 'good and *twice* wounded'. Brennan subsequently had his right leg amputated below the knee, according to the Staff Officer of Pensions at Stockport. And the subject of amputation brings us to Edward Repton (Ripton on his discharge papers), who lost his leg at Waterloo. Fifteen years later he wrote to the commissioners of Chelsea Hospital:

> Your petitioner's name is Edw. Ripton has been a private soldier in the Second Battalion of the 30th Regiment of Foot commanded by General Manners – and on the 18th Day of June 1815, I lost my right thy and Leg at Waterloo, and since that time has never got but one Wooden Leg, I applied to Richard Nave Secretary and Register of Chelsey for a Leg and he wrote Mr Woid that he sant me one in October 1829 which never came to me I wrote to him twice since to no how I migt make it off and he will not answer my Letters and now if youre Lordships will be so good to order me one it will prevent me of Wearing a Crutch.

History does not record whether his request was granted.

All the wounds mentioned so far were received in action. Home service could also prove dangerous, as we saw with Charles Adams, who was a victim of the popular sport of hamstringing soldiers. A year later John Maloney, a man in his forties,

> was assaulted on his post at the Commissariat stores at Athlone between the hours of nine and ten o'clock by four ruffians, unknown, who after maltreating him in a most inhuman manner left him on the high road in a state of insensibility and with his arm fractured in several places so as to endanger his life since which his arm has been amputated.

Minet, commanding the battalion, continued, 'I have to add that the said John Maloney is a man of most excellent character', thus forestalling any suspicion that Maloney might have been in league with the unknown ruffians.

Fatalities are far more difficult to assess, beyond the simple distinction recorded in the casualty returns between natural and unnatural deaths, the latter being deaths in action or 'died of wounds'. The records do not specify whether a natural death was the result of disease, constitutional failure or some other medical condition. For example, the casualty returns of the first battalion record the deaths of Lieutenants John Rumley and Richard Harrison as natural. Thanks to Macready's journal, however, we know that Rumley died of chronic liver failure which he struggled in vain to overcome, while Harrison was victim of a sudden outbreak of cholera morbus.

Liver failure and cholera were scourges that afflicted the first battalion throughout the years spent in India. Benjamin Nicholson, for example, was suffering so severely through his court martial that a member of the court had to read his speech for the defence. Nicholson, however, survived and lived for many years, although his departure from India, three years after his court martial, was 'for recovery of health'. Similarly, the discharge papers instance twenty-four men suffering from hepatitis and sixteen from chronic affection of the liver. All of them had served in India.

Other conditions were even more prevalent. Across the two battalions, sixty-five men were discharged for eyesight problems: three for 'loss of vision', eighteen for 'impaired vision' and, most significantly, forty-four for ophthalmia. This was initially recorded in Egypt, where the 30th served in 1801. According to a staff officer,

> The ophthalmia, or inflammation of the eyes, may be looked upon as truly endemic in Egypt. In all the towns and villages, and indeed all over the country, the natives are distressingly subject to this disease, so that eyes perfectly sound and uninjured are very seldom to be seen. Even the women, who keep their faces so carefully and jealousy concealed, have their eyes uncovered, certain of not being admired or coveted for the brilliancy of them.
>
> Our army, both near Alexandria, and on the banks of the Nile, was affected to a very great degree with an ophthalmia, attended with exquisite pain. Various reasons are assigned for this great prevalence of inflammation in the eyes, and often consequent blindness, but what seem the most probable causes are the excessive heat and strong light reflected from the sands, the air everywhere impregnated with saline particles, the night air, and, lastly, the fine sand and burning dust, which are blown about by the winds, and fill the eye.
>
> Blisters applied on each temple, and bathing the eyes in salt water, were found the best cure for this painful and distressing disease. It is worthy of remark, that many persons, whose eyes had withstood the burning heat and pernicious glare of the Egyptian sands, were afflicted with this complaint when at sea, on their return home.[157]

In fact, the condition is caused by an intercellular bacterium, *chlamydia trachomatis*. It is also highly contagious and spread relentlessly through the army, affecting all ranks. General Graham was invalided home from the Peninsula as a result of contracting ophthalmia, and it cost Elkington an eye. As the statistics suggest, it shortened many soldiers' service. Until 1814 it seemed more prevalent in the second battalion, but the inspection return for the first battalion in May that year included the observation, 'I am sorry to say that the ophthalmia has lately made its appearance to an alarming extent in this Regiment, there be no less than twenty-four men labouring under the disease.' In 1813 drafts from the returning six companies were sent to India, and probably carried the contagion with them.

Also of interest are the figures for rheumatism and asthma. The former appears on sixty-three discharge papers, nearly all of them men who had served in India rather than the Peninsula. This high incidence of rheumatism in relatively young men, particularly those who had not suffered the cold, damp conditions of winter service in Spain, Portugal and Flanders, is somewhat surprising, but the term may cover a variety of ailments, including rheumatic arthritis and the after-effects of rheumatic fever. Asthma, of which there were thirty-two cases, seems to have affected only those who served in the Peninsula and may have been triggered by the same conditions that are usually associated with rheumatism.

The conditions may also explain the high incidence of chronic dysentery and diarrhoea, thirty-three and seven respectively (both were often associated with hepatitis) and the frequency of diseased, ulcerated and sore legs (twenty-six cases). Apart from the men who were described simply as 'worn out' (164), the two most numerous categories were a breakdown in health, described variously as 'debility', 'constitution impaired, decayed or exhausted' or general ill-health (64) and wounds (103). Although all wounds had to be noted, this did not necessarily lead to discharge. There are papers which refer to wounds received many years before the man left the army, as far back as the period of marine service during the Revolutionary War (1793) and even, in one case, during service in the West Indies, twenty years before discharge. Nevertheless, the frequency of wounds as a direct cause of discharge is high, and two actions dominate, Badajoz and Waterloo.

Although there is some confusion about the total numbers wounded at Quatre Bras and Waterloo, 156 can be identified as certainly having taken wounds but surviving the battle. What happened to them, in terms of survival, provides evidence of the surgeons' skills. Obviously, the wounds themselves would vary between the potentially life-threatening to the relatively minor, but even a minor wound was subject to infection. Appended to the muster rolls for 1815 is a list of 'men who served at Waterloo or any immediately preceding action and are entitled to extra rates', which was the notional two years' extra service with which they would be credited when their pensions were assessed. This list includes the men who died of their wounds, twenty-six in total through to November, after which no man is recorded as having died of wounds. This figure suggests a rather higher level of skill than surgeons of the period are generally thought to have possessed. Significantly, ten of the wounded, more than a third, died on the 24th June, six days after the battle of Waterloo. This would be the point when infection would become life-threatening and sepsis, combined with shock, was the condition that no surgeon of the early nineteenth century could treat.

Some reasons for discharge read strangely to the modern eye. The seven cases of scrofula (tuberculosis of the lymphatic glands), more popularly known as 'the king's evil', seem to belong to an earlier age when the royal touch was thought to be a cure. On the other hand, the case of corpulence seems oddly modern. In the first decades of the nineteenth century, obesity might affect the rich, but it was unlikely to be experienced by a soldier dependent upon army rations. Surprisingly, though, remembering the figures from regimental courts martial, there were only two drink-related discharges.

Mental breakdown was not unknown. John Sharpe, who tried to hang himself, was the same man eventually discharged for 'mental alienation' and held in the asylum at Fort Clarence (India). Even sadder was the fate of Richard Hill, who 'died in the Lunatic Hospital Madras on the 19th May 1812 but no report [was] made of his death until an enquiry was made the 24th instant', this being the 24th May 1816. More fortunate was William Wanlass, who spent a year in the lunatic hospital but then returned to the ranks.

One complaint that was rarely cited as a reason for discharge but which affected both officers and men was venereal disease. Macready had already suffered once, in Belgium, before succumbing again in India, where he found himself sharing the company of a fellow-sufferer, Ensign Charles Warren, under the attention of Dr Pearse. Macready's mistake was that he 'patronised the native talent of India to a very liberal extent till at length one of my favourite Hindostanees – the pagan reprobate! – put an effectual end to my largesse'.[158] Among the men the problem was widespread.

The other statistics that make interesting reading are those from the monthly returns which indicate the number of men in hospital and the casualty figures during the existence of the second battalion. Taking just three years, 1805, 1811 and 1815, some significant conclusions may be drawn. 1805 can be considered a year of home service. The sickness figures are fairly constant for most of the year, although the last three months of the year were definitely unhealthy, with an increased rate of both sickness and death. 1811 was a period of hard marching in the Peninsula, and this seems to have taken its toll on men unused to the terrain and the climate, and with no immunity against local fevers. Most of the sick were returned as 'in hospital', which means the general hospital, rather than 'sick present' (in quarters). In comparison, Flanders and France were relatively healthy places (except for Walcheren, of course) and the sickness figures are distorted by the actions of Quatre Bras and Waterloo. Two points emerge from this survey. Firstly, a soldier was far more likely to die from disease than from wounds received in action. Secondly, when the sickness figures and the fatalities are compared, it emerges clearly that despite their handicaps of limited knowledge and difficult conditions, the military surgeons did well to keep so many men alive.

Chapter 13

Women, Children and Other Miscellaneous Matters

There can be no doubt that the army preferred unmarried soldiers, but women and children were a fact of army life which regiments somewhat reluctantly accommodated. As the *Rules and Regulations for the Cavalry* made clear, in the first instance pressure would be applied to persuade a man to rethink his intention to marry. 'Marriage must be discouraged as much as possible. Officers must explain to the men the many miseries that women are exposed to and by every sort of persuasion they must prevent them from marrying if possible.' Furthermore, men could only marry with the consent of their commanding officer. There is no evidence to suggest the attitude of the commanding officers of the 30th but it seems safe to assume that they would have shared the general attitude of the time.

One senior officer explained:

> I was not so well convinced of it at the time, but now, from all that I have seen, heard and witnessed, I am fully and decidedly of opinion, that married men have no business whatever in the army. The moment that important step is taken, the moment the trouble of military life should be exchanged for quiet and retirement…In time of war matrimony is a serious drawback to a soldier. Constant uneasiness about the family he has left at home, when he himself is called abroad, and their anxiety for him, are painful things to think of; his happiness and peace of mind are marred, and all his best exertions paralyzed, by reflecting on his situation; and he hinders his advancement in the service.[159]

Nevertheless, women were very much part of the military world. They were useful as cooks, laundrywomen and seamstresses, and were even recognised as such by some regiments, who paid them for laundering and mending the men's clothes. In fact, one officer complained bitterly that when there were no women around he was dependent upon the services of his soldier-servant, who had no idea how to look after an officer's clothes. As we have seen, they also had an unofficial role in the nursing of the sick and wounded. Whereas the general hospitals in Britain had matrons and female nurses, soldiers' wives could fulfil this function abroad.

When a battalion was on home service, some of the wives would be allowed to stay in the barracks. There was no privacy, however; only a blanket arrangement around the marital bed, where any children would also be sleeping. Although this was unpleasant for the married couple, it also provoked the disgust of those in command. Arthur Trevor, lieutenant-colonel of the 33rd, explained how the evil began

> when these wretched creatures [soldiers' wives] are allowed to crowd into Barracks, with their starving children – some with families of 5, 6, 7 & 8 (I have this last number in the depot) taking up all the room, bedding, tables, fires of the men – destroying their comfort, and all attempts at cleanliness – making the Soldiers discontented and driving them to the Canteen or Beer Shop and frequently to Desertion. Soldiers' wives are generally the greatest nuisances.[160]

Only one of the diarists of the 30th, Macready, makes any reference to soldiers' wives, which suggests that in general terms their presence was not the problem that Lieutenant-Colonel Trevor describes. Macready, however, had a similarly jaundiced opinion of them. As the light company raced towards Quatre Bras they had to pass through Nivelles where they found

> considerable difficulty in forcing [their] way thro' the crowds of baggage animals, commissaries, quartermasters and women, who thronged the streets. Some of our regimental wives came up, blessed us, and kissed their husbands – many for the last time. Such memories agitate the hearts even of soldiers' wives, the most callous and insensible creatures in existence.[161]

Significantly, the women encountered by the light company were the ones without children, because Hamilton had taken the decision to leave married men with children at the depot when the battalion sailed to Flanders in January 1814 to join Graham's expedition. Hamilton had brought his own wife out to the Peninsula, however, although it is not clear how long she remained there. She joined him behind the Lines of Torres Vedras in January 1811, having travelled from England with Mrs Kingsley, the quartermaster's wife, and seems to have quickly joined in with the rather convivial social life that her husband and his friends were enjoying as they waited for Masséna to retreat. Stewart records an evening spent with Major and Mrs Hamilton and Mr and Mrs Kingsley when 'a book offered some amusement'. The book in question was not considered suitable for the ladies, who were then teased about its contents.

Mrs Kingsley accompanied her husband to India and seems to have made such an impression on the officers that when she died some theatricals were immediately cancelled out of respect, even though, as Macready somewhat bitterly remarked, the death of a remarkably fine officer (Lieutenant McDougall) had not been a reason for interrupting the general flow of social life. Another officer's wife was

Mrs Grey, married to Major George Grey, who undoubtedly made life more pleasant for the young men of the second battalion in the winter of 1811–1812. Ensign Carter recorded that he dined with Major and Mrs Grey on the 21st December and, as we have seen, he also enjoyed a Christmas celebration at the Major's after General Walker had given the battalion a hard time at drill. Mrs Grey, heavily pregnant, was in Lisbon three months later when news arrived that her husband had been killed during the assault on Badajoz. In a state of shock, she gave birth prematurely.

Officers, as these examples demonstrate, could take their wives with them on campaign without restriction, although at their own expense. For the men, though, the regulation that allowed only six wives per company meant that everything depended upon the drawing of lots. Nowhere do the records of the 30th name the women who travelled to India or to Portugal, except incidentally in casualty returns. There exists, however, a list of the women who did not sail to Portugal with the second battalion in 1809. This makes a distinction between English and Irish wives, and includes the amount each was given to return to her home. Once there, they had to fend for themselves.

Before this, the women would have suffered the kind of scene that Donaldson so vividly described.

> The women in the company to which I belonged were assembled in the pay-sergeant's room for the purpose. The men of the company had gathered round them, to see the result, with various degrees of interest depicted on their countenances. The proportionate number of tickets were made with 'to go' or 'not to go' written on them. They were then placed in a hat, and the women were called by their seniority to draw their tickets. I looked round me before they began. It was an interesting scene. The sergeant stood in the middle with a hat in his hands, the women around him, with their hearts palpitating, and anxiety and suspense in every countenance. Here and there you would see the head of a married man pushed forward, from amongst the crowd, in the attitude of intense anxiety and concentration.

Donaldson then described some of the results of this drawing of lots; when a sergeant's wife drew 'not to go' there was little concern because she was not popular in the company. Similarly, when a corporal's wife drew 'to go' the response was much the same, for the same reason. 'The next was an old hand, a most outrageous virago, who thought nothing of giving her husband a knock down when he offended her, and who used to make great disturbance about the fire in the cooking way.' Just the sort of woman, therefore, that aroused the ire of Arthur Trevor. 'Everyone uttered their wishes audibly that she would lose, and her husband, if we could judge from his countenance, wished so too.' Inevitably, this [virago] drew a 'to go' ticket. Then came the wife of a young man, who was much respected in the company for his steadiness and good behaviour. She was remarkable for her affection for her husband, and loved by the whole company for her modest and obliging disposition.

When she drew 'not to go', she fainted in her husband's arms and even when she had recovered from her swoon

> she awoke only to a sense of her misery…The scene drew tears from every eye in the room, with the exception of the termagant whom I have already mentioned, who said, 'what are ye a' makin' sie a wark about? let the babie get her greet out. I suppose she thinks there's naebody ever parted with their man but her, wi' her faintin', and her airs, and her wark.'

The drawing of lots continued, and 'the barrack, through the rest of that day, was one continued scene of lamentation.'[162] The women who were to be left behind had their own bleak future to contemplate but they must also have realised that they could be left a widow without ever knowing what had become of their husband.

Even for the women fortunate enough to have drawn 'to go', life would not prove easy or comfortable. The only concession the army made to their presence was a half-ration allowance (with a quarter for children). Not surprisingly, the women became expert foragers, often beating the commissary to scarce stores of food. This drove Wellington to threaten, in a moment of exasperation, that he would punish any woman caught plundering with the lash. Yet from a woman's point of view, her first duty was to her husband. As Biddy Skiddy, wife of Dan Skiddy of the 34th, so pertinently expressed it, 'We must risk something to be in before the men, to have the fire and a dhrop of tay ready for the poor crathers after their load an' their labour.'[163]

When the army went into action, the women stayed with the baggage, but there are plenty of tales of wives searching for their husbands even while a battle still raged. Their need to know what had happened was desperate; there was no place and no allowance for a widow, even if she had children. Consequently, her only option, unless she had the means to travel home, was to remarry. Such a remarriage is implied by the will of Sergeant-Major Thomas Dancer who died in the regimental hospital, Madras, in 1827. In his will he gave particular instructions:

> I bequeath and request of Major Dalrymple and Captain and Adjutant Atkinson to take my affairs in hand as executors, and put all the best advantage for my orphan boy Robert Morgan to whom I bequeath all my wordly affairs…I also bequeath that the above Robert Morgan will be put under the charge of Sergeant Gavinn who promises that he will not see him wronged and in whose promise I place the utmost confidence.

The boy signed his name to the £5.3.4d that he inherited as Robert Morgan, suggesting that he was, in fact, a (much beloved) stepson of Sergeant Dancer.

Most of the men who made wills, a practice encouraged by the army, left their money to fellow soldiers, but in India at least when wives were 'at the regiment' they were beneficiaries. Almost an equal number of wills, though, directed that money should be given to 'my native woman'. For example, John Atkins directed:

> I do bequeath to my native Girl whom I have in keeping and she having four Children by me, Consider I am duty bound, she going by the name of Chooby, all my Pay arrears of Pay Knapsack Necessaries and all monies that is or may become Due at my decease or any payments – after legally intitling me to the same…

The worst physical experiences for women seem to have occurred when the army was retreating. Both the retreat to Corunna in the winter of 1809/1810 and the retreat from Burgos in the very wet autumn of 1812 created vivid memories, recalled long after the events. The latter retreat, which saw wives of men in the 30th struggling to keep up, set up images in the mind of Sergeant Douglas of the Royals that he later set down in his memoirs:

> Every movable article, being in front, had so cut up the roads…or any opening through the woods, that we were not only mid-leg, but knee-deep in mud…It occurred to my mind that the region resembled the land where Cain went to reside after the curse was invoked, for certainly very few footprints were visible and some places, I am certain, never bore such an impress. On the 2nd day's march from Salamanca, a woman a little to the right of the column had sunk under the hardships and expired, but her infant was still alive; and a little further on the left a Portuguese soldier, worn with hunger and fatigue, had also sunk in the mud and was totally unable to extricate himself.[164]

Donaldson remembered in harrowing detail the fate of one young woman

> who had endeavoured to be present with her husband on every occasion, if possible, having kept up with us amidst all our sufferings, from Salamanca, was at length so overcome by fatigue and want, that she could go no farther; for some distance, with the assistance of her husband's arm, she had managed to drag her weary limbs along, but at length she became so exhausted, that she stood still unable to move; her husband was allowed to fall out with her, for the purpose of getting her into one of the spring waggons, but when they came up, they were already loaded in such a manner that she could not be admitted, and numbers in the same predicament were left lying on the road side. The poor fellow was now in a dreadful dilemma, being necessitated either to leave her to the mercy of the French soldiers, or by remaining with her to be taken prisoner – and even then

perhaps being unable to protect her...In despairing accents she begged him not to leave her, and at one time he had taken the resolution to remain, but the fear of being considered as a deserter urged him to proceed, and with feelings easier imagined than described, he left her to her fate, and never saw her again; but many a time afterwards did he deprecate his conduct on that occaasion, and the recollection of it embittered him for life.[165]

Donaldson was particularly sensitive to the sufferings of women:

during our campaigns in the Peninsula, it is almost incredible what the poor women who followed us had to endure, marching often in a state of pregnancy, and frequently bearing their children in the open air, in some instances on the line of march, by the road side, suffering, at the same time, all the privations to which the army was liable. In quarters, on the other hand, they were assailed by every temptation which could be thrown in their way, and every scheme laid by those who had rank and money, to rob them of their virtue which was all they had left to congratulate themselves upon.[166]

A less familiar setting for army wives, perhaps, is on board the ships of the Royal Navy when their husbands were serving as marines. The muster books of these ships, however, reveal that between 1793 and 1801 a number of women experienced life at sea. For example, in 1795, on board three ships, *Egremont, Princess Royal* and *Terrible*, there were nine women and one child. For once, their names are given. Thus the child, on board the *Princess Royal*, was Peggy McCewan, daughter of Private James McCewan and his wife Elizabeth. On board *Terrible* was Sergeant Henry Murphy, with his wife, Mary. Murphy was one of the first colour sergeants with the first battalion and when he died in 1820 he willed his money to Mary, who had accompanied him to India. It is possible that the two drummer boys with the same surname were children of Henry and Mary Murphy.

In one respect, the women fared rather better on board ship than they did when with the army, receiving a two-thirds ration, while children received half. Compared even with the less than satisfactory arrangements for married couples in barracks, though, life on board ship must have been totally devoid of privacy. Nor would their presence have been popular, neither with the many captains of the day who regarded the presence of women on board as a threat to discipline and the smooth running of their ships, nor to those sailors who superstitiously believed that women on board were unlucky.

In 1847 a general service medal was belatedly authorised for both military and naval actions during the 'Great War' against the French. Queen Victoria originally directed that all who were present in the nominated actions should receive the medal, irrespective of gender, but the Medal Committee decided that 'Upon further consideration this [a specific claim] cannot be allowed. There were many women in the fleet equally useful, and it will leave the Army exposed to *innumerable* applications of the same nature.' Although it is possible to understand this decision, given the gender prejudices of the mid-nineteenth century, it is nonetheless questionable whether some women, like Mrs Reston, wife of a sergeant in the 94th, did not have as much right to a medal as any man who served in the army. Mrs Reston was with her husband when a detachment of the 94th were sent to man the guns at Matagorda, a fort vital to the defence of Cadiz in 1810. During the French bombardment she helped the surgeon dress wounds and then, when water was desperately needed, braved the shells to fetch it from the well. She also carried sandbags into position, and passed ammunition, wine and water to the gunners. There were many men who subsequently claimed a GSM that did less.

Where there were women, there were children and their experiences of army life were as challenging as their mothers'. Yet all the evidence suggests that within the regiment they were regarded as a responsibility that could not be shirked. Just as John Laughron, orphaned by his father's murder of his mother (and subsequent execution), was enlisted into the second battalion to save him from destitution, so there is a pattern in the first battalion of men dying and their sons joining up almost immediately afterwards. Others were not so lucky, however. When a woman died on the march, her baby or young child was likely to perish with her. Yet the humanity of the 'scum of the earth' might be demonstrated in such circumstances. For the women trudging along behind the army through the snow to Corunna, their suffering took on horrendous proportions. Many of them collapsed and died. One woman, who had given birth to twins only a few days before lay dead in the snow beside another woman, also nursing a baby. Yet the children survived thanks to the humanity of some passing infantry soldiers. Similarly, some men of the 30th stayed as long as they could with an abandoned child after Masséna withdrew from the Lines. They knew the women were coming up and trusted that one of them would take the child into her care.

Nor were the officers indifferent to the fate of orphaned children. When Elijah Fletcher was killed at the assault of Badajoz, his credits were 'appropriated together with a liberal subscription from the Officers for the maintenance of his child'.

In this case, it would seem that Fletcher was a widower, since there is no mention of a wife still living, either in Spain or in England. Judging by the men's wills, though, this was a not uncommon situation. Sergeant Joseph Shaller had three children, with no evidence of a wife. When he died he left his money, the amount unspecified, to Sophia, Frederic and Charles. Some idea of their ages is suggested by the childish signatures of Sophia and Frederic, while Charles made his mark. Sergeant David Hasquath willed £20.14.4d 'to his daughter Catherine Hasquath aged 4 years and the amount paid into the hands of William Ledge, Quarter Master, John Brown Sgt Major and John Ferguson, Sgt, 30th Regt, in charge of the child'. Again, there is no suggestion that Catherine's mother was alive to care for her. Nor can there be any doubt that all those nominated to care for orphaned children would have performed this duty conscientiously. The regiment would have tolerated nothing less of them.

Children with the regiment enjoyed one advantage over children from a similar civilian level of society. After the introduction of schoolmaster sergeants, the army educated them. Most of the boys, as the inspection returns demonstrated, would enlist at the age of ten. The girls stayed with the regiment beyond that age and many of them, in all probability, became soldiers' wives. They would certainly have an advantage over the young women who married soldiers without having had any experience of army life.

Nevertheless, as the war dragged on, there was an increasing number of orphans who could not be accommodated by units on active service. The Royal Hibernian Military School had been established in Dublin in 1765 for the orphaned children of men who had served in the regular army. In 1801 the Duke of York proposed a similar asylum for England, and by 1803 the Royal Military Asylum had been established in Chelsea. It was designed to accommodate 700 boys and 300 girls, giving them a basic education in reading, writing and arithmetic, and sometimes a trade, although the boys were encouraged to join the army. These children were easily identified, the boys by their red jackets and blue trousers, and the girls by their red gowns, blue petticoats, white aprons and straw bonnets.

If family was an aspect of life that many men desired, religion was something that most of them seem to have dispensed with, at least until they found themselves in action. A large number of memoirs are informed by strong religious convictions, but these often came about after the man's military career had ended. Sergeant Anthony Hamilton of the 43rd, for example, was settled in Vermont when he

> began to read the bible and commenced going to meetings. My conviction increased, as light broke into my mind, for several months, when one morning, as I was praying for mercy, in a squestered spot near the house, I found peace and pardon through faith in Jesus Christ.[167]

Hamilton needed to undergo a second conversion, after a period of drunkenness before his faith was established, but he is typical of those who discovered a different way of life after leaving the army.

The Duke of York was aware of the godlessness of the average soldier and in 1796 instituted general chaplains, who were paid a daily rate of ten shillings, to replace the regimental chaplains who had rarely been present with their regiments. The general chaplains came under the authority of the Army Chaplains Department. The

> Chaplain-General [was] a situation made out by order of the Duke of York, when commander-in-chief, for the government of brigade and regimental chaplains. The chaplain-general is responsible to head-quarters for the recommendation and good conduct of all such persons.[168]

One satirist advised chaplains, who were 'of no small importance in a regiment, though many gentlemen of the army think otherwise', that if they were

> ambitious of being thought a good preacher by your scarlet flock, you must take care that your sermons be very short. That is the first excellence in the idea of

a soldier. Never preach any practical morality to the regiment. That would be only throwing away your time. To a man, they all know, as well as you do, that they ought not to get drunk or commit adultery; but preach to them on the Trinity, the attributes of the Deity, and other mystical and abstruse subjects, which they may never before have thought or heard of. This will give them a high idea of your learning: besides, your life might otherwise give the lie to your preaching.[169]

That chaplains did not enjoy a good reputation is borne out by the story told, and much enjoyed, of a young clergyman who, about to conduct his first Sunday service, was directed to the big drum, which had been placed in the centre of the square of assembled soldiers. It was to serve as a marker, but the unfortunate young man assumed it was his pulpit and tried to climb on it, with inevitably embarrassing results.[170] Macready had a similarly ridiculous story to tell. During the blockade of Antwerp in 1814 there were many false alarms of French sallies:

On one occasion, Mrs MacKenzie [General MacKenzie's wife] was riding, and came back 'haste post haste' as if the whole ravishing French army were behind her, swearing (I beg her pardon) that she had seen them. The Assembly was sounded, and in five minutes we were on the march. We approached within two miles of Merxem, and finding no enemy to fight withal, returned laughing at the fond credulity of our gallant General.

   This circumstance, tho' ridiculous enough, was not without its beneficial effects as it ameliorated the style and corrected the hasty decision of our worthy Chaplain, Mr S. This gentleman had recently favoured us with a sermon in which he depicted the crimes of our soldiers as excessive, surpassed only by the more inexcusable culpability of the officers who winked at their enormities. But on this alarm the pious man hurried together his worldly goods and, placing them in charge of our baggage guard, was enraptured at the alacrity and good-will of our fellows. He called us together on the following Sunday and, after painting the whole affair in the most glowing colours, concluded by trusting 'that we should henceforth continue true soldiers and fight the good fight of faith'. Our good-natured fellows freely forgave him his former abuse, but couldn't help observing they thought 'the Parson a very rum bitch'.[171]

Stewart's journal suggests that he took the practice of religion rather more seriously than Macready. On the 24th February 1811 he recorded that 'Ensign N[eville, a vicar's son] read divine service to the battalion', while four days later

Lt Killet & Balfour of the 1st Foot with us in the evening after we had all attended prayers at a House where two officers of the 9th Regt preached every night – one named Lt Watson the other Ensign Whitley.

These two officers were of particular concern to Wellington, who had a deep-rooted dislike of Methodism. In a letter to Henry Calvert, the Adjutant-General, written at Cartaxo in February 1811, he explained how

> It has besides come to my knowledge that methodism is spreading very fast in the army. There are two, if not three, methodist meetings in this town, of which one is in the Guards. The men meet in the evening, and sing psalms; and I believe a serjeant (Stephens) now and then gives them a sermon…These meetings likewise prevail in other parts of the army. In the 9th regiment there is one, at which two officers attend…and the commanding officer of the regiment has not yet been able to prevail upon them to discontinue this practice. Here, and in similar circumstances, we want the assistance of a respectable clergyman. By his personal influence and advice, and by that of true religion, he would moderate the zeal and enthusiasm of these gentlemen, and would prevent their meetings from being mischievous, if he did not prevail upon them to discontinue them entirely.
>
> This is the only mode in which, in my opinion, we can touch these meetings. The meetings of soldiers in their cantonments to sing psalms, or hear a sermon read by one of their comrades, is, in the abstract, perfectly innocent; and it is a better way of spending their time than many others to which they are addicted; but it may become otherwise; and yet till the abuse has made some progress, the commanding officer would have no knowledge of it, nor could he interfere. Even at last his interference must be guided by discretion, otherwise he will do more harm than good; and it can in no case be so effectual as that of a respectable clergyman.[172]

The Church of England, of course, was a hierarchy, as was the army. Methodism preached a more individual relationship between God and man which Wellington seems to have feared as something akin to Jacobinism. As early as 1810 he tried to organise a system of brigade chaplains and he also wanted regular Sunday brigade worship. The problem was the limited manpower available; in 1814 the Chaplain General had only thirty-six chaplains at his disposal. Furthermore, there was a reluctance to accompany the army on active service, so that men like Samuel Briscall, whom Wellington admired sufficiently to appoint his chaplain at headquarters, remained the exception rather than the rule. As a result, Private Wheeler could write:

> It is true that there are chaplains with the army who sometimes perform divine service, but of what use are they, the service they perform has no effect, for their mode of life do not agree with the doctrine they preach. I have often heard the remark that a Chaplain is no more use to an army than a town pump without a handle.[173]

Wellington seems to have been less troubled by the Catholic presence in his army, perhaps because of the perception that his Irish Catholic soldiers wore their religion lightly. In a general order of 1811 which was directed at the militia but had implications for the regular army,

> His Royal Highness the Commander in Chief [York] is pleased to direct, that the commanding officers of regiments shall be particularly attentive, that no soldier professing the Roman Catholic religion, shall be subject to any punishment for not attending the divine worship of the Church of England, and that every such soldier shall be at full liberty to attend the worship of Almighty God according to the forms prescribed by his religion, when military duty does not interfere.[174]

Whether or not this order was taken seriously by the second battalion in Spain (and by other regiments presumably) or even whether the general perception of the men was wrong, there is evidence that Catholic soldiers went to church. Ensign Carter wrote in his diary for the 1st December 1811,

> the next day being Sunday we halted and had division divine service after which to my great astonishment I saw my old padrone come into the square [at Guarda] & present a paper to General Hay which [stated] Lieutenant Brisac who owed him 17 dollars not being able to pay it, had given him a letter to send to his wife who was in Lisbon, ordering her to hand over the money to one of his associates there; the general was very angry & asked for him. He was told that he had been sent to mass with the Catholics, the general made reply that he would have him even if he was on the altar…[175]

If the fact that Catholic soldiers had gone to hear mass was a rare or unexpected event, Carter would certainly have made more of it. As it is merely a small detail in the story about Brisac, included without comment, it can be assumed that sending the Catholic soldiers to mass was usual enough not to be worthy of particular mention. There certainly was more accommodation of Catholic soldiers towards the end of the war, perhaps in response to the growing agitation for full Catholic emancipation. By 1817, for instance, witnesses giving evidence at a court martial were able to swear their oath on a Catholic bible, a point which the court martial papers carefully record. Also, in India, soldiers' wills sometimes direct bequests to a Catholic priest, probably in acknowledgement of the priest's ministrations.

Women, children and chaplains all inhabit a rather shadowy half-world in the life of the army and of a regiment like the 30th. They were there in person; their presence would have been recognised and acknowledged by everyone in the regiment. But they have no real place in the public life of the regiment, as instanced by all the returns and records that the War Office demanded. Another figure whose presence, although crucial, was rarely acknowledged in the day-to-day life of the regiment was the agent. Indeed, his name appears only on the back cover of each monthly return.

James defines a regimental agent as

> a person in the civil department of the army, between the pay-master general and the paymaster of the regiment, through whom every regimental concern of a pecuniary nature must be transacted. He gives security to government, or to the colonels of regiments, who are responsible to government, for all monies that may pass through his hands in the capacity of an Agent – and by the Mutiny Act it is provided, That if an agent shall withhold the Pay of Officers or Soldiers for the space of one Month, he shall be dismissed from his Office and forfeit 100*l*.[176]

This financial responsibility was a vital part of the agent's function, but he served many other purposes. As we have seen, he had a part to play in the obtaining of a first commission, since he was the first point of contact for the aspirant officer. He was the conduit through which general orders reached the regiment. These are usually appended to the end of the monthly returns and concern matters like circulars relative to courts martial, losses specific to the battalion sustained on foreign service, boys receiving men's pay, the appointment of an officer to the staff, or money owing to an officer in connection with a commission or a promotion. Thus much of the official life of a regiment was managed by the agent. He would also, when in a two-battalion regiment both battalions were on active service, keep each informed about officers who properly belonged to them but were serving with the other battalion. Deaths, resignations and transfers (or the rarer instances of cashiering) all had implications for promotion. Linked to this, he also requested the names of officers wanting to effect a transfer to another regiment, since he could set up the exchange. The agent also dealt with the affairs of the men in the ranks, such as the effects of a deceased private soldier or transfers to the veteran and garrison battalions.

A man might seek the assistance of the agent in unsual circumstances. When Private John Riley finally returned to England after what was either a four-year period of desertion or a bizarre story of imprisonment and repatriation, he made his way to the agent, Mr Croasdaile, in London and received an advance of £2 in respect of the money he was owed. Mr Croasdaile also gave him printed forms which he could fill in to claim remuneration for clothing and arrears of pay. It was these which led to his court martial because he insisted that he should not be transferred to the first battalion until his claims had been settled. It is also the evidence, incidentally, that the prisoners who returned in 1814 were able to claim their back pay and other dues.

The agent could also prove valuable to an impecunious officer since he would, on occasion and under strict conditions, advance money against pay. Macready definitely had money problems, which he must have conveyed to his father because in March 1815 he wrote to thank his father for lodging ten pounds with Mr Croasdaile. Unfortunately, he had already spent eight pounds on a share of a horse, while the remaining two pounds were to pay for some hide-covered panniers. It seems, however, that his request to his father for more money was not met because a few months later he was writing again, aggrieved that Mr Croasdaile would not allow him a sub against his pay. Although it is unlikely either Macready's father or Mr Croasdaile knew that Macready himself was spending time and money at the *Palais Royale* in Paris, they both probably recognised that he was finding it all too easy to get into debt.

Women, children and the other miscellaneous matters discussed here were, strictly speaking, outside rather than inside the regiment. There can be no doubt, however, that they were a part of army life for the men who served the colours. Appreciated to a greater or lesser degree, like the regimental sergeant-major with the power to arrest or the recruiting sergeant with the power to bamboozle, the colonel who flogged or the colonel who was regarded as a good luck talisman, the soldier in the ranks who would happily steal your necessaries or the soldier who on his death-bed willed you all his money, they were just one more element in the complex system that determined a soldier's life as he marched against Napoleon.

Appendix
Surgeons and Assistant Surgeons in Order of Appointment

	Previous military service	*Period with the 30th*	*Later service*
Ebeneezer Brown	Surgeon's mate, 79th 24.12.96 Assistant surgeon	Surgeon 4.4.00–22.10.03	Staff surgeon 1812 Dep.Insp.of Hospitals 1816 Half-pay 1835 Brevet Insp.of Hospitals 1828 Died in Madras
Henry Dewar	No information	Assistant Surgeon 1801–1803	No information
Daniel O'Flaherty	No information	Assistant Surgeon 1.8.03–18.12.06	Assistant Surgeon 9th Garrison Battalion 1808 Ass.Surg. 5th Garr.Bn 1811 Ass.Surg. 1st Garr.Bn 1816 Half-pay 1816 Surg. 14th Dragoons 1824 Surg. 46th 1825 Died Cannanore
Robert Pearse	15.6.98 Hospital Mate 30.8.99 Ass. Surgeon, 9th	Surgeon 10.9.03–11.9.28	Half-pay 1839 No longer in Army List
James Kennedy	7.2.99 Hospital mate 24.8.00 Ass.Surg. 3rd W.I.Regt 28.3.01 Ass.Surg. 39th	Surgeon 22.10.03–2.1.08	Surgeon 7th Garr. Bn 27.4.08 Died in Ireland
Nicholas Gernon	Hospital Mate	Ass.Surg. Oct 1803–Mar 1804	Superseded
Robert Anderson	No information	1803 Assistant Surgeon	Superseded
Fabricius (Patrick) Timon	2.5.03 Hospital Mate	Ass.Surg. 25.10.03–30.5.05	Resigned and joined East India Company, Madras 1806 Ass.Surg. 22nd Dragoons 1807 Resigned 1812 Died in Java
William Dowell Fry	Oct 1803 Hospital Mate	Ass.Surg. 1803–Dec 1805	Resigned for 'private motives' 1812 Hosp.Mate

Appendix: Surgeons and Assistant Surgeons in Order of Appointment

	Previous military service	*Period with the 30th*	*Later service*
Frederick O'Heighan	No information	Ass.Surg. 17.3.04–1.8.05	1817 half-pay 1831 Ass.Surg. 41st 1832 Half-pay 1837 Dead Died
R.Maxwell	No information	Ass.Surg. 1804–1806	Died Cape of Good Hope
William Griffin	Sept 1803 Ass.Surg. 3rd Irish Light Infantry Battalion	Ass.Surg. May 1805–Feb.1813	Ass.Surg. 85th 1813 Surgeon, 5th 1813 Retired on full pay 1813 Dead
Edward Purdon	25.9.03 Ass.Surg. 1st Irish Light Infantry Battalion	Ass.Surg. 9.12.05–12.4.10	8th Royal Veteran Battalion 12.12.10 Died
Samuel Ayrault Piper	May 1806 Ass.Surg. East India Company	Ass.Surg. 2.12.06–20.2.23 Surgeon 19.11.30–5.12.34	Surgeon 83rd Surg. Royal Staff Corps 1846 Half-pay 1867 Dead
Edward Brett	Hospital mate	Ass.Surg. 9.12.05–12.4.10	Died in England
John Hennen	24.3.00 Hospital Mate 4.4.00 Ass.Surg. 40th Nov 1801 Ass.Surg. 3rd Dragoons 12.11.03 Surg. 3rd Irish Light Infantry Battalion 24.8.06 Half-pay 8.11.06 Surg. 7th Garr.Bn.	Surgeon 31.12.07–24.10.11	Staff Surgeon 1814 Half-pay 1815 Full pay 1815 Dep.Insp. of Hospitals 1823 Brevet Insp. Of Hospitals 1828 Died in Gibraltar
Thomas Irwin	28.12.09 Hospital Mate	Ass.Surg. 18.10.10–2.2.11	Died in Portugal
John Evans	Mar. 1810 Hospital Mate	Ass.Surg. Oct 1811–July 1821	Died in India
Dennis Hughes	17.3.04 Ass.Surg. 28th 18.12.06 Ass.Surg. 7th Garrison battalion	Surgeon 24.10.11–13.1.13	Died in Portugal
Patrick Clarke	July 1810 Hospital Mate	Ass.Surg. June 1812–Jan 1816	Half-pay 82nd 1823 No longer on Army List
James Goodall Elkington	6.8.07 Hospital Mate July 1808 Ass.Surg. 24th	Surgeon Mar 1813–June 1817	Half-pay 1821 Surgeon 1st 1821 Surg. 21st Lancers (until 1829) 1841 Royal Military School Dublin 1853 Dead
John Huggins	10.1.14 Hospital Mate	Ass. Surg. 28.12.15–15.4.17 24.4.18 Hospital Assistant to the Forces	Half-pay 1817 Ass. Surg. 92nd 1831 Ass.Surg. 58th 1833 Half-pay 1877 Dead
John Rose Palmer	26.11.07 Ass. Surg. 11th 27.12.10 Resigned 30.5.11 Ass.Surg. 103rd	Ass.Surg. 19.9.16–25.6.17	Half-pay 1824 Staff Surgeon 1824 Resigned

Notes

Chapter One: Portrait of a Regiment
1. The second battalion was inspected on the 2nd April, the first battalion on the 4th May, and the depot on the 10th May. These three inspections encapsulate the whole regiment within five weeks (WO27/126).
2. WO27/91. The inspection was carried out by Major-General Hatton at Grouville Barracks, Jersey in November 1813.

Chapter Two: In Command
3. Stanhope, *Notes of Conversations with the Duke of Wellington*, p. 18.
4. Thomas Carter, *Historical Records of the Forty-Fourth or the East Essex Regiment*, p. 70.
5. *The Journal of Edward Neville Macready*, chapter 9.
6. James Aytoun, *Redcoats in the Caribbean*, p. 9.
7. For a fuller discussion of the British army of the period, see R. Glover, *Peninsular Preparation*, pp. 14–45.
8. *General Regulations and Orders 1805*, p. 3.
9. Charles James, *An Universal Dictionary*, p. 434.
10. Ibid., p. 117.
11. Quoted in Thomas Walsh, *Journal of the Late Campaign in Egypt*, pp. 117–118.
12. Macready's Journal, chapter 70.
13. James, *Dictionary*, p. 455.
14. Ibid., p. 5.
15. Ibid., p. 697.
16. WO71/224.
17. Aytoun, pp. 35–36.

Chapter Three: Scum of the Earth
18. McGuffie, 'Recruiting the Ranks of the Regular British Army during the French Wars', p. 50.
19. Oman, *Wellington's Army 1809–1814*, p. 211.
20. John Shipp, *Memoirs*, Vol. I, p. 12.
21. *The Letters of Private Wheeler*, p. 17.
22. *The Recollections of Sergeant Morris*, pp. 2–4.
23. Bannatyne, *History of the Thirtieth Regiment*, p. 228. Bannatyne seems to have been looking at total losses, rather than those of men from the Army of Reserve.
24. Paul M. Kerrigan, 'Garrisons and Barracks in the Irish Midlands, 1704–1828', p. 105.
25. Macready, chapter 33.
26. Maurice Harvey, *Gibraltar – a History* (Spellmount 1996), p. 105.
27. *The Journal of J.G. Elkington*.
28. *General Orders* Vol. II, 26/11/10, p. 211.

29. Ibid., Vol. II, p. 208.
30. Ibid., Vol. II, p. 213.
31. Ibid., Vol. II, p. 179.
32. Ibid., Vol. II, p. 207.
33. Charles James, *The Officer's Companion*, Vol. I, pp. 198–199.
34. *A Soldier of the 71st*, pp. 76–77.
35. See *Redcoats Against Napoleon*, pp. 196–198.
36. *General Orders*, Vol. II, pp. 172–173.
37. Grattan, *Adventures with the Connaught Rangers*, Vol. II, p. 141.
38. *General Orders*, Vol. VII, 23/6/15, p. 135.

Chapter Four: Or Fine Fellows?
39. The first departure occurred in January 1806, followed by twenty-eight in September and nine in October. These may have been men who met the original criterion, unfit for active service but fit for garrison work. The largest number went in January 1807, three sergeants and 239 rank and file to the 9th Garrison Battalion. A month later they were joined by Lieutenant Browne and Assistant Surgeon Flaherty. The last detachment to join were twenty-six rank and file who went to the second Garrison Battalion in December 1807.
40. John Yorke's career has been researched in detail by Colin Yorke (see *Gone for a Soldier*, privately published 2006).

Chapter Five: Raw Recruit to Rough Soldier
41. Quoted in Butler, *Wellington's Operations in the Peninsula*, Vol. 1, p. 405.
42. Foy, *History of the War in the Peninsula*, Vol. 1, p. 157.
43. Ibid., pp. 196–197.
44. Stephen Morley, *Memoirs of a Sergeant in the 5th Regiment of Foot*, p. 40.
45. McGuffie, p. 57.
46. James, *Dictionary*, p. 144.
47. WO72/23.
48. McGuffie, p. 54.
49. Macready, chapter 36.
50. Shipp, Vol. I, p. 238.
51. Donaldson, *Life of a Soldier*, pp. 59–60.
52. *Rules and Regulations for the Manual and Platoon Exercises etc*, p. 1.
53. James, *Military Dictionary*, p. 257.
54. *Rules and Regulations*, p. 1.
55. *Rules and Regulations*, p. 2.
56. *Rules and Regulations*, p. 22.
57. WO27/121.

Chapter Six: The Backbone of the Regiment
58. James, *Dictionary*, p. 803.
59. James, *Regimental Companion*, Vol. I, p. 258.
60. James, *Dictionary*, p. 803.
61. When the remnants of the second battalion arrived in India and found themselves subjected to extra drill, Macready, in one of his anti-drill moods, ascribed this insulting treatment of a battle-hardened and efficient unit to the vindictiveness of Lieutenant-Colonel Vaumorel.
62. WO27/94.
63. WO27/98 (Cadiz); WO27/121 (Jersey).
64. James, *Dictionary*, p. 803.
65. James, *Dictionary*, p. 804.

66. James, *Dictionary*, p. 804.
67. Lydon bequeathed a traditional association with the regiment to his son, Dominic, who was wounded at the battle of the Alma during the Crimean War, and his grandson, Patrick, RSM in the 1st Battalion of the East Lancashire Regiment (as the 30th had become) in the second Boer War.
68. James, *Dictionary*, p. 804.
69. James, *Dictionary*, p. 134.

Chapter Seven: Officers and Gentlemen
70. Two other officers appointed by order of the Commander-in-Chief, India also served with the first battalion, William Stanhope and William Ledge, but neither appears in the Army List.
71. Macready, chapter 20.
72. Macready, chapter 43.
73. Bannatyne suggested that Ninian and Henry Craig were father and son. Both were quartermaster sergeants promoted to quartermaster and then to ensign, although Ninian is given as Scottish and Henry as Irish. That Henry had a son called Ninian certainly suggests the possibility of a relationship, however.
74. James, *Officers' Companion*, Vol. 1, pp. xii–xiii.
75. *The Royal Military Chronicle*, Vol. III, p. 8.
76. James, *Regimental Companion*, Vol. I, p. 63.
77. *The Royal Military Chronicle*, Vol. III, p. 269.
78. Ibid., Vol. III, p. 8.
79. Ibid., Vol. V, p. 438.
80. James, *Dictionary*, p. 691.
81. James, *Regimental Companion*, Vol. III, p. 473.
82. *The Royal Military Chronicle*, Vol. III, p. 77.
83. Ibid., Vol. III, p. 269–271.
84. Ibid., Vol. III, p. 77–78.
85. Ibid., Vol. II, p. 253.
86. Ibid., Vol. II, pp. 133–134.

Chapter Eight: An Officer's Life – Work and Play
87. *The Royal Military Chronicle*, Vol. II, p. 84.
88. See *Redcoats Against Napoleon*, pp. 133–134.
89. Macready, chapters 2 and 43.
90. Macready, chapter 26.
91. Thomas Reide, *A Treatise on the Duty of Infantry Officers*, p. 6.
92. *The Royal Military Chronicle*, Vol. II, pp. 135–136.
93. Reide, p. 7.
94. James, *Regimental Companion*, Vol. I, p. 176.
95. Ibid., pp. 159–163.
96. Ibid., p. 183.
97. *Standing Orders for the Garrison of Gibraltar, 1803*.
98. Ibid.
99. Reide, p. 49.
100. *Rules and Regulations*, Part II, p. 26.
101. Dundas, *Principles of Military Movements*, p. 23.
102. Reide, p. 161.
103. *The Journal of Ensign John Carter*, pp. 8–10.
104. Ibid., p. 11.
105. Ibid., pp. 20–21.

106. Ibid., p. 106.
107. Macready, chapter 6.
108. Ibid., chapter 13.
109. Ibid., chapter 42.
110. Carter, p. 20.
111. Ibid., p. 10.
112. Macready, chapter 58.
113. Macready, chapter 47.

Chapter Nine: Crime and Punishment
114. E. Samuel, *An Historical Account of the British Army, and of the Law Military*, pp. 179–180.
115. Blackstone, *Commentaries on the Laws of England*, p. 1400 (quoted in Glover, *Peninsular Preparation*).
116. James, *Dictionary*, p. 25.
117. Samuel, p. 321.
118. Ibid., pp. 350–351.
119. Ibid., p. 489.
120. Ibid., p. 539.
121. Ibid., p. 703.
122. Ibid., p. 705.
123. *The Royal Military Chronicle*, Vol. I, No. 6, p. 491.
124. James, *Regimental Companion*, Vol. I, p. 209.
125. Shipp, Vol. III, p. 204.
126. *The Recollections of Rifleman Harris*, ed. Hibbert, p. 92.
127. *The Private Journal of F.S. Larpent*, Vol. I, p. 52.
128. James, *Dictionary*, p. 685.
129. Wellington, *Despatches*, Vol. 4, p. 380.
130. Ibid., pp. 432–434.

Chapter Ten: You Stand Charged…
131. WO71/245.
132. WO71/245.
133. WO71/245.
134. Alexander Fraser Tytler, *An Essay on Military Law*, pp. 237–238.
135. WO71/224.
136. WO71/254.

Chapter Eleven: The Law of the Lash
137. Macready, chapter 33.
138. WO27/137.
139. Macready, chapter 15.
140. WO91/10.
141. See *Redcoats Against Napoleon*, pp. 196–198.
142. WO71/219.
143. *The Autobiography of William Lawrence*, pp. 48–49.

Chapter Twelve: Disease and Death
144. Grattan, *Adventures with the Connaught Rangers*, Vol. 1, p. 105.
145. James, *Regimental Companion*, Vol. 2, p. 18.
146. *A Collection of Orders, Regulations, and Instructions for the Army (1807)*, p. 354.
147. James, *Dictionary*, p. 874.
148. Wellington, *Despatches*, Volume 9, pp. 356–357.

149. Carter, p. 9.
150. William Dent, *A Young Surgeon in Wellington's Army*, p. 20.
151. James, *Regimental Companion*, Vol. 1, pp. 56–57.
152. John Hennen, *Principles of Military Surgery*, pp. 25–27.
153. James, *Regimental Companion*, Vol. 2, pp. 33–34.
154. James, *Regimental Companion*, Vol. 2, pp. 40–41.
155. *A Collection of Orders*, pp. 381–382.
156. Hennen, p. 33.
157. Thomas Walsh, *Journal of the Late Campaign in Egypt*, Appendix, p. 189.
158. Macready, chapter 34.

Chapter Thirteen: Women, Children and Other Miscellaneous Matters
159. Major John Patterson, *Camp and Quarters*, Vol. I, pp. 113–114.
160. Arthur Trevor, 'Leaves from My Log-Book' (quoted in Haythorthwaite, *The Armies of Wellington*, p. 126).
161. Macready, chapter 9.
162. Donaldson, pp. 80–84.
163. Harris, p. 138.
164. Douglas, *Tale of the Peninsula and Waterloo*, p. 62.
165. Donaldson, pp. 283–284.
166. Donaldson, p. 219.
167. *Hamilton's Campaign with Moore and Wellington*, p. 161.
168. James, *Dictionary*, p. 100.
169. Francis Grose, *Advice to the Officers of the British and Irish Armies*, pp. 68–70.
170. Oman, *Wellington's Army*, p. 329.
171. Macready, chapter 4.
172. *Despatches*, Vol. VII, pp. 231–232.
173. Wheeler, p. 153.
174. Quoted in James, *Regimental Companion*, Vol. III, p. 422.
175. Carter, p. 5.
176. James, *Dictionary*, p. 7.

Select Bibliography

National Army Museum
NAM 6112 – 33 Journal of Captain William Stewart 1810–1811
NAM 6807 – 209 Journal of Edward Neville Macready

The National Archives
WO12 Pay Lists and Muster Rolls
WO17 Monthly Returns
WO23 Register of Half-Pay Officers
WO25 Casualty Returns
WO27 Inspection Returns
WO71 Court Martial Proceedings
WO97 Men discharged and awarded Chelsea pensions
WO119 Men discharged and awarded Kilmainham pensions

Primary Sources
A Collection of Orders, Regulations and Instructions for the Army 1807
Despatches of the Duke of Wellington
General Orders, Spain and Portugal, Volumes II–V (London 1811–1814)
General Regulations and Orders 1805
Military Instructions for the Drill, Manual and Platoon Exercises (Edinburgh 1803)
The Royal Military Calendar 1820
The Royal Military Chronicle, Volumes I-VI
Rules and Regulations for the Manual and Platoon Exercises 1805
A Soldier of the 71st in *Memorials of the Late War* (Edinburgh 1828)
Standing Orders for the Garrison of Gibraltar 1803 (Edinburgh 1803)
The Volunteer and Intelligent Soldier's Companion
Adye, S. Payne, *Treatise on Courts Martial* (London 1799)
Aytoun, James, *Redcoats in the Caribbean* (Blackburn Recreation Services Dept 1984)
Carter, John (Gareth Glover ed.), *Ensign Carter's Journal 1812* (Ken Trotman Publishing 2006)
Dent, William, *A Young Surgeon in Wellington's Army* (Surrey 1976)
Donaldson, Joseph, *The Eventful Life of a Soldier* (Edinburgh 1827)
Douglas, John, (Stanley Monick ed.), *Douglas's Tale of the Peninsula and Waterloo* (Leo Cooper 1997)
Dundas, General David, *Principles of Military Movements Chiefly Applied to the Infantry* (Ken Trotman reprint)
Elkington, James Goodall, *The Journal of J.G. Elkington* (Extracts published in 'XXX', the magazine of the East Lancashire Regiment)
Foy, General Maximilien, *History of the Peninsular War* (London 1827)

Grattan, William, *Adventures of the Connaught Rangers* (London 1847)
Grose, Francis, *Advice to the Officers of the British and Irish Armies* (London and Dublin 1806)
Hamilton, Anthony, *Hamilton's Campaigns with Moore and Wellington during the Peninsular War* (Spellmount 1998)
Harris, Benjamin, (C. Hibbert ed.), *The Recollections of Rifleman Harris* (London 1970)
Hennen, John, *Principles of Military Surgery* (Edinburgh 1820)
James, Charles, *A Regimental Companion in Three Volumes* (London 1811)
James, Charles, *An Universal Dictionary* (London 1816)
Larpent, F.S., *The Private Journal of F.S. Larpent* (London 1853)
Lawrence, William, (G.N. Bankes ed.), *The Autobiography of Sergeant William Lawrence* (London 1886)
Morley, Stephen, *Memoirs of a Serjeant of the 5th Regiment* (Ken Trotman reprint)
Morris, Thomas, (John Selby ed.), *The Recollections of Sergeant Morris* (The Windrush Press 1998)
Patterson, John, *Camp and Quarters* (2 Volumes, London 1840)
Reide, Thomas, *A Treatise on the Duty of Infantry Officers* (London 1806)
Samuel, E., *An Historical Account of the British Army, and of the Law Military* (London 1816)
Shipp, John, *Memoirs of the Extraordinary Military Career of John Shipp* (London 1829)
Tytler, Alexander Fraser, *An Essay on Military Law* (3rd edition by Charles James, London 1814)
Walsh, Thomas, *Journal of the Late Campaign in Egypt* (London, 1803)
Wheeler, William, (B.H. Liddell Hart ed.), *The Letters of Private Wheeler* (Michael Joseph Ltd 1951)

Secondary Sources
Bailey, D.W., *British Military Longarms 1715–1815* (Arms and Armour Press 1971)
Bannatyne, Lt. Col. Neil, *History of the Thirtieth Regiment* (Littlebury Bros 1923)
Brett-James, Antony, *Life in Wellington's Army* (Tom Donovan 1994)
Butler, Captain Lewis, *Wellington's Operations in the Peninsula* (London 1904)
Carter, Thomas, *Historical Records of the Forty-Fourth, or the East Essex Regiment* (1887, Naval and Military reprint)
Claver, Scott, *Under the Lash* (Touchstream Books 1954)
Crumplin, Michael, *Men of Steel: Surgery in the Napoleonic Wars* (Quiller Press 2007)
Dalton, Charles, *The Waterloo Roll Call* (The Naval & Military Press reprint)
Divall, Carole, *Redcoats Against Napoleon* (Pen & Sword 2009)
Douet, James, *British Barracks 1600–1914* (The Stationery Office 1998)
Fortescue, The Hon. J.W., *The County Lieutenancies and the Army 1803–1814* (The Naval & Military Press Ltd reprint)
Gerrigan, Paul M., 'Garrisons and Barracks in the Irish Midlands, 1704–1828' (Old Athlone Society)
Glover, Michael, *Wellington's Army in the Peninsula 1808–1814* (David & Charles 1977)
Glover, Richard, *Peninsular Preparation – The Reform of the British Army 1795–1809* (Cambridge University Press 1970)
Harvey, Maurice, *Gibraltar, a History* (Spellmount 1996)
Haythornthwaite, Philip, *The Armies of Wellington* (Arms and Armour 1994)
Howard, Martin, *Wellington's Doctors* (Spellmount 2002)
McAnally, Sir Henry, *The Irish Militia 1793–1816, A Social and Military History* (Dublin and London 1949)
McGuffie, T.H., 'Recruiting the Ranks of the Regular British Army during the French Wars' (The Journal of Army Historical Research)
Mullen, A.L.T., *The General Military Service Roll 1793–1814* (The London Stamp Exchange Ltd 2000)
Oman, Sir Charles, *Wellington's Army 1809–1814* (Greenhill Books 1986)

Page, Brigadier F.C.G., *Following the Drum: Women in Wellington's Wars* (André Deutsch 1986)
Park, S.J. and Nafziger, G.F., *The British Military, its System and Organization 1803–1815* (Rafm Co. Inc. 1983)
Rogers, Colonel H.B.C., *Wellington's Army* (Ian Allen Ltd 1979)
Stanhope, Philip Henry, 5th Earl, *Notes of Conversations with the Duke of Wellington 1831–1851* (The World Classics 1938)
Tyler, *Bloody Provost* (Phillimore 1980)
Yorke, Colin, *Gone for a Soldier* (privately published 2006)

Index

Abbott, William, 30th Foot, 131
Abrantes, Portugal:
  general hospital, 187
Accommodation, 37–43
  barracks, 38; Berwick, 41; billeting arrangements, 42–3; Bromswell Camp, 38; Chelmsford, 37–8; Colchester, 38; Fort St George (Madras), 40; Grouville (Jersey), 41; hygiene, 42; Irish, 38–40; Limerick, 42; Royal Barracks Dublin, 38–9; South Barracks Gibraltar, 41; Tralee, 42; Woodbridge, 37
Acland, Maj-Gen Wroth Palmer, inspecting officer, 1, 10–11
Adams, Charles, 30th Foot, 52, 193
Adjutant:
  duties of, 27; responsibilities for courts martial, 146–7
Adjutant-General, 138
Allen, Thomas, 30th Foot, 134
  court martial, 170
Amicus curiae, 154
Amiens, peace of, 96, 132
Anderson, Assistant Surgeon Robert, 30th Foot, 184
Anderson, Lt John, 1st Foot (Royals), 109, 110
Andrews, Matthias, officer, 30th Foot, 66, 123
  career of, 28
Apothecaries, military, 180
Apothecary General, 178
Armourer sergeants, 82
Army, strength of, 67
Army Chaplains' Department, 204
Army Medical Board, 178, 183, 184, 186
Arrest and confinement, 144
Articles of War, 130, 138
  administration of justice, 136; desertion, 132; divine worship, 131; duties, 135–6; five summative articles, 136–8; musters and returns, 131–2; mutiny, 131; punishable crimes, 133–4; quarrels and challenges, 132–3; redressing wrongs, 134; stores, ammunition etc., 134–5; troops in the East Indies, 136; troops on board ships of war, 136
Artis, Nathaniel, 30th Foot, 82
Ashbrooke, Lord, officer, 30th Foot, 100
Assistant surgeons:
  duties of, 190
Asthma, 195
Asylum, Madras, 196
Atherstone, Warwickshire, 60
Athlone, Co. Westmeath, 38, 41
Atkins, John, 30th Foot:
  will of, 201
Atkinson, William, officer, 30th Foot, 28, 200
Attestation, 70–1
Auchmaly, General Sir Samuel, 150

Aylesbury, Buckinghamshire, 60
Aytoun, James, 30th Foot, 14, 15, 31

Backhouse, George, officer, 30th Foot, 128
Badajoz, assault of, 54, 55, 60, 61, 62, 69, 86, 87, 89, 91, 93, 108, 114, 181, 191, 192, 195
  escalade of San Vincente, 58
Bailey, Norris William, officer, 30th Foot, 10, 25, 96, 112, 127, 186
Baillie, Andrew, officer, 30th Foot, 112
Baker, John, 30th Foot, 169
Baker, Narborough, officer, 30th Foot, 111
Balfour, Lt, 1st Foot (Royals), 122, 206
Bamford, Samuel, officer, 30th Foot, 25, 29, 122, 128, 129
Barfield, Essex, 60
Barnwell, Christopher, 30th Foot, 87, 90
Barrow, Maj, Deputy Judge Advocate General, 150
Barry, Gen John, 14
Bathurst, Lord, Secretary of State for War and the Colonies, 182
Battalion strength, theoretical, 15–6
Battles:
  of Barossa, 60, 66
  of Buçaco, 46
  of Eutah Spring, America, 116
  of Fuentes de Oñoro, 54, 61, 87, 89, 101, 177, 191
  of Orthez, 60
  of Quatre Bras, 3, 11, 44, 54, 57, 60, 61, 78, 88, 94, 99, 101, 114, 121, 191, 195, 198
  of Salamanca, 54, 58, 59, 61, 62, 86, 87, 89, 93, 114
  of The Nive, 60
  of Toulouse, 60
  of Vitoria, 32, 60
  of Waterloo, 11, 54, 57, 60, 61, 78, 87, 88, 89, 90, 93, 96, 97, 99, 101, 112, 114, 138, 143, 191, 192, 195; survival rates of wounded men, 195–6
Beaumont, Percival, officer, 30th Foot, 111, 113
Beere, Henry, officer, 30th Foot, 97, 101
Beere, Lt Hercules, 61st Foot, 101
Beeston, Nottingham, 60
Belem General Hospital, Lisbon, 187
Belem Rangers, 179
Bell, Joseph, 30th Foot, 52
Belsdin, Lt-Col, 3rd Portuguese, 122
Berridge, Joseph, officer, 30th Foot, 85, 88, 94
Berry, Luke, 30th Foot, 83
Berwick-on-Tweed, 182
Bibby, Thomas, 30th Foot, 52
  gives evidence at court martial, 149
Billingborough, Lincolnshire, 68, 69, 70
Bilson, Col Sir Charles Philip, 28th Foot, 137

Index 221

Bircham, Samuel, officer, 30th Foot, 9, 79
  career of, 116–7; president of a court martial, 147–50
Black, Andrew, 30th Foot, 52
Blackstone, Sir William, 130
Blacktown, Madras, 146
Bloxholme, Lincolnshire, 17
Bonaparte, Napoleon, 13
  first abdication, 1
Boston, Lincolnshire, 69
Bottesham, Cambridgeshire, 87
Bourke, Richard, 30th Foot:
  gives evidence at Ensign Herring's court martial, 156; court martial of, 171
Bourne, Lincolnshire, 69
Boyd, Edward, officer, 30th Foot, 97, 112
Boyd, Lt, 4th Foot, 129
Bradley, Thomas, 30th Foot, 131
Bradshaw, formerly Capt, 60th Foot, 68
Brady, Francis, 30th Foot, 88
Brasschaat, Belgium, 1
Brennan, Daniel, 30th Foot:
  wounds received, 193
Brett, Asst Surg Edward, 30th Foot, 181
Brevet system, 107–08
Brian, *see* Brien
Brien, William, 30th Foot, 85, 87, 88–9, 92, 136, 171
Brisac, George, officer, 30th Foot, 112, 124, 207
Briscall, Rev Samuel, appointed Chaplain to Duke of Wellington, 206
Bristow, William, 30th Foot, 52
Brokers:
  army, 106–07; commissions, 106–07
Brooke, John Edmond, officer, 30th Foot, 97, 111, 113
Brown Bess, 74–5
Brown, John, 30th Foot, 156, 203
Brown, Joseph, 30th Foot, 57
Brown, Surgeon Ebeneezer, 30th Foot, 180, 184, 185
Bruce, Lt-Col, 19th Foot, 150
Brussels, 90
Brydges, J.W., officer, 30th Foot, 97, 113, 114
Bullen, James, 30th Foot, 97
  death of, 177
Burdett, Sir Charles, officer, 30th Foot, 19, 100
Burdett, Sir Francis, 140
Burgos, 191
  retreat from, 44, 49, 54, 77, 97, 192, 201
Burke, William, 30th Foot, 93
Burne, Lt-Col, 36th Foot, 161
Butler, James, 30th Foot, 190

Cadiz, 59, 60, 66, 81, 86, 98, 99, 181, 192, 203
  Fort Puntales, 16; 30th Foot arrives, 41
Callinan, Anthony, 30th Foot, 58
Calvert, Sir Harry, Adjutant-General, 141, 206
Cambridge, 65, 138
Camms, Co. Tyrone, 62
Campbell, Capt R.N., later Vice-Admiral, 22
Campbell, William, officer, 30th Foot, 123, 125
Cannanore, India, 1, 50, 137
Cape of Good Hope, 57
Carden, Washington, officer, 30th Foot, 147
  stands court martial, 174
Carroll, John, 30th Foot, 91, 92

Cartaxo, Portugal, 206
Carter, John, officer, 30th Foot, 96, 97, 118, 122, 123, 124, 125, 127, 173, 184, 207
Cashell, Tipperary, 85
Castello Branco, Portugal, 135
Castlebar, Co. Mayo, 66, 88
Castlereagh, Robert Stewart, Viscount, 35, 142
Cathcart, Gen Lord:
  expedition to North Germany, 2, 20, 40
Catholic soldiers:
  permitted to attend Mass, 207; permitted to swear oath on Catholic Bible, 207
Ceylon Rifles, 117
Chambers, Thomas Walker, officer, 30th Foot, 7, 59, 97, 98, 102, 114, 138, 174, 175
Chaplain-General, 204, 206
Chaplains, advice to, 204–05
Charleston, South Carolina, 116
Chelsea, 62, 83, 90
Chelsea, York Military Hospital, 187, 193
Children, with the army, 203
Ciudad Rodrigo, 69, 70
  siege of, 58; claim for Peninsula Medal bar at, 60; assault of, 108
Clancarty, Lord, Ambassador at The Hague, 127
Clara, Co. Offaly, 40
Clarke, Asst Surg Patrick, 30th Foot, 181
Clarke, Mary Ann, 107
Claybrook, Leicestershire, 86
Cleavely, Mary, 59
Cleavely, William, 30th Foot, 59
Cline, Brien, 30th Foot, 91, 92, 136
Clinton, Arthur, 30th Foot, 59–60
Clonmel, Co. Tipperary, 192
Cochrane, Thomas, 30th Foot, 52
Coimbra, 99
  general hospital at, 187
Colborne, John, later Lord Seaton, 36, 171
Colchester, regimental depot, 1, 59
Colonels, duties of, 18
Colonial Secretary, 15
Colour Sergeant, institution of, 84
Commission brokers, 106–07
Commissioned Sergeants, 114–17
Commissions:
  purchase of, 103–06; price of, 104, 109
Condron, Peter, 30th Foot, 135
Connell, Charles, 30th Foot, 131
Connolly, Thomas, 30th Foot, 86, 88
Coombs, Capt, 25th Native Infantry, deputy judge advocate, 150–4
Cordovilla, Spain, 44
Coria, Portugal, 141
Corporal punishment, 139–40
Corporals:
  demotion of, 94; duties of, 95
Corsica, 69, 116
Corunna, retreat to, 201, 203
Costello, Edward, 30th Foot, 91
Courts martial, regimental, powers of, 163
Covering Sergeant, 84
Cox, Jeremiah, 30th Foot, 137
  stands court martial, 171
Cox, William, 30th Foot, 46
Craan, Willem Benjamin, cartographer, 96

Craig, Henry, officer, 30th Foot, 31, 83, 116
Craig, Ninian, 30th Foot, 83
Cramer, Henry, officer, 30th Foot, 134, 147, 170
Crawford, Lt Alexander, 16th Dragoons:
 gives evidence at Capt Leach's court martial, 161
Crimping, 67–8
Crimps, 67–8
Croasdaile, Mr, regimental agent to 30th Foot, 209
Cuellar, Spain, 26
Cummins, Robert, 30th Foot, 82
Curragh, the camp, 82
Cuthbert, Thomas, 30th Foot, 82–3

Dalrymple, John, officer, 30th Foot, 129, 200
Dancer, Thomas, 30th Foot:
 will of, 200–01
Daniell, Robert, officer, 30th Foot, 83, 112, 114, 115
Dankerts, Mr, Commissary, 30
Darling, George, officer, 30th Foot, 72, 112
Davison, Thomas, 30th Foot, 90–1
Davy, Patrick, 30th Foot, king's hard bargain, 172
Dawson, George, 30th Foot, 92–3
De Jose, Tomas, 30th Foot (see also De Joseph), 61–2
De Joseph, Thomas, 30th Foot (see also De Jose), 61–2
Deal, military hospital, 187
Delft, Netherlands, 127
Dent, Surgeon William, 9th Foot:
 reasons for entering army, 185–6
Deputy Judge Advocate, duties of, 147, 151
Derby, 66
Derby, Derbyshire, 61
Derry, William, 30th Foot, 131, 169
Dewar, Charles, 30th Foot, 92
Discipline, 37
Doman, John, 30th Foot, 156
Dominica, 13
Donaldson, Sgt Joseph, 94th Foot, 73
 describes women drawing lots, 199–200;
 describes suffering of soldiers' wives, 201–02
Donellan, Matthew, 30th Foot, 4, 27, 57, 85, 86, 87, 89
Douglas, Robert, officer, 30th Foot, 72, 111, 113
Douglas, Sgt John, 1st Foot (Royals):
 describes suffering of women, 201
Dover, 90
Doyle, Gen John, 22
Drill Sergeant, duties of, 84
Dublin, 65, 68
Duelling, 173–4
Duke of York, 101, 105, 107, 138, 178, 207
Dumfries, 52
Duncan, Ensign Robert, 82nd Foot:
 gives evidence at Capt Leach's court martial, 161
Dundas, Gen Sir David, 18, 121
Dungannon Fort, 68
Dunton, Bucks., 85
Dupree, Charles, 30th Foot, 2, 3
Dyer, Moses, 30th Foot, 177, 192
Dysentery, 195

Eades, Michael, officer, 30th Foot, 123
Eagar, James, officer, 30th Foot, 25, 112

East India Company, 136
Edinburgh, 65
Edward, Duke of Kent, 41
Egerton, Col, 44th Foot, 128
Egremont, HMS, 202
Egypt, 69
 1801 campaign, 3, 82, 89, 93
Elkington, Surgeon James Goodall, 30th Foot, 28, 41, 42, 96, 122, 125, 127, 167, 173, 181, 183, 184, 185, 186, 187, 191, 195
Elliot, Richard C., officer, 30th Foot, 72, 112
Elvas General Hospital, 187
Enniscorthy, Co. Wexford, 65
Evans, John, Asst Surg, 30th Foot, 124, 127, 181, 183, 184
Exchange, 113–4
Executions, 144

Fahey, Francis, 30th Foot, 56, 132
Farrell, Brian, 30th Foot:
 stands court martial, 169
Farrell, Dennis, 30th Foot, 92–3
Farrell, Michael, 30th Foot, 55
Farrell, Peter, 30th Foot, 52
Fawcett, Sir William, Adjutant-General, 141
Ferguson, John, 30th Foot, 203
Fettes, Alexander, officer, 30th Foot, 97, 113, 114
Field exercises, 121
Field hospitals, 191
Field manoeuvres, 119
Fielding, William, 30th Foot, 52
Figuera, Portugal, 99
Finlay, Daniel, 36th Foot:
 gives evidence at Captain Leach's court martial, 159–60
Flanders, 50
Fleming, Thomas, 30th Foot:
 stands court martial, 169
Fletcher, Elijah, 30th Foot, 203
Flowers, George, 30th Foot, 94
Flude, Jonathan, officer, 30th Foot, 97, 100, 112
Food, rations, 49–50
Forbes, Lord, later Viscount Granard, officer, 30th Foot, 100
Foreign Secretary, 15
Fort Clarence, Madras, 52, 196
Fort St George, Madras, 146, 148, 150
Fox, Samuel, officer, 30th Foot, 123
Foy, General Maximilien, 63–4
Franck, James, Inspector General of Hospitals, 179, 189
Freear, Arthur W., officer, 30th Foot, 112
French, Samuel, officer, 30th Foot, 133
 court martial of, 174
Freneda, Portugal, 141
Frost, Daniel, 30th Foot, 131
Fry, Asst Surg William, 30th Foot, 185
Fuentes de Oñoro, Spain, 86
Fullerton, James, officer, 30th Foot, 61, 66, 69

Galway, 65, 82, 83
Garland, Francis, 30th Foot, 156
Garland, John, officer, 30th Foot, 28, 112, 123, 125
Garrison battalions, 56
Garvey, John, officer, 30th Foot, 26, 111

Index   223

Gavinn, Martin, 30th Foot, 200
General Don, 41
General orders:
　destruction of civilian property, 43; destruction of olive trees, 43; hygiene, 43, 44
Gernon, Asst Surg Nicholas, 30th Foot, 184
Ghent, Belgium, 127
Glasgow, 65
Glass, RSM David, 79
Goodship, John, 30th Foot, 57
Gore, Arthur, officer, 30th Foot, 96, 100
Gosport (Haslar), military hospital, 187
Gould, John, 30th Foot, 93
Govea, Portugal, 141
Graham, Gen Sir Thomas, 1, 18, 60, 61, 66, 89, 118
　contracts ophthalmia, 195
Grantham, Lincolnshire, 69
Grattan, Lt William, 88th Foot (Connaught Rangers), 191
　describes aftermath of battle, 177
Gravelines, France, 58–9
Green, Lt-Colonel Charles, 30th Foot, 19
　promoted to general list, 20
Gregg, James Nesbit, officer, 30th Foot, 129
Grellis, William, 30th Foot, 82
Gressie, Java, 116
Grey, George, officer, 30th Foot, 101, 123, 124, 199
　death of, 187
Grey, Mrs:
　with husband in Portugal, 199
Grey, Owen Wynne, officer, 30th Foot, 101
Griffin, Asst Surg Samuel, 30th Foot, 169, 181
　stands court martial, 173
Guard duties, 120
Guarda, Portugal, 126, 207
Gunning, Patrick, 30th Foot, 93

Half-pay, 114
Hall, James, 30th Foot:
　stands court martial, 167
Hamilton, Lt-Col Alexander, 5, 6, 10, 24, 30, 52, 57, 58, 61, 81, 85, 86, 87, 88, 90, 96, 97, 100, 112, 116, 122, 123, 163, 168, 173
　career of, 22–3; comparison with Vaumorel, 166; joined by his wife in Portugal, 198
Hamilton, Mrs, 198
Hamilton, Sgt Anthony, 43rd Foot:
　religious conversion of, 204
Harpur, William, officer, 30th Foot, 147
　court martial, 174
Harris, Pte Benjamin, 95th Rifles, 140
Harris, Thomas, 30th Foot, 85
Harrison, Joseph (or Josiah), 30th Foot, 87, 88
Harrison, Richard, officer, 30th Foot:
　death of, 194
Hart, Edward, 30th Foot:
　commutes punishment, 167–8
Hasquath, David, 30th Foot:
　will of, 203
Hatton, General John, 137
Haughey, Charles, 30th Foot, 62, 92
Hawker, Peter, officer, 30th Foot, 134
Hay, General Andrew, 77, 207
Haydon, William, 30th Foot, 91
Heaviside, Richard, officer, 30th Foot, 133
　stands court martial, 173; supports Daniel Rohan's claim to a pension, 192
Henley-on-Thames, 52
Hennen, Surgeon John, 30th Foot, 96, 123, 181, 184, 185
　advice to young surgeons, 186–7; on wounds, 191
Herring, John, officer, 30th Foot, 139, 169
　stands court martial, 150–7, 173
Hertford, 58
Hill, Ensign, 82nd Foot:
　gives evidence at Captain Leach's court martial, 160–1
Hill, John (1), 30th Foot, 60
Hill, John (2), 30th Foot, 60
Hill, John (3), 30th Foot, 60
Hill, Richard, 30th Foot, 196
Hislop, Gen Sir Thomas, 21
Hitchin, John, officer, 30th Foot, 102, 114, 123, 128, 129
Home Secretary, 15
Hood, Admiral, 18
Hospital, mates, 179–80
　sergeant duties of, 190; ward masters, 188; (general) organisation of, 187–8; (general) hygiene, 188; (regimental) equipment, 189
Hotham, Admiral William, R.N., 116
Houghton, Brig Gen Daniel, inspecting officer, 7
Howard, Robert, officer, 30th Foot, 25
Hughes, Surgeon Dennis, 30th Foot, 181
Hughes, Jeremiah, 30th Foot:
　commutes punishment, 168
Hughes, Robert, officer, 30th Foot, 111, 115, 116
Hull, Yorkshire, 30th Foot depot at, 72, 73, 138
Hungerford, Berkshire, 32
Hutchinson, Emmanuel, officer, 30th Foot, 153, 157
　gives evidence at Ensign Herring's court martial, 155–6
Hutchinson, Hely, General, 20

Infantry, number of regiments, 13
Inspection, regimental, 1–12
Inspector General of Hospitals, 178–9
Inspector of Hospitals, 183
Inspector of Regimental Hospitals, 178
Irish Light Infantry Battalion, 184
Irwin, Asst Surg Thomas, 30th Foot, 181, 184
Irwin, William, 30th Foot, 52, 135

Jackson, George, 30th Foot, 52
Jackson, Thomas, officer, 30th Foot, 174
　gives evidence at Ensign Herring's court martial, 151–2, 154, 157
Jacob, Michael, 30th Foot, 91
James, John, officer, 30th Foot, 97, 128
James, Maj (retd.) Charles, 108, 109, 119, 139
　on colonels, 18; on majors, 24; on adjutants, 27; on barracks and quarters, 42; on marching, 44; on fluglemen, 73; on sergeants, 79–80; on RSMs, 80; on drill sergeants, 84; on Roman Catholic officers, 102–03; on applying for a commission, 103–04; on sale of commissions, 106; on surgeons' instruments, 186; describes regimental agents, 208

James, Richard, 36th Foot, 160, 161
Jarry, Gen François, 117
Java, (see Gressie), 116
Jenny, transport:
   wreck of, 58, 102, 134
Jersey, Channel Islands, 50
   Fort Regent (St Helier), 41
Jones, Michael, 30th Foot:
   career of, 25
Jones, Thomas, 30th Foot, 136
   king's hard bargain, 171
Jones, Thomas, officer, 30th Foot, 133, 147
   court martial, 174
Judge Advocate General, 136, 141

Keith, Francis, 30th Foot, 93
Kelly, Thomas, officer, 30th Foot, 72, 97
   death of, 77
Kennedy, Joseph, 30th Foot, 131
   king's hard bargain, 172
Kennedy, Surgeon James, 30th Foot, 184
Kertland, William, 30th Foot, 131
Key, Richard, 30th Foot, 164
   trial of, 146–50
Keys, Edward, 30th Foot, 68–9, 70, 72–6, 78
Kilbeggan, Co. Westmeath, Locke's distillery, 40
Killet, Lt, 1st Foot (Royals), 122, 206
Kilmainham Hospital, 61, 192, 193
Kilmartin, Charles, 30th Foot, 88
Kilmore, Co. Armagh, 52
King George III, 102
King William III, 38
King's hard bargains, 36, 171–2
Kingsley, John Foster QM, 30th Foot, 10, 46, 83, 123, 125
   career of, 29–30; court martial of, 30–1, 173; joined by wife in Portugal, 198
Kingsley, Mrs, 198
Kinsale, Ireland, 181
Knapsacks, 44–5
Knede, John, 30th Foot, 55

Lancaster, 52
Lance Sergeant, 84
L'Anversoise (French 74-gun), 10
Larpent, Francis Seymour, Judge Advocate to the forces in the Peninsula, 141, 144
Latouche, David, officer, 30th Foot, 102
Latouche, David, banker, 104
Laughey, Michael, 30th Foot, 169
Laughron, Edward, 30th Foot, 4, 93, 134
Laughron, John, 30th Foot, 203
   career of, 53
Lawrence, William, 40th Foot:
   flogged, 175–6
Leach, Thomas, officer, 30th Foot, 174
   trial of, 157–62
Leaney, Co. Antrim, 86
Leardet, Frederick, officer, 30th Foot, 147
Ledge, William, officer, 30th Foot, 79, 203, 115, 147, 150
   irregular appointment as Quartermaster, 29
Lee, James, 30th Foot:
   king's hard bargain, 172
Leicester, 65

Leith, Gen James, 47, 157
Leitrim, Ireland, 94
Leslie, Robert, Judge Marshal, 157
Lickler, Samuel, 30th Foot:
   court martial, 148–9, 170
Light, James, officer, 30th Foot, 139, 154, 155, 157
   gives evidence at Ensign Herring's court martial, 153
Lilley, John, 30th Foot, 57
Limerick, Ireland, 14, 57, 125
Lines of Torres Vedras, 93, 99, 181, 198
Linhares, Portugal, 126
Lisbon, 61, 62, 87, 101, 125, 141, 181, 207
Lisbon, Belem General Hospital, 187
Liver diseases, 194
Locke's distillery, 40
Lockhart, Lt-Col William, 30th Foot, 116, 172
   career of, 19–20
Lockwood, Asst Surg Augustus, 30th Foot, 101
Lockwood, Purefoy, officer, 30th Foot, 101, 102, 111, 112, 125
Lole, Joseph, 30th Foot, 131
Londonderry, 39
Longford, Ireland, 16, 38, 41
Louvain, Belgium, 127
Lowestoft, Suffolk, 102
Lunatic hospital, Madras, 196
Lydon, Luke, 30th Foot:
   career of, 83–4
Lynch, Michael, 30th Foot, 45
Lynch, Robert Blosse, officer, 30th Foot, 123, 170

Machell, Lt Lancelot, Royal Engineers, 25
Machell, Richard, officer, 30th Foot, 123, 129, 184
   financial affairs of, 25–6
Mackenzie, Maj-Gen Kenneth, inspecting officer, 1, 6, 10, 11
Mackenzie, Mrs, wife of Gen Mackenzie, 205
Macready, Edward Neville, officer, 30th Foot, 7, 14, 24, 47, 62, 66, 69, 94, 96, 99, 102, 109, 112, 115, 118, 120, 122, 126, 127, 128, 129, 134, 140, 173, 184, 194
   describes Fort St George, Madras, 40; visits battlefields of Assaye, Crécy, Fontenoy, Malplaquet, Oudenarde, 126–7; impressions of 1st Battalion, 164; praise of 2nd Battalion, 165; contracts venereal disease, 196; opinions of soldiers' wives, 198; incident at Antwerp, 205; lent money by regimental agent, 208–09
Macready, Richard, 30th Foot, 68
Macready, William, actor, 102, 115
Madden, George, officer, 30th Foot, 72
Madras, 85, 200
Mafra, Portugal, 125
Majors, duties of, 24–5
Malhada Sorda, Spain, 26
Maloney, John, 30th Foot:
   attacked at Athlone, 193–4
Malta, 69, 89, 93
Manners, Gen Robert, 71, 183
   career of, 17–8
Mansel, George, officer, 30th Foot, 128
Marbot, Gen, Baron Jean Baptiste de, 63, 64
Marriage, discouragement of, 197
Masséna, Marshal, 125, 126, 203

Masters, Stephen, officer, 30th Foot, 66
Matagorda Fort, Cadiz, 203
Maxwell, David (1), officer, 30th Foot, 101
Maxwell, David (2), officer, 30th Foot, 101
Maxwell, Christopher (1), officer, 30th Foot, 101
Maxwell, Christopher (2), officer, 30th Foot, 9, 101, 154
  prosecutes at court martial of Richard Key, 149; prosecutes at court martial of Ensign John Herring, 150–1
Maxwell, William, officer, 30th Foot, 101
Mayne, Lt Richard, 30th Foot, 102
Mayne, Richard, officer, 30th Foot, 55, 123, 125
McCann, George, 30th Foot, 86, 87, 91
McCewan, James, 30th Foot, 202
McCewan, Mrs, 202
McDonald, Major James, 17th Dragoons:
  gives evidence at Captain Leach's court martial, 161
McDonald, William, 30th Foot, 167
  charged with murder, 169
McDougall, Alexander, officer, 30th Foot, 198
McGrady, Pte Barnet, 82nd Foot, 158, 160
McGrigor, James, Inspector General of Hospitals, 182, 187
  improvements made by, 178–9; brings about improvements, 189
McNabb, Alexander, officer, 30th Foot, 97, 123, 125, 138
  career of, 99
McNabb, Joseph, 30th Foot, 169
McQuain, John, 30th Foot, 55
Medical knowledge, extent of, 177
Medical officers, staff, pay, 180
Men under arrest, 144
Mental breakdown, 196
Menzies, Capt Archibald, 42nd Foot, 191
Merxem, Belgium, 205
Messing, officers', 109
Military Courts, 144–5
Military Hospitals, 187
Military purveyors, 180
Militia, 35
  quality of, 35–6
Mills, Robert, 30th Foot, 24, 57, 86, 172
Minet, Lt-Col William, 30th Foot, 114, 116, 123, 125, 172
  career of, 21–2
Moate, 16, 38, 40, 52
Moira, Gen Lord, 97
Mont St Jean (Waterloo), 191
Moore, Gen Sir John, 22, 116, 142
Moore, Lawrence, 30th Foot, 55
Moore, William, 30th Foot, 57
Moran, Martin, 30th Foot, king's hard bargain, 171
Moran, Michael, 30th Foot, 133
Morgan, Robert, 200–01
Morris, Sgt Tom, 73rd Foot, 35
Morrisey, Michael, 30th Foot, 52
Morrissey, Morris, 30th Foot:
  court martial, 170
Mountford, Lt Lewis, 47th Foot, 133
  killed in a duel, 173
Mulgrave, Brig Gen Lord, 116

Mullingar, Co. Westmeath, 38, 134
Murder, court martial for, 169, 173
Murphy, Henry, 30th Foot, 85, 202
Murphy, Mrs Mary, 202
Murray, Gen, 60
Murray, Robert, officer, 30th Foot:
  prosecutes Richard Key, 147–9
Musket, 74–5
Mutiny Act, 130, 131, 136, 138, 141

Napper, John, officer, 30th Foot, 112
Navas Frias, Portugal, 47
Necessaries, 49, 72
Neville, Parke Percy, officer, 30th Foot, 98, 102, 112, 129, 205
New Brunswick, 86
Newton, Hospital Mate (attached), 30th Foot, 181
Nicholson, Benjamin Walker, officer, 30th Foot, 7, 19, 104, 144, 169, 194
  stands court martial, 174–5
Nivelle, Belgium, 198
Nowlan, Brian, 30th Foot, 58
  king's hard bargain, 172
Nunn, Benjamin, officer, 30th Foot, 28

O'Brien, Mr Daniel:
  supports Rohan's claim for a pension, 193
Offences, incidence of, 163–4
  drunkenness, 164; absence without leave, 164–5; disobedience, 165; making away with regimental necessaries, 165; unsoldierlike conduct, 165; theft, 165–6; miscellaneous, 166
Officers:
  length of service with 30th Foot, 96–7; social backgrounds, 98; geographical origins, 99; social backgrounds, 100–02; family connections, 101; Catholic, 102–03, 108–09; rates of pay, 108–09; messing, 109; commissions, costs of, 109; methods of appointment, 111–3; commissions, exchange of, 113–4; training, 117–21; dining, 122–4; sightseeing, 126–7; walking expeditions, 127–8; hunting, 128; learning foreign languages, 129; theatricals, 129; under arrest, 144; incidence of courts martial involving charges against officers, 168–9; trial by court martial, 173–5
O'Flaherty, Asst Surg Daniel, 30th Foot, 184, 185
Ogg, Col, 148, 149, 150
  inspecting officer, 164
O'Halloran, Theophilus, officer, 30th Foot, 77, 112
O'Heighen, Asst Surg Frederick, 30th Foot, 184
Olmeda, Spain, 26
Omagh, Co. Tyrone, 39, 41
On the march:
  arrangements for, 44–7; departure, 45; order of march, 45–6; stragglers, 46–7
O'Neil, Terence, 30th Foot, 94–5
Ophthalmia, 19, 52, 194–5
Oporto, general hospital, 187

Packenham, Gen Edward, 183
  inspects hospitals, 190
Palmer, Asst Surg John Rose, 30th Foot, 184
Palmerstone, Lord, Secretary of State for War, 140
Pamplona, siege of, 11

226 Inside the Regiment

Pardons, 168
Parry, Edward, officer, 30th Foot, 112
Pay, 50
Paymaster sergeant, duties of, 82
Paymaster's clerk, duties of, *see* Paymaster sergeant
Paymasters, duties of 25–6
Peale, Joseph, 30th Foot, 82
Pearse, Julian, 30th Foot, 55
Pearse, Surgeon Robert, 30th Foot, 6, 181, 183, 184, 196
Pellew, Admiral Sir Edward, R.N., 20, 116
Peñaparda, Portugal, 47
Pennefather, William, officer, 30th Foot, 112
Perry, Andrew, officer, 30th Foot, 138–9
Perry, John, officer, 30th Foot, 156
Physician General, 178
Physicians Military, 179
Picton, Gen Thomas, 99
Pilgrim, John, 4th Foot, 169
Piper, Asst Surg Samuel Ayrault, 30th Foot, 181, 183
Plymouth, military hospital, 187
  bad conditions, 188–9
Policing the army, 141–4
Pollock, Sgt Robert, Tyrone Militia:
  gives evidence at Captain Leach's court martial, 158–9
Poonamallee, India, 85
Portugal, general hospitals, 187
Poyntz, Arthur (jr.), officer, 30th Foot, 29, 101
Poyntz, Arthur (snr.), officer, 30th Foot, 83, 101, 112, 151, 155, 157
  career of, 29; gives evidence at Ensign Herring's court martial, 153
Poyntz, James, officer, 30th Foot, 29, 97, 101
Poyntz, Samuel Robert, officer, 30th Foot, 29, 72, 76, 101, 112
Pratt, William, 30th Foot, 136
Prendergast, Edmund, officer, 30th Foot, 97
Preston, Samuel, 30th Foot, 131
Prigmore, William, 30th Foot:
  gives evidence at Ensign Herring's court martial, 156
Prince of Wales, 101
Prince Regent, 87
  institutes rank of Colour Sergeant, 79
Princess Royal, HMS, 202
Private soldiers:
  public perception of, 32; geographical origins of, 32–3; motives for enlisting, 33–5; pay of, 50; occupations, 51; age at enlistment, 51–2; length of service, 52–3; causes of death, 53–5; desertion of, 55; transfer of, 56–7; conduct of, 57–8; prisoners of war, 58–60; French views of, 63–4
Provost Marshal, 142, 143, 144
Punishment:
  corporal punishment, 139–40; flogging, 166–7; solitary confinement, 167; commutation of, 167–8
Purchase of commissions, 103–06
Purdon, Asst Surg Edward, 30th Foot, 181

Quartermasters, duties of, 28–9
Queen, transport, wreck of, 54
Queen Victoria, 202
Queen's Regiment (Canadian Regiment), 99

Rae, Lt, 1st Foot (Royals), 30, 31, 122
Ralph, John, officer, 30th Foot, 129
Ramsden, Robert, 30th Foot, 52
Ramsey, Samuel, 30th Foot, 52
Rank, brevet, 107–08
Rations, 49–50
Rawdon, George, 30th Foot, 54, 59
Reading, Berkshire, 66
Recruitment, parties, 32, 65, 67
  districts, 65–6; parties, composition of, 66; bounty, 68; attestation, 70–1; training (general), 73–8; training (platoon exercises), 75–6; training (marching), 76–7
Regiment, infantry, numbers of, 13
Regimental agents, 208–09
  responsibilities of, 208
Regimental courts martial, 163
Regimental inspection, 1–12, 77–8, 81
Regimental Sergeant-Major, duties of, 80–1
Regimental Surgeons, 30th Foot, 180–1
Reide, Thomas, 118, 120, 121
Repton, Edward, 30th Foot:
  applies for wooden leg, 193
Reston, Mrs Agnes, 203
Reynolds, Michael, 30th Foot, 57
Rheumatism, 195
Rice, Daniel, 30th Foot, 136–7
Riley, Francis, 30th Foot, 135
Riley, John, 30th Foot, 46
  court martial of, 27, 169; given money by regimental agent, 208
Ripton, Edward, 30th Foot, *see* Repton, 193
Roberts, Thomas, officer, 30th Foot, 114
Robertson, Robert, 30th Foot:
  gives evidence at Private Richard Key's court martial, 149
Robinson, Gen Frederick P., 183
  inspects hospitals, 190
Roche, Benjamin, officer, 30th Foot, 125
Rodwell, Thomas, 30th Foot, 54
Roe, John, officer, 30th Foot, 112
Rohan, Daniel, 30th Foot:
  consequences of a fall at Badajoz, 192–3
Roscommon, Ireland, 85
Rotterdam, Netherlands, 127
Royal College of Surgeons, 184, 185
Royal Hibernian Military School, Dublin, 204
Royal Military Asylum, Chelsea, 204
Royal Military College, 96, 100, 101, 112, 117, 118
Royal Veterans Battalions, 82, 92
Rugby School, 102
Rumley, George, officer, 30th Foot, 101
Rumley, John, officer, 30th Foot, 101, 112
  death of, 194
Runa, Palace of, Portugal, 126
Rutland, William, 30th Foot, 52

Sabugal, Portugal, 50
Salamanca, 181

San Sebastian, 60
Scott, William, 30th Foot, 82
Scotton, Joseph, 30th Foot, 65
  career of, 86, 90, 93
Scotton, William, 30th Foot, 136
Scrofula, 196
Sergeants:
  duties of, 79–80; demotion of, 90–1; punishment of, 91; desertion by, 93–4; resignation of, 94; commissioning of, 114–7
Shaller, Joseph, 30th Foot:
  will of, 203
Sharpe, John, 30th Foot, 52, 137, 196
Shipp, John, 34–5, 69, 140
  views on flogging, 172
Siborne, William, 96
Sickness rates, 196
Siege of Ciudad Rodrigo, 60
Siege of San Sebastian, 60
Simpson, John, 30th Foot:
  court martial of, 169
Sinclair, Donald, officer, 30th Foot, 7, 113, 114, 156
Skiddy, Mrs Biddy, 200
Skirrow, James, officer, 30th Foot, 72, 147
Sleaford, Lincolnshire, 61, 65, 66, 69, 72, 146
Sloane, William, 30th Foot, 55
Smallpox, inoculation against, 183
Smith, Bailey, 30th Foot:
  court martial of, 169–70
Smith, Robert, 30th Foot, 92
Smith, Robert, officer, 30th Foot, 125
Social change, 34
Soldiers' children:
  with the army, 203–04; education of, 203
Soldiers' wives:
  in barracks, 197; tasks performed by, 197; drawing lots to accompany husbands, 199–200; remarriage, 200; sufferings of, 201–02; on board ship, 202
Spalding, Lincolnshire, 69
Sparkes, Michael, officer, 30th Foot, 66
Spawforth, James, officer, 30th Foot, 72, 113
Spencer, Col Brent, 40th Foot, 20
Spencer, Deputy Assistant Commissary General, 49
St Helier, Jersey, 41
Stafford, Staffordshire, 52
Stanhope, the Hon. Philip, officer, 30th Foot, 97, 100
Stanhope, William, officer, 30th Foot, 99
Steinkerk, Belgium, 167
Stephens, officer, 30th Foot, 112
Stephenson, George, officer, 30th Foot, 28, 79, 112, 146, 149, 154, 157
  gives evidence at Ensign John Herring's court martial, 152
Stephenson, William, 30th Foot:
  court martial, 169
Stewart, William, officer, 30th Foot, 22, 43, 44, 47, 93, 96, 100, 102, 112, 114, 118, 122, 125, 127, 128, 129, 173, 184, 198
  career of, 27–8; in command of the depot, 10, 11, 12
Stilton, Huntingdon, (now Cambridgeshire), 82

Stone, Thomas, 30th Foot:
  career of, 60–1
Strabane, Co. Tyrone, 39, 59, 62
Straddling, Charles, 30th Foot, 92
Stuart, John, officer, 30th Foot, 128
Suicide, attempted, 171
Sullivan, William, officer, 30th Foot, 102
Surety, John, 30th Foot, 91
Surgeon General, 178, 179, 180
Surgeons, Military, 179
  reputation of, 177; pay, 182; duties of, 183; length of service, 183–4; training of, 184–5; uniform, 186
Syston, Leicestershire, 54

Taunton, Somerset, 65
Templemore, Co. Tipperary, 59
Terrible, HMS, 202
Teulon, George, officer, 30th Foot, 112
The Hague, Netherlands, 127
Tincombe, Francis, officer, 30th Foot, 112, 123
Tinsley, William, 30th Foot, 52
Toner, Dennis, 30th Foot:
  accused of desertion, 147–8
Tongue, John, officer, 30th Foot, 147, 156
Toronto, 99
Torquemada, Spain, 44
Torres Vedras, lines of, 60
Torres Vedras, Portugal, 128, 129
Toulon, 15, 69, 79, 114, 116
  fall of Fort Mulgrave, 20–1
Trevor, Lt-Col Arthur, 33rd Foot, 199
  opinion of soldiers' wives, 198
Tribe, Capt Richard, 82nd Foot:
  gives evidence at Captain Leach's court martial, 161–2
Trichinopoly, India, 81, 150
Tullamore, Co. Offaly, 16, 39–40, 65
Tully, John, 30th Foot, 93
Turner, Lt-Col Charles, Royal West India Rangers, 112
Turville, 30th Foot:
  court martial, 170
Twite, John, 30th Foot, 45
Tynaart, Netherlands, 135
Tyrrell, Pte Joseph, 82nd Foot, 161
  gives evidence at Captain Leach's court martial, 160
Tytler, Alexander Fraser, 148

Uncle, William, 30th Foot, 58
Uniform, 47–9
  cost of, 108–09; for surgeons, 186

Valenciennes, France, 59
Valverde, Portugal, 47
Vaumorel, Lt-Col Philip, 30th Foot, 1, 7, 8–10, 50, 68, 85, 90, 137, 146, 168, 174–5, 183
  career of, 20–1; attitude to discipline, 23–4; compared with Hamilton, 166
Venereal disease, 196
Verdun, 102, 114, 125, 134
Vigoureux, Lt-Col Charles, 30th Foot, 10
Vila Nova del Rey, Portugal, 77

Villa de Toro, Spain, 26
Villamuriel, Spain, 44
　action at, 54, 58, 59, 60, 61, 62, 77, 87, 93, 101, 114
Vimeiro, Count of, 126
Vipond, Thomas, 30th Foot, 54

Wade, Lt-Col George, 30th Foot, 17
Wainhouse, Corp William, 82nd Foot, 160, 162
　gives evidence at Captain Leach's court martial, 159
Wakefield, Yorkshire, 69
Walker, Adam, 30th Foot:
　court martial, 171
Walker, Gen George Townsend, 123, 177
Wanlass, William, 30th Foot, 196
War of American Independence, 99
Ward, John, 30th Foot, 85, 87
Warren, Charles, officer, 30th Foot, 102, 196
Waterloo, survival rates of wounded men, 195–6
Watson, Charles, 30th Foot, 93
Watson, Lt, 9th Foot, 206
Wellington, Duke of, 32, 46–7, 49, 79, 102, 105, 125, 128, 135, 139, 141, 142, 143, 145, 147
　opinion of troops, 13; general orders of, 43–4; on promotion of surgeons, 182; on Chaplains, 206; on Methodism, 206
Wellington, Somerset, 92
Westen, Sgt John, 82nd Foot, 159, 160, 161, 162
　gives evidence at Captain Leach's court martial, 157–8
Wetherall, Gen Frederick, inspecting officer, 9, 137
Wheele, Jacob, 30th Foot, king's hard bargain, 171–2
Wheeler, Pte William, 51st Foot, 35, 96
　on chaplains, 206
White, John Lorraine, officer, 30th Foot, 7, 127
White, Robert, 30th Foot, 57, 58, 88
White, William, 30th Foot, 52
Whitley, Ensign, 9th Foot, 206
Wier, Patrick, 30th Foot (see also Wire), 167
Wigston, Leicestershire, 85
Wilkinson, William, General and officer in 30th Foot, 81, 96, 97, 100, 172, 175
　inspecting officer, 8; career of, 18–9; attitude to discipline, 23
Williamson, John, 30th Foot, 29
Williamson, Thomas, officer, 30th Foot, 123
Wilson, Capt, 1st Foot (Royals), 122
Wilson, John, 30th Foot, 93
　court martial, 170
Wilson, Nicholas, 30th Foot, 29, 83
Winrow, John, officer, 30th Foot:
　court martial, 173
Wire, Patrick, 30th Foot (see also Wier), 124
　court martial, 167
Women, *see* soldiers' wives, 197
Woodhouse, William, 30th Foot:
　court martial, 169
Woods, James, 30th Foot, 79, 81, 94
Wounds, nature of, 192
Wray, Hugh Boyd, officer, 30th Foot, 127
　career of, 25–6

York, Duke of, 17, 204
　as Commander-in-Chief, British Army, 15
Yorke, John, 30th Foot, 58
Young, Alexander, officer, 30th Foot, 28

British Army:
Royal Horse Guards (The Blues), 65, 86
3rd Dragoons, 184
10th Light Dragoons, 65, 86
14th Light Dragoons, 113
16th Dragoons, 157
17th Dragoons, 157

The Guards, 56
1st Foot (Royals), 46
3rd Foot, 115
9th Foot, 46
16th Foot, 14
17th Foot, 102
26th Foot, 56, 57, 157
30th Foot, battalion strength 16–7
33rd Foot, 69
35th Foot, 46
36th Foot, 72, 111, 113, 147
37th Foot, 100
43rd Foot, 56
44th Foot, 14
47th Foot, 56, 57
51st Foot, 35
54th Foot, 77, 112
56th Foot, 100
60th Foot, 14
61st Foot, 112
69th Foot, 92
73rd Foot, 35
79th Foot, 92, 180
80th Foot, 111
94th Foot, 203

7th Garrison Battalion, 181, 184
8th Garrison Battalion, 113
9th Garrison Battalion, 59, 66

1st Battalion Royal Veterans, 117
4th Battalion Royal Veterans, 79
8th Battalion Royal Veterans, 181

Staff Corps, 97
Army of Reserve, 33, 56, 57, 59, 64, 65, 85, 86
　quality of, 36
Army of Defence, 33, 57
Loyal Volunteers of St George's Middlesex, 35
Antrim Militia, 57
Carlow Militia, 57
Tipperary Militia, 65, 111

Foreign and Colonial Regiments:
Brunswick Oels Jaegers, 14
Queen's Regiment (Canadian Regiment), 99
Royal African Corps, 66
2nd Ceylon, 66
De Meuron's Regiment, 112